Lecture Notes
in Business Information Processing

576

Series Editors

Wil van der Aalst, *RWTH Aachen University, Aachen, Germany*

Sudha Ram, *University of Arizona, Tucson, USA*

Michael Rosemann, *Queensland University of Technology, Brisbane, Australia*

Clemens Szyperski, *Microsoft Research, Redmond, USA*

Giancarlo Guizzardi, *University of Twente, Enschede, The Netherlands*

LNBIP reports state-of-the-art results in areas related to business information systems and industrial application software development – timely, at a high level, and in both printed and electronic form.

The type of material published includes

- Proceedings (published in time for the respective event)
- Postproceedings (consisting of thoroughly revised and/or extended final papers)
- Other edited monographs (such as, for example, project reports or invited volumes)
- Tutorials (coherently integrated collections of lectures given at advanced courses, seminars, schools, etc.)
- Award-winning or exceptional theses

LNBIP is abstracted/indexed in DBLP, EI and Scopus. LNBIP volumes are also submitted for the inclusion in ISI Proceedings.

Charlotte Verbruggen

Advancing Multi-modelling in MDE for Integrated Domain and Business Process Modelling

 Springer

Charlotte Verbruggen
Business Informatics Group
Institute of Information Systems Engineering
TU Wien
Vienna, Austria

ISSN 1865-1348   ISSN 1865-1356 (electronic)
Lecture Notes in Business Information Processing
ISBN 978-3-032-13875-0   ISBN 978-3-032-13876-7 (eBook)
https://doi.org/10.1007/978-3-032-13876-7

Voor opa

Preface

This book encompasses a revised version of the Ph.D. dissertation written by the author, at the Research Centre for Information Systems Engineering (LIRIS) at KU Leuven (Belgium). In 2025, the Ph.D. dissertation won the "CAiSE Ph.D. Award," granted to outstanding Ph.D. theses in the field of information systems engineering. This book presents various research efforts on the topic of integration of domain and process modelling, covering a broad perspective of model-driven engineering (MDE) and information systems engineering. More specifically, this dissertation covers a literature review on modelling and MDE by practitioners, empirical research on students' understanding of modelling tasks, modelling method development and evaluation, and modelling tool development and evaluation.

This dissertation addresses the integration of domain and process modelling using the domain modeling approach Merode and the process modeling language BPMN, focusing on three key quality dimensions: abstract syntax, concrete syntax, and semantics. In modeling languages, abstract syntax defines the possible elements of a model and their interrelations, as represented in a meta-model. Concrete syntax specifies how these elements are represented. Semantics convey the meaning of each element and their relationships. Addressing this integration challenge will support the development of tools for modeling and code generation or model execution that combine Merode and BPMN models. The solution, therefore, aims to formalize the abstract syntax, concrete syntax, and semantics of the Merode-BPMN integration.

The first part provides an introduction to the research topic, the applied methodology, and the dissertation structure, along with the identification of research objectives.

The second part addresses the identification and motivation of the problem. It includes a literature review of empirical findings on model-driven engineering in practice, and two empirical studies exploring how well students perform in combined data and process modeling, and how they experience this task.

The third part focuses on the design and development of artifacts. The fourth chapter presents the MERODExBPMN meta-model for integrating abstract syntax and basic semantics of the data and process perspectives. The fifth chapter advances this integration by identifying the semantic gaps in the Information System Services Layer of Merode and proposing a proof of concept for a solution. This chapter also addresses the additional concrete syntax that is required. The sixth chapter demonstrates the application of the MERODExBPMN meta-model, aiming to align conceptual modeling terminology with that of process mining and event logging.

The fourth part evaluates the developed artifact. The seventh chapter details an evaluation framework and taxonomy for modelling approaches, which is applied on the proposed integration, while the eighth chapter evaluates the prototype tool from a user perspective. The fifth part concludes this dissertation with a chapter on conclusions, lessons learned, limitations, and directions for future research.

Charlotte Verbruggen

Acknowledgements

I have truly enjoyed these 4 years of working on my Ph.D. thanks to many different people that I would like to thank here.

First and foremost, I would like to thank my supervisor, Monique, for everything she has taught me as a researcher and teacher, but also as a mentor in life. I am very grateful for her support, guidance, and encouragement. In addition to being a great promotor, you make LIRIS a warm and welcoming place to work, and I have really enjoyed our many conversations.

I would also like to thank the other members of my Ph.D. committee. Johannes and Fani, your feedback has guided my research since the beginning of my Ph.D., and your input and suggestions have led to great improvements in my work. Dominik, thank you for your constructive feedback at various conferences, and for your continued support in my academic career. Oscar, thank you for hosting me in Valencia and giving me the opportunity to run an experiment with you and your students. I really enjoyed meeting your team and exploring the city. Finally, I would like to thank Prof. Hande Yaman Paternotte for agreeing to chair my Ph.D. committee.

I would also like to thank the other professors at LIRIS for their encouragement, support and feedback, especially Bart, Jan, Ferdi, Wouter and Jochen. My thanks also go to all my colleagues at LIRIS for their friendship: Daria, Galina, Raf, Bjorn, Ziboud, Hans, Pavani, Jari, Carlos, Alexander, Philipp, Toon, Yannis, Alexandre, Simon, Felix, Elena, Manon, Margot, Kseniya, Zahra, Xiaomeng, Aurélie, Chris, Bruno, Brecht, Yanyi, Marco, Victor, Jakob, Mathis, Daan, Yongbo, Almer, Adir and Jente.

Finally, I would like to thank my friends and family who have encouraged me along the way, whether it was once, twice, or every day. Thank you for taking an interest in my work and filling my free time with great conversations. To my brother Hendrik, thank you for being my sounding board. And especially to my parents, thank you for your endless support and encouragement. I could not have reached this milestone without your great example and belief in me. Thank you for everything.

November 2024   Charlotte Verbruggen

Committee

Promoter

Monique Snoeck	KU Leuven

Doctoral Committee

Johannes De Smedt	KU Leuven
Estefanía Serral Asensio	KU Leuven
Dominik Bork	TU Wien
Oscar Pastor	Universitat Politècnica de València

Chair

Hande Yaman Paternotte	KU Leuven

Contents

**Part III   Design and Demonstration of the Integration of MERODE
and BPMN**

Part V   Epilogue

Part I
Prologue

Chapter 1
Introduction

Business information systems play an important role in the day-to-day business operations of most companies. They are used to support work processes (within departments as well as across departments) and store data. As technology progresses, more and more aspects of running businesses that were traditionally executed manually, are now supported by business information systems. Today, these information systems are used for a variety of business processes, such as supply chain management, sales, customer relationship management, payroll, HR management etc. Each of these processes requires (potentially large amounts of) data, stored in databases. These processes do not stand on their own but most often interact. For example, in a business applying lean supply chain principles, sales have an immediate effect on the supply chain management process as products are made to order and only a limited amount of raw materials are kept in stock to reduce operating costs. Therefore, capturing all business processes, their corresponding data and interactions is needed. However, given the large number of processes, combining the support for all business processes including their data needs in a single business information system can quickly become very complex. To master this complexity and ensure smooth operations, maintainability and adaptability, it is therefore crucial that the business information system of a company is based on solid design principles that provide an integrated view on both the data and the process perspectives.

1.1 Model-Driven Engineering

The Object Management Group is a consortium that was founded in 1989 for the development of standards providing specifications for modelling languages (e.g., UML and BPMN have OMG standards). In 2000, the Object Management Group (OMG) published the standard for a Model-Driven Architecture [1]. The research domain of the underlying principle of Model-Driven Engineering (MDE) addresses the complexity of designing complex systems by creating conceptual models of the to-be-build software which can be translated to code by means for formally defined transformations. The basic idea of MDE is to base software development on computational and platform independent models that leave out many technical details and are at a higher abstraction level compared to code or technical designs. Therefore, these models can be more easily used to communicate with stakeholders during the requirements engineering phase when the requirements of the software are collected and finalized, as the models provide a visual representation of the system which can help clarify the effect of a requirement on the overall design of the system. Additionally, models can be used to perform quality checks on the system's design before it is implemented. Doing quality checks on the

© The Author(s), under exclusive license to Springer Nature Switzerland AG 2026
C. Verbruggen, *Advancing Multi-modelling in MDE for Integrated Domain
and Business Process Modelling*, Lecture Notes in Business Information Processing 576,
https://doi.org/10.1007/978-3-032-13876-7_1

models and making adaptions to the design is much more cost effective than performing these checks and making changes to the finished code. However, the models still need to be transformed to code, which is itself still a complex process. Generally speaking, MDE practitioners start from a set of platform-independent models (PIMs) capturing the concepts and functionalities of the system independent of the platform on which it will be deployed. These PIMs can then be transformed to Platform-specific models (PSMs) that capture how these concepts and functionalities are to be implemented for the chosen platform. Finally, the PSMs can be transformed to code. This approach transforms the stakeholders' requirements (which are usually informal and difficult to interpret) to a formal specification in a step-by-step manner. An added benefit of this approach is that it facilitates moving the implementation of business software to a new platform if required, given that the platform independent requirements are already captured by the PIM and only the transformation to a new PSM and code are required.

1.2   General problem

Currently, the adoption of MDE in industry is lacking, although recently there has been an uptake in low-code/no-code platforms allowing citizen programmers to develop applications based on graphical representations. Low-code/no-code platforms often use drag-and-drop mechanisms for the visual design of the user interface, in combination with a workflow model and/or a data model. While this can be categorized as part of MDE, applications developed with low-code/no-code platforms usually focus on the interaction between humans (customers or employees) with the system, rather than the formal specification of a business information system. Further adoption of MDE in the creation of business information systems would allow companies to invest more resources in designing systems rather than writing code, but for MDE of business information systems to see the same uptake as low-code/no-code platforms, several challenges need to be addressed [2], [3]. The main challenge addressed in this dissertation is the *integrated* modelling and design of the data and process perspective for the purpose of MDE and code generation. In order to model a complete business information system addressing several or all of the aspects of running a business, several models need to be created to address the different aspects, usually in different modelling languages. These models should be correct independently, but the integration between different models should also be correct and consistent. It is therefore important that the modelling languages used are compatible and that consistency between models can be ensured.

To ensure this integration, two avenues are possible: choose one language that addresses multiple perspectives and enhance that language to address the missing elements, or combine different languages. UML covers different perspectives with different diagram types, but lacks clear semantics, both for the diagram types themselves as for the integration between diagram types. BPMN covers the process perspectives and includes references to data elements, but lacks a model (type) for the data perspective. In this dissertation we choose not to enhance one language, but rather opt to combine two languages, one for each perspective. We focus on data and process modelling as they are the core components of business information systems, as demonstrated by the fact that many low-code/no-code platforms focus on one or both of these perspectives.

We start with a broad view by identifying the challenges of MDE faced by practitioners through an extensive literature review in Chapter 2. We identify several benefits and issues practitioners experience when applying MDE. The most commonly reported benefits are improved understanding of the system, improved quality of the system and increased productivity. On the other hand, the most commonly reported problems are missing tool functionalities, followed by the high effort required to acquire MBSE skills, the high effort required to use MDE tools and the organization's culture inhibiting the adoption of modelling practices. In Chapter 3, we will narrow down the scope to the combined modelling of the data and process perspective with two case studies with student participants to investigate the more narrow topic of novice modelers' understanding of multi-perspective modelling. The pilot experiment in Leuven shows promising results including a potential correlation between the understanding of multi-perspective modelling and overall model quality, and between the understanding of multi-perspective modelling and the time distribution across the two models. Another result of the pilot experiment is that the correct modelling of actors in the system can be a challenge for novice modelers. The second study, carried out at the University of Valencia, uses an adapted version of the experimental setup from the pilot experiment. In this study, we find that the participants' overall grade on the UML class diagram and the BPMN process model seem to be correlated. We see two potential explanations for this correlation. One explanation is that participants need the same ability to abstract for both models. So it could be that the grade is mostly explained by the participant's abstract thinking skills. On the other hand, the interaction between the two models could also be a factor: If the participant is good at identifying which requirement should be included in which model, and how the models can interact, in theory, the overall quality of both models increases because the models contain the correct elements. This second explanation is also supported by the observation from the pilot experiment that the two participants with a good understanding of multi-perspective modelling produce models of a higher quality.

The findings that overlap from the literature review in Chapter 2 and from the studies in Chapter 3, are related to the integration of modelling languages (i.e. students with a good understanding of multi-perspective modelling seem to produce better models) and tools (tool integration is one of the few concrete examples of missing tool functionality, and it is mentioned in two separate publications). The main challenge when integrating modelling languages that address different perspectives is that they need to be integrated on all three quality dimension levels: abstract syntax, concrete syntax & semantics. The quality dimensions are defined as follows:

- The **abstract syntax** of a modelling language defines the elements that constitute a model and how these are related to each other via a meta-model [4].
- The **concrete syntax** of a modelling language specifies the representation of the abstract syntax, i.e. the notation [4], [5]. A modelling language has only one abstract syntax, but can have multiple concrete syntaxes, for example a visual notation and an XML notation.

- While the abstract syntax specifies all possible model elements and their relationships, **semantics** express the meaning of each model element and each relationship. Semantics consist of *type semantics* and *inherent semantics* [6]. Type semantics provide meaning for the elements of the meta-model while inherent semantics provide meaning for the instances of a model. In other words, the type semantics are the same for each model in a given modelling language, while the inherent semantics can differ among models in the same modelling language.

Defining the integration for these three quality dimensions is specific to the modelling languages in question, and is very difficult to generalise. Therefore, the overarching problem of integrating modelling languages on the three quality dimensions is further narrowed down to integrating a data modelling language and a process modelling language in this dissertation. The first step is to select two modelling languages that are compatible to a certain extent, to ensure the feasibility of the integration.

We identify two specific modelling approaches as the best suited for this specific integration (Merode and BPMN). BPMN was chosen as the modelling language for the business process perspective, because it is supported by the OMG with a meta-model and specification [7] and it is a popular process modelling language in education, the research community and industry [8]. For the data modelling perspective, we chose the Merode approach. Merode is a modelling approach for Information Systems Engineering that is based on a layered architecture with an artefact-centric domain model – consisting of UML class diagrams and state charts – at its core. The top layer is the Business Process layer, where business processes can be included. However, a formal specification defining how such a process is modelled and integrated with the other layers is not yet realized. Merode is thus a modelling approach for Information Systems with potential for integration with BPMN. The OO-method is an object-oriented domain modelling approach that is very similar to Merode and would also be a good candidate for this integration. Both methods make use of the UML standard, but add to that methodological guidelines that are missing from UML. We chose to develop the integration with Merode since it is event-driven, meaning that the interaction between objects is inherently driven by event invocations. Compared to OO-Method, the use of events facilitates connecting the process layer to the information system layer as the interaction between Merode and business comes down to the interaction between domain events and business processes. This is explained in detail in sections 4.4.1 and 5.4.1.

The problem addressed in this dissertation is therefore the integration of Merode with BPMN for the three quality dimensions of abstract syntax, concrete syntax and semantics. Once this integration problem has been addressed, there will be a solid basis for the creating of a modelling tool and a code generation or model execution tool for combined Merode and BPMN models. This leads to three clear objectives for a solution:

1) Formalize the abstract syntax of the integration between Merode and BPMN
2) Formalize the concrete syntax of the integration between Merode and BPMN
3) Formalize the semantics of the integration between Merode and BPMN

These three objectives will be addressed in Part III. Objective 1 is addressed by the development of an integrated meta-model in Chapter 4. This meta-model is first evaluated with a theoretical example that demonstrates its instantiation. Objectives 2 and 3 are addressed in Chapter 5. In addition, the usefulness of the meta-model is demonstrated in Chapter 6 by using it as a basis for aligning the terminology (i.e. abstract syntax) of the domain of data-aware process modelling and the domain of process mining and event logging. A detailed framework for the evaluation of the three research objectives is presented in Chapter 7, and the framework is also applied to validate the proposed integration of Merode and BPMN. The results of Chapter 5 are applied in a prototype implementation which is evaluated by students in Chapter 8.

1.3   Research Methodology

The structure of this dissertation follows the design science research methodology by Peffers et al. [9], depicted in Figure 1.1. This methodology consists of a research process that has six activities. Activity 1 consists of identifying the problem and motivating it. This is followed by defining the objectives of a solution in activity 2. The next activity consists of designing and developing an artefact that fulfils the objectives identified in activity 2. The fourth activity consists of demonstrating how the artefact solves the problem, and the fifth activity consists of evaluating the artefact. The final activity is communication of the research that has been conducted. From the fifth and the sixth activity, researchers can iterate back to activity 2 and 3 to define new objectives or improve the design of the artefact. Peffers et al. [9] also include four different entry points to their design science process. A problem-centred initiation uses the identification of the problem as an entry point. An objective-centred solution uses the definition of objectives for a solution as an entry point. A design and development centred initiation uses the design of the artefact as an entry point, and finally, a client/context initiated project uses a demonstration as entry point. In all four cases, the six activities do not need to be executed in sequential order, but should all be addressed at some point. This dissertation follows the problem-centred initiation approach.

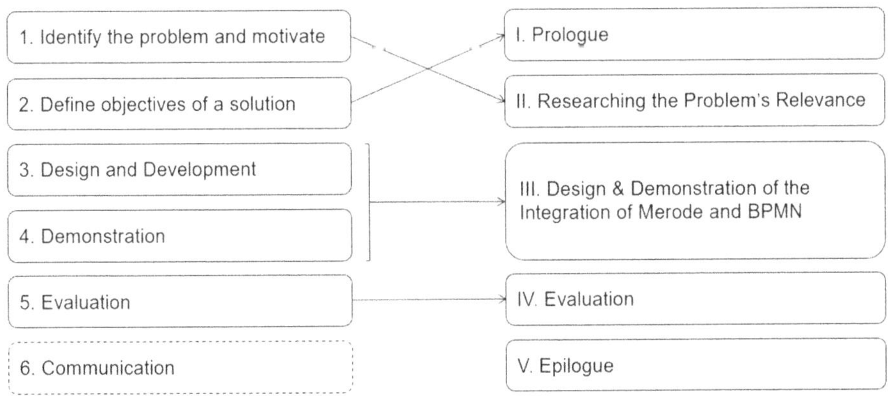

Figure 1.1 The Design Science methodology for Information Systems Research by Peffers et al., adapted from [9] (left) and how it corresponds to the structure of this dissertation.

1.4 Dissertation structure

Part I introduces the research topic of this dissertation, the applied methodology, and the structure that is followed. It also includes the identification of the research objectives, addressing activity 2 of the Design Science methodology.

Part II of this dissertation addresses the first activity of Peffers's design science methodology: the problem identification and motivation. This part consists of two chapters. Chapter 2 consists of a literature review on the use of model-driven engineering by practitioners, consolidating empirical research findings published since 2015. This work was previously published in the following papers:

– Verbruggen, C., Snoeck, M. (2021). Model-Driven Engineering: A State of Affairs and Research Agenda. In: *Lecture Notes in Business Information Processing book series (LNBIP, volume 421)*: *vol. LNBIP 421*, (335-349). Presented at the International Conference on Evaluation and Modeling Methods for Systems Analysis and Development, Melbourne, VIC, Australia. doi: https://doi.org/10.1007/978-3-030-79186-5_22
– Verbruggen, C., Snoeck, M. (2022). Practitioners' experiences with model-driven engineering: a meta-review. *Software And Systems Modeling*. doi: https://doi.org/10.1007/s10270-022-01020-1

Chapter 3 consists of two empirical studies on how students experience the combined modelling of the data and process perspective, and how well they perform. The first study has been published in the paper listed below.

– Verbruggen, C., Snoeck, M. (2022). Exploratory Study on Students' Understanding of Multi-perspective Modelling. In: *Enterprise, Business-Process and Information Systems Modeling*: *vol. 450*, (321-335). Presented at the International Conference on Evaluation and Modeling Methods for Systems Analysis and Development, Leuven, 06 Jun 2022-10 Jun 2022. ISBN: 978-3-031-07474-5. doi: https://doi.org/10.1007/978-3-031-07475-2_22

Part III reports on the Design and Development of the artefacts, covering the third and fourth activity of the design science methodology by Peffers. Chapter 4 presents the MERODExBPMN meta-model, addressing the integration of the abstract syntax of the data perspective and the process perspective. Chapter 5 addresses the semantic integration of both perspectives by formalizing the Information System Services Layer of Merode. Chapter 6 demonstrates the use of the MERODExBPMN meta-model in an effort to align the terminology of the conceptual modelling domain with the terminology of the process mining and event logging domain. This work has been published in the following papers:

– Goossens, A., Verbruggen, C., Snoeck, M., De Smedt, J., Vanthienen, J. with Goossens, A. (corresp. author), Verbruggen, C. (corresp. author) (2023). Aligning Object-Centric Event Logs with Data-Centric Conceptual Models. In: *Lecture Notes in Business Information Processing*, (479), (44-59). Presented at the Enterprise, Business-Process and Information Systems Modeling, Zaragosa, 12 Jun 2023-13 Jun 2023. Cham (Germany). ISBN: 978-3-031-34241-7. doi: https://doi.org/10.1007/978-3-031-34241-7

– Verbruggen, C., Goossens, A., De Smedt, J. et al. iDOCEM: defining a common terminology for object-centric event logging and data-centric process modelling. Softw Syst Model (2024). doi: https://doi.org/10.1007/s10270-024-01191-z

Part IV addresses the fifth activity of the design science methodology: the evaluation of the artefact. This part consists of two chapters. Chapter 7 presents the development of an evaluation framework and taxonomy. A first iteration of this work has received a best paper award at the EMMSAD 2023 working conference and the extended version presented in this dissertation has been accepted for publication in the SoSyM journal. This work has been published in the following papers:

– Verbruggen, C., Snoeck, M. (2023). TEC-MAP: A Taxonomy of Evaluation Criteria for Multi-modelling Approaches. In: *Enterprise, Business-Process and Information Systems Modeling. BPMDS EMMSAD 2023 2023. Lecture Notes in Business Information Processing, vol 479. Springer*, (259-273). Presented at the International Conference on Evaluation and Modeling Methods for Systems Analysis and Development, Zaragoza, 12 Jun 2023-13 Jun 2023. Cham. ISBN: 978-3-031-34241-7. doi: https://doi.org/10.1007/978-3-031-34241-7_18
– Verbruggen, C., Snoeck, M. TEC-MAP: a taxonomy of evaluation criteria and its application to the multi-modelling of data and processes. Softw Syst Model (2024). doi: https://doi.org/10.1007/s10270-024-01198-6

Chapter 8 addresses the evaluation of the prototype presented in Chapter 5.6 from the perspective of the user.

Part II, III and IV can be mapped onto Hevner's Design Science Framework (Figure 1.2).

Part V concludes the dissertation with a chapter on conclusions, lessons learned, limitations and future work.

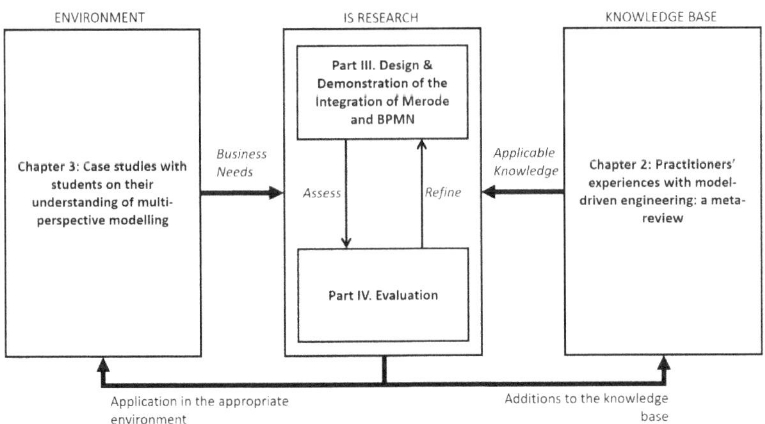

Fig. 1.2 The Design Science Framework, adapted from Hevner [10]

Part II
Researching the Problem's Relevance

This part presents the research done to identify and motivate the relevance of the problem, addressing the first activity in Peffers's design science methodology [9]. At the end of this part, the objectives for a solution are defined, addressing the second activity of Peffers's methodology.

This part consists of two chapters that approach the problem from different sides, as done in Hevner's framework for design science in information systems research [10]. In this framework, information systems research is informed by the knowledge base on the one hand and the environment on the other hand. The knowledge base covers existing research, such as frameworks, models, methods, methodologies etc. The environment covers the people and organizations that experience the problem, as well as their existing technologies. To address the knowledge base, the second chapter presents a systematic literature review compiling an overview of empirical research on the experience of practitioners with model-driven engineering. To address the environment, the third chapter presents two experiments on the capability of students to create a data model and a process model for a combined case description, and their experience during this exercise.

Chapter 2
Practitioners' experiences with model-driven engineering: a meta-review

This chapter was previously published in [11] and [12].

2.1   Introduction

The Model-Driven Architecture was launched in 2001 by the Object Management Group (OMG). Since then, the research community has embraced model-driven engineering (MDE), but to a lesser extent than practitioners had hoped. MDE develops software systems through platform-independent models [1]; platform-specific models and code can then be obtained through transformations. Van der Linden et al. [8] addressed the necessity to "pull" research topics from practitioner demands rather than "pushing" research solutions to the industry. This motivates researchers to conduct practitioner surveys to identify research paths that will solve problems the industry faces. Several surveys of practitioners' problems have been conducted in the past, and as will be obvious from their discussion in this review, their reported results all varied. The differences may be due to the studies focusing on different aspects, having different demographics, being performed at a different time, or analysing the results through a different lens. Badreddin et al. [13], for example, conducted a survey that discussed the evolution of modelling in software design over a decade, whereas Ho-Quang et al. [14] focused on the use of UML in open source projects. These differences will be addressed throughout this review. While this conveniently allows a researcher to cherry-pick a survey that best demonstrates a specific gap, the main drawback is that knowledge about the state of practice remains dispersed. To adequately address practitioners' problems, a good understanding of their problems is required, and it is interesting to know what problems appear consistently across surveys in order to set priorities.

To further set the scope of this study, it intends to focus on the work of business and functional analysts (BFAs) and the modelling languages they use during the requirements engineering (RE) process. This choice is primarily justified by the fact that BFAs serve as a bridge between users and developers and provide the first translation of (informal) requirements into (more formal) models. This bridging role of BFAs is important: stakeholder involvement (e.g., through agile development) is considered a significant success factor for projects [15]. While stakeholder requirements are mostly expressed in textual formats, transforming them into a conceptual model is needed as the first step to MDE. Furthermore, clear conceptual thinking about a system is important for its successful design [16]. In making conceptual models based on requirements, the BFAs

© The Author(s), under exclusive license to Springer Nature Switzerland AG 2026
C. Verbruggen, *Advancing Multi-modelling in MDE for Integrated Domain and Business Process Modelling*, Lecture Notes in Business Information Processing 576,
https://doi.org/10.1007/978-3-032-13876-7_2

thus contribute to the quality of a software project while providing essential input to the model-driven software engineering process.

This study conducts a meta-review to obtain a general overview of the needs of BFAs. Therefore, the research questions will be broad to capture all relevant information from recent research. Since the research questions are very broad, we focus on papers published since 2015, up to 2021. The time limit is chosen for two reasons. First, surveys published in this period span a period of approximately 10 years since the surveys themselves look to the past relative to their year of publication. Second, since the industry is rapidly expanding, and therefore the use of modelling languages may differ drastically now compared to nine or more years ago.

A previous study [11] describes the preliminary findings of this research. To improve the reliability and expand the results, the review query is re-executed to include more recent studies, and a larger set of related studies is reviewed to better position and discuss the findings of the meta-review.

The rest of this chapter is arranged as follows: Section 2.2 discusses the related research; Section 2.3 presents the review methodology; Section 2.4 reports the results of the review; Section 2.5 discusses the findings from the results; Section 2.6 concludes the chapter. The data used for the selection procedure and the data analysis for the meta-review can be accessed online.[1]

2.2 Related Research

Web of Science and Scopus were searched for meta-surveys on MDE, and all editions of the SoSyM Journal were browsed to find existing research related to modelling in practice. This study kept an open mind for this initial investigation and considered papers not specifically focusing on conceptual modelling. Fourteen publications were found that were either a meta-survey on modelling or MDE, studies that focus on the challenges of MDE, or surveys that did not qualify for inclusion as a meta-review source but provided interesting insights. Six of the seven surveys were published before 2015, with one survey focusing on modelling tool adoption.

The related work can be grouped into three categories: surveys on UML, surveys on modelling (not UML), and articles on MDE. These categories will be discussed in Sections 2.2.1, 2.2.2 and 2.2.3, respectively.

2.2.1 Identified Surveys on UML

Four related studies report on a practitioners' survey in their use of UML. Grossman et al. [17] published a survey on how software developers used UML in 2005. Their survey results reveal that the most used UML diagram types are the use case diagram, the class diagram and the sequence diagram. According to the survey, some issues were identified: UML "is too big and complex, it is semantically imprecise, it is implemented in a non-standard manner, it has limited customizability, it has inadequate support for component-based development, and that it is unable to easily interchange model diagrams" [17]. The

---

[1] The data can be accessed on Zenodo: https://doi.org/10.5281/zenodo.6727785

survey also used Fowler's categories [18] to report the different approaches practitioners take while using UML. They discovered that most practitioners use "UML by sketch" rather than "UML by blueprint" or "UML as a programming language." Given that UML 2.0 was published in 2005, the results of this survey apply to UML1.x.

In 2008, Dobing and Parsons [19] published a survey on the practical use of UML diagrams. Their results reveal that the class, use case, and sequence diagrams are the most used diagram types. In their study, participants who used a given diagram were asked to rate on a 5-point scale to what extent they use these diagrams for a given purpose and how useful they believe them to be. UML class diagrams were most frequently used for "clarifying understanding of application among technical members of the project team" (average score of 4.35). They were also frequently used for "specifying system requirements for programmers" and "documenting for future maintenance and other enhancements" (4.06 and 4.18, respectively). However, they were less used for "verifying and validating requirements with client representatives on the project team" (2.90). The results for sequence diagrams are similar to those of class diagrams. They were mostly used for "clarifying understanding of application among technical members of the project team" (4.14). They were also frequently used for "specifying system requirements for programmers" and "documenting for future maintenance and other enhancements" (3.71 and 3.76, respectively). However, they were less used for "verifying and validating requirements with client representatives on the project team" (2.91). Use case diagrams were mostly used for "verifying and validating requirements with client representatives on the project team" (3.36). They were also frequently used for "clarifying understanding of application among technical members of the project team" (4.14) and "specifying system requirements for programmers" (3.06). However, they were less used for "documenting for future maintenance and other enhancements" (2.90). This is reflected in the perceived usefulness of the diagrams, with 93% of participants finding UML class diagrams at least moderately useful for "clarifying understanding of application among technical members of the project team" and 92% of participants finding UML sequence diagrams at least moderately useful for this purpose. In contrast, 74% of participants believed that UML use case diagrams are at least moderately useful for "verifying and validating requirements with client representatives on the project team." One of the main issues reported in this survey is a lack of understanding of the notation by analysts or clients.

Nugroho and Chaudron [20] conducted a survey to determine the influence of UML on productivity and quality. The survey specifically examined the impact of the model's completeness and the level of detail. Regarding the impact of completeness, they concluded that "the respondents indicated that incomplete models, amongst the other given factors, has led them to implementation problems and deviations more frequently" [20]. This is an intriguing finding, given that they also reported that developers discovered a low level of model completeness in their projects. Their results also show that "the majority of the respondents agreed that a model should put more emphasis on parts of a system that are more critical and complex, instead of specifying all parts of a system equally", given that ensuring model completeness increases the required modelling effort.

Petre [21] reported the responses to an earlier survey on the levels of use of UML. In this survey, most participants did not use UML due to lack of context, understanding, synchronization, and consistency. The participants who used UML used it selectively and only as long as it was useful to them. The vast majority of tasks for which UML is considered useful are related to communication with stakeholders: requirements elicitation, negotiation, and communication. Nonetheless, some people use UML throughout the design and development process. They adapt their use of the language to fit their needs. The most common diagram types used by participants were class, activity, and sequence diagrams. Many participants used UML in a multi-modelling setting. They combine different modelling languages to capture all aspects of the system. Finally, some participants noticed a contradiction between the two roles of a modelling notation: abstraction and formalism. The authors got feedback on the survey results after the research was published. The results did not surprise professional developers, but the academic community reacted differently. Some academics that answered the survey questioned the methodology and sample of participants, while others reached similar conclusions based on literature and personal experience [21].

2.2.2 Identified Surveys on Modelling (not UML)

Three related studies report practitioners' surveys on other topics related to modelling. Fettke [22] conducted a survey on the use of conceptual modelling. This survey reported that ER modelling and UML are the most frequently used languages. The results reveal that "database design and management, improvement of internal business processes, and software development are […] the highest prioritized purposes for conceptual modelling." The survey also identified several aspects as success factors or barriers. The four barriers are "plethora of modelling methods," "price [of tools]," "investment risk [related to the market position of the tool vendor]," and "complexity [of the tool]." The survey identified 23 success factors spread over the categories "language," "method," "model," "tool," and "miscellaneous."

Malavolta et al. [23] conducted a survey on architectural languages. They found that 93% of participants use semiformal notations like UML, UML profiles, SysML and Archimate. Out of 48 participants, 25 indicated that they believe the tools lack some features. The most prominent feature was "analysis and simulation support," which was missed by seven participants. Other missing features mentioned by five or more participants are better visualization, usability features, integration with other tools, and multiple viewpoints. Only five participants had used architectural languages in the past and stopped using them. Four of those five participants found the languages were too formal. One of their main findings is that architectural languages should support communication between stakeholders and formal development. The authors called this the extrovert and introvert role of the architect. Other findings are that practitioners "prefer semiformal and generic ALs" that are not too complex and that analysis features and support for multiple views are among the top-required features in the tools.

Whittle et al. [24] surveyed "tool-related issues affecting the adoption of model-driven engineering" by interviewing practitioners. The participants' main problems were "tool immaturity, complexity and lack of usability." The authors concluded that these issues are caused by lack of consideration for the cognitive process of the end-user of the tool. The survey also identified internal support by the company as an important factor in the successful adoption of MDE tools.

2.2.3 Research on MDE

The remaining seven related studies address the broader scope of MDE and the challenges that the community faces. In [25], Bran Selic identified several factors that determine the success of a computer language: the language should be technically sound, expressive, understandable, familiar to its target users, efficient, and well supported. Furthermore, in [26], he highlighted the factors that determine the success of the adoption of model-based methods. Apart from technical factors, he emphasized the importance of the social and economic factors, such as the "technology-centric mindset" that many developers adopt or the resources required to adopt a new methodology.

Zheng and Taylor [27] presented an overview of model-based software development approaches and noted three challenges. The first challenge is multi-aspect modelling, or providing models from different viewpoints to develop a full system specification. The second challenge is code generation, more specifically, ensuring the correctness of the code generation templates. The third challenge is model-code consistency management. The authors identified techniques of MBSE that can help meet these challenges: "exploitation of domain specificity, meta-modelling and iterative transformation."

Giraldo et al. [28] conducted a literature review to investigate "the mismatch between the research field of modelling language quality evaluation and the actual MDE practice in industry." They identified eight challenges that the industry faced, and that the research did not address: "language/model according to MDE (MDE compliance)," "multiple modelling languages," "explicit management of abstraction levels," "metrics over models," "model transformations as a managed process," "semantic in the diagram (diagram as a user-interface)," "agile ontological analysis," and "incorporation of quality in models as technical debt issues in MDE managed process."

Dermeval et al. [29] performed a systematic literature review of the "applications of ontologies in RE," selecting publications from 2007 to 2013, thus addressing a different time frame than this study's aim. Some of their conclusions are that most studies used OWL as an ontology-related language to support RE, and the three main benefits of ontologies in the RE process are that they "reduce ambiguity, inconsistency or/and incompleteness," "aid requirements management," and improve "domain knowledge representation for guiding requirements elicitation."

Bucchiarone et al. [2] identified and classified MDE challenges as foundation (e.g., agile development), domain (e.g., sociotechnical integration and adaptation), tool (e.g., consistency, scalability, and synchronization), community (e.g., teachability and sharing), and social challenges (e.g., co-engineering, and example-based modelling).

Wortmann et al. [30] conducted a systematic mapping study of modelling languages in relation to industry 4.0. They found that the main benefits of modelling languages are reduced time and costs and improved sustainability and international competitiveness.

The challenges addressed by modelling languages in industry 4.0 are "digital representation, integration, and processes." Finally, the modelling languages most often used according to the included publications are variants of UML.

Van der Linden et al. [8] investigated the requirements of conceptual modelling practitioners in their professional work. They found that the primary visual notations used in practice are regulated by standardization bodies. The predominant visual notations used by practitioners (RQ3a) are UML and BPMN, followed by SysML and Archimate, although the latter two are used by less than 20% of the respondents. Furthermore, the authors provided evidence for the Physics of Notation (PoN) framework [31] as a guiding theory for designing visual notations that are well-aligned with practitioners' requirements. They see this as the most important takeaway: "*academic research should stop 'pushing' new notations to industry, because there is little to no data showing they achieve any significant adoption.*"

2.2.4 Summary of the Related Research

In summary, we can draw the following conclusions from the related research. Most surveys focus on UML or identify UML as the most used modelling language. The UML diagram types most often mentioned are the class and sequence diagrams. Several surveys mention that practitioners use modelling languages in an informal or semi-formal way or adapt UML to their needs. An observation mentioned in two different studies [21], [23] is that models have two conflicting roles. On the one hand, they should provide a useful abstraction to facilitate communication between stakeholders with different levels of expertise. On the other hand, they need to be formal enough to contain all the necessary information. Several publications also indicate that modelling languages lack understandability/usability and that the social and cultural environment within an organization can determine the success rate of adopting modelling approaches.

2.3 Methodology

This study adhered to Kitchenham's guidelines for a systematic literature review [32]. First, the research questions are defined, then the search strategy for finding relevant publications is discussed. Sections 2.3.3 and 2.3.4 explain the inclusion and exclusion criteria and the selection procedure, respectively. In the final section, a set of quality criteria is discussed. These quality criteria were not used to select the publications, but to provide insight into the overall quality of the selected publications. Figure 2.1 shows the process of the search and selection procedures.

2.3.1 Defining Research Questions

The first step in conducting a systematic literature review is identifying the research questions. Architecting systems requires dealing with various concerns (also known as viewpoints) and many tasks related to phases of a development lifecycle and goals of the RE process. While this study focuses on modelling as it is used by BFAs, it is still useful

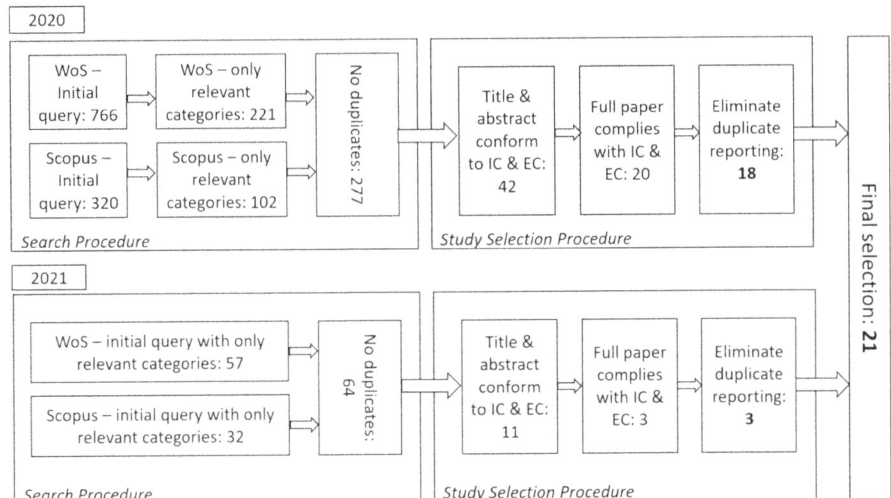

Figure 2.1 Overview of the search and selection procedures (IC = inclusion criteria, EC = exclusion criteria)

to have a broader understanding of what modelling is used for in software development. This raises the following question:

RQ1 - For which aspects (type of activities) of software development do practitioners use modelling languages?

The research by van der Linden et al. [8] reinforces the belief that this study should focus on the use of the standard languages UML and BPMN. As a general-purpose language, UML can be used for a wide range of goals. The use of BPMN is constrained to the domain of business process management. As the popularity of these languages is growing, an interesting question is to what extent other research confirms that these two languages dominate the field. This leads to the second research question:

RQ2 - Which other modelling languages are in use next to BPMN and UML, and how often are they used?

The first two research questions discuss how modelling languages are currently used. The final two research questions identify practitioners' negative and positive experiences with MDE.

RQ3 - Which problems/difficulties/requirements do practitioners experience with MDE?

RQ4 - What are the benefits of MDE according to the practitioners?

2.3.2 Search Strategy for Finding Relevant Papers

Before identifying the search query, a set of five publications were selected as a golden standard. These are surveys that would ideally be included in the meta-review. The goal of this golden standard is to check whether the query finds all these surveys: [8],

[13], [21], [33], [34]. The query was executed on Web of Science & Scopus. These two databases were chosen because they cover a wide selection of publishers, including Springer, Elsevier, IEEE and ACM. The initial query executed on both databases was:

topic = [(conceptual modelling OR UML OR BPMN) AND (practice OR use OR practitioner* OR professional*) AND (review OR survey OR summary OR summarize*)] AND LANGUAGE = English*[2]

Because this study focuses on BFAs, "conceptual modelling" rather than "modelling" is chosen. Moreover, the use of the latter results in an unmanageable number of publications. As the golden standard includes publications with no exclusive focus on conceptual modelling, this ensures that the query is not too narrow.

The query resulted in 766 Web of Science and 320 Scopus publications. The document type was restricted to "review" to filter more thoroughly. This resulted in 66 Web of Science and 92 Scopus publications. There were still many results related to different fields. Therefore, the results were additionally filtered for the categories that seemed irrelevant. Checking the filtering confirmed that only irrelevant publications were excluded through this additional filtering.

The initial query was executed again (end of October 2020), excluding publications with a publication date before 2015 or in the irrelevant categories. This resulted in 221 Web of Science and 102 Scopus publications. This selection included all 4 of the 5 golden standard publications published after 2014. Removing the duplicate publications in both databases led to a final query result of 277 publications for the next step.

In October 2021, the query was executed again to add any relevant publications that were recently published. This time, the publication dates were restricted to 2020 and 2021. This resulted in 57 Web of Science and 32 Scopus publications. The publications with a publication date before September 2020 were excluded for duplicating the initial query's result. After removing the duplicate publications, 64 were left for the next step.

2.3.3 Inclusion and Exclusion Criteria

The inclusion and exclusion criteria determine which publication will be discussed in the review. A publication is included if (1) it is an empirical study with practitioners or a literature review of empirical studies with practitioners, (2) it addresses at least one of the research questions, and (3) its topic is information systems modelling, not statistical or mathematical modelling or simulation. A publication is excluded if (1) it is an empirical study with only students or academics as participants or (2) it is a theoretical study.

2.3.4 Study Selection Procedure

The study selection procedure used in 2020, as reported in the previous study [11], consists of three iterations. In the first iteration, two researchers assessed each publication

---

[2] It should be noted that the search engines of Web of Science and Scopus automatically apply lemmatization rules to search queries, see https://images-webofknowledge-com.webvpn.bjtu. edu.cn/data/images/help/WOK/hs_title.html and https://service.elsevier.com/app/answers/det ail/a_id/15137/supporthub/scopus/. Hence, both "modelling" and "modeling" will be searched for.

against the inclusion and exclusion criteria using the title and abstract. When there was doubt or disagreement, the publications were included in the next iteration. Forty-two publications were selected after this iteration. In the second iteration, one researcher read the full publications and reassessed the inclusion and exclusion criteria. The final decision was taken jointly by the two researchers. This second iteration resulted in a set of 20 publications. In the final iteration, the authors of the publications and data used were analysed, and two more publications were discarded to eliminate duplicate reporting on the same data.

In 2021, one researcher followed the same procedure. Sixty-four publications were evaluated in the first iteration based on their title and abstract, leading to a selection of 14 publications. Three of these publications were discarded since they were already included in the results discussed in [11]. After reading the remaining 11 publications, 3 publications were selected to augment the initial set [35], [36], [37]. One of these three publications [35] repeated the findings of a publication already included in the selection [13]. However, the authors conducted a new survey and compared the findings with their previous findings. This meta-review included only the new findings in its analysis to avoid duplicate reporting.

The final selection of the 21 publications is shown in Table 2.1. Since this meta-review focuses on practitioners' experience, most selected publications were surveys. Table 2.2 summarizes the demographic information of all surveys included in this meta-review. When demographic information was not reported in the survey, the category "unknown" was used to avoid making assumptions about the nationalities of the participants. Publications [48], [49], [50], [51] are not surveys, but they were included because they focus on the perspective of practitioners. Publication [48] analyses modelling tools and how they comply with a set of requirements. Publication [49] is a literature review that focuses on primary studies on business process modelling formalisms. Publication [50] analyses architectural languages and how they comply with a set of requirements, and publication [51] is a literature review of empirical studies on BPMN.

2.3.5 Quality Criteria

The quality criteria were not used for selecting the publications but were useful for indicating their overall quality. For each type of publication, a set of criteria was defined. The quality criteria for systematic literature reviews are (1) the publication has a clear search strategy based on Kitchenham's guidelines [24], and (2) the publication has a clear selection strategy based on Kitchenham's guidelines [32]. The quality criterion for systematic mapping studies is (3) the publication reports the protocol used. Furthermore, surveys should comply with the following criteria: (4) the survey design is reported in the publication, (5) detailed survey results are included in the publication, and (6) the demographics of the survey participants are discussed. Finally, all publications should comply with the following criteria: (7) a discussion of the threats to validity is included. Most publications fulfilled the quality criteria. Two surveys [36], [40] did not fulfil criterion 6. The two literature reviews [49], [51] and one survey [44] did not fulfil criterion 7.

Table 2.1 Overview of selected papers

Nr.	Citation	Ref.
1	M. Ozkaya and F. Erata, "A survey on the practical use of UML for different software architecture viewpoints," Inf Softw Technol, vol. 121, May 2020, doi: https://doi.org/10.1016/j.infsof.2020.106275.	[34]
2	D. van der Linden, I. Hadar, and A. Zamansky, "What practitioners really want: requirements for visual notations in conceptual modeling," Softw Syst Model, vol. 18, no. 3, pp. 1813–1831, Jun. 2019, https://doi.org/10.1007/s10270-018-0667-4.	[8]
3	M. Ozkaya, "Do the informal & formal software modeling notations satisfy practitioners for software architecture modeling?," Inf Softw Technol, vol. 95, pp. 15–33, Mar. 2018, doi: https://doi.org/10.1016/j.infsof.2017.10.008.	[38]
4	G. Liebel, N. Marko, M. Tichy, A. Leitner, and J. Hansson, "Model-based engineering in the embedded systems domain: an industrial survey on the state-of-practice," Softw Syst Model, vol. 17, no. 1, pp. 91–113, Feb. 2018, doi: https://doi.org/10.1007/s10270-016-0523-3.	[39]
5	O. Badreddin, R. Khandoker, A. Forward, O. Masmali, and T. C. Lethbridge, "A decade of software design and modeling: A survey to uncover trends of the practice," in Proceedings - 21st ACM/IEEE International Conference on Model Driven Engineering Languages and Systems, MODELS 2018, Association for Computing Machinery, Inc, Oct. 2018, pp. 245–256. doi: https://doi.org/10.1145/3239372.3239389.	[13]
6	T. Ho-Quang, R. Hebig, G. Robles, M. R. V. Chaudron, and M. A. Fernandez, "Practices and perceptions of UML use in open source projects," in Proceedings - 2017 IEEE/ACM 39th International Conference on Software Engineering: Software Engineering in Practice Track, ICSE-SEIP 2017, Institute of Electrical and Electronics Engineers Inc., Jun. 2017, pp. 203–212. doi: https://doi.org/10.1109/ICSE-SEIP.2017.28.	[14]
7	M. Ozkaya, "What is software architecture to practitioners: A survey," in MODELSWARD 2016 - Proceedings of the 4th International Conference on Model-Driven Engineering and Software Development, SciTePress, 2016, pp. 677–686. doi: https://doi.org/10.5220/0005826006770686.	[40]
8	F. Saleh and M. El-Attar, "A scientific evaluation of the misuse case diagrams visual syntax," Inf Softw Technol, vol. 66, pp. 73–96, Oct. 2015, doi: https://doi.org/10.1016/j.infsof.2015.05.002.	[41]
9	T. Huldt and I. Stenius, "State-of-practice survey of model-based systems engineering," Systems Engineering, vol. 22, no. 2, pp. 134–145, Mar. 2019, doi: https://doi.org/10.1002/sys.21466.	[42]
10	D. Akdur, V. Garousi, and O. Demirörs, "A survey on modeling and model-driven engineering practices in the embedded software industry," Journal of Systems Architecture, vol. 91, pp. 62–82, Nov. 2018, doi: https://doi.org/10.1016/j.sysarc.2018.09.007.	[43]

(continued)

Table 2.1 (*continued*)

Nr.	Citation	Ref.
11	K. Farias, L. Gonçales, V. Bischoff, B. Da Silval, E. Guimarães, and J. Nogle, "On the UML use in the brazilian industry: A state of the practice survey," in Proceedings of the International Conference on Software Engineering and Knowledge Engineering, SEKE, Knowledge Systems Institute Graduate School, 2018, pp. 372–375. doi: https://doi.org/10.18293/SEKE2018-183.	[44]
12	H. Störrle, "How are conceptual models used in industrial software development? A descriptive survey," in ACM International Conference Proceeding Series, Association for Computing Machinery, Jun. 2017, pp. 160–169. doi: https://doi.org/10.1145/3084226.3084256.	[45]
13	A. M. Fernández-Sáez, D. Caivano, M. Genero, and M. R. V. Chaudron, "On the Use of UML Documentation in Software Maintenance: Results from a Survey in Industry," in MODELS, Ottawa, ON, Canada, 2015, pp. 292–301.	[46]
14	C. Monsalve, A. April, and A. Abran, "Business Process Modeling with Levels of Abstraction," in IEEE COLCOM, 2015.	[47]
15	O. Badreddin, K. Rahad, A. Forward, and T. Lethbridge, "The Evolution of Software Design Practices Over a Decade: A Long Term Study of Practitioners," Journal of Object Technology, vol. 20, no. 2, pp. 1:1-19, 2021, doi: https://doi.org/10.5381/jot.2021.20.2.a1.	[35]
16	I. Routis, C. Bardaki, G. Dede, M. Nikolaidou, T. Kamalakis, and D. Anagnostopoulos, "CMMN evaluation: the modelers' perceptions of the main notation elements," Softw Syst Model, 2021, doi: https://doi.org/10.1007/s10 270-021-00880-3.	[36]
17	A. Albaghajati and J. Hassine, "A use case driven approach to game modeling," Requir Eng, 2021, doi:https://doi.org/10.1007/s00766-021-00362-4.	[37]
18	M. Ozkaya, "Are the UML modelling tools powerful enough for practitioners? A literature review," Oct. 01, 2019, Institution of Engineering and Technology. doi: https://doi.org/10.1049/iet-sen.2018.5409.	[48]
19	A. Awadid, S. Nurcan, and S. Ayachi Ghannouchi, "On leveraging the fruits of research efforts in the arena of business process modeling formalisms: a map-driven approach for decision making," Softw Syst Model, vol. 18, no. 3, pp. 1905–1930, Jun. 2019, doi: https://doi.org/10.1007/s10270-018-0689-y.	[49]
20	M. Ozkaya, "The analysis of architectural languages for the needs of practitioners," Softw Pract Exp, vol. 48, no. 5, pp. 985–1018, May 2018, doi: https://doi.org/10.1002/spe.2561.	[50]
21	M. Kocbek, G. Jošt, M. Heričko, and G. Polančič, "Business process model and notation: The current state of affairs," Computer Science and Information Systems, vol. 12, no. 2, pp. 509–539, Jul. 2015, doi: https://doi.org/10.2298/CSIS140610006K	[51]

Table 2.2 summary of demographic information of the surveys

Paper	Year of survey	Nr of responden	Europe	Americas	Asia/ Pacific	Middle East	Africa	Largest group reported
1	March '18–June '18	109	34 countries; USA is the top-popular country, followed by India, France, UK, and Turkey.					USA
2	Oct '16–March '17	108	33%	20%	8%	5%	2%	
3	June–Dec 2016	115	28 countries					
4	Oct 2013	113	unknown					
5	unknown	228	10,3%	70,5%	19,2%			USA/Canada 70%
6	July 2016	485	91 countries.					
7	unknown	50	unknown					
8	unknown	52	5,8%	15,40%	55,80%	0%	23,1%	Asia/Pacific 55.80%
9	Jan 2016 to June 2016.	66	Worldwide					USA 37% Unknown 39%
10	Apr–May 2015	627	66%	14%	19%		1%	Europe 66%
11	unknown	222		Brazil				
12	Sept 2014–April 2016	96	67%	8%	4%			Germany 40%
13	Feb–April 2013	178	86,5%	8,90%	3,40%	0,60%	0,60%	Europe 86,5% (Italy 61,8%)
14	Unknown	17	unknown					
15	Nov 2018	10	EU and USA					
16	Unknown	24	Unknown					
17	Apr 2019	29	Unknown					

2.4 Results

The selected publications used various data collection methodologies. Therefore, summarizing the data is challenging. The publications are discussed in separate groups depending on how the results were reported to make meaningful data summaries for each research question.

2.4.1 RQ1 - For which aspects (type of activities) of software development do practitioners use modelling languages?

Participants in two surveys [13], [45] were asked to respond using a 5-point Likert scale. To combine the results of these publications with the results of the other surveys that do not use a Likert scale, the 5-point Likert scale data needed to be transformed into binary data. In this meta-review, the general approach is to identify the survey questions that correspond to the research question and sum the percentages for the points of the Likert scale that indicate an agreement. For example, in Störrle's [45] survey, a Likert scale was used to determine how often participants used models for a set of specified software development activities (never & rarely–sometimes–often & always). Here, only one column indicated agreement with the suggested activities (often & always). Regarding the activity "discuss with colleagues," 79% of participants indicated "often & always" and considered this an activity for which they use models. These percentages can now be compared to the results of surveys that did not use Likert scale data ([8], [14], [34], [39], [43], [50], [51]).

The surveys that address the first research question base their survey questions on various frameworks. The first framework is the software architecture viewpoints of Rozanski & Woods [52]: the context, functional, information, concurrency, development, deployment, and operational viewpoints. According to Ozkaya et al. [34], the information and functional viewpoints are modelled by the highest number of participants (99% and 96%, respectively). Many participants also modelled the deployment, concurrency, and development viewpoints (75%, 66%, and 64%, respectively). The operational viewpoint was modelled by only 29% of the participants. In a different study, Ozkaya [50] presented an evaluation of 113 architectural languages. Their findings reveal that most architectural languages support the logical and information viewpoints (91% and 78%, respectively). The concurrency viewpoint is supported by 45% of the languages, but the development, deployment, and operational viewpoints are supported by relatively few architectural languages (26%, 15%, and 10%, respectively). The behavioural and physical viewpoints, which were supported by 46% and 15% of the architectural languages, were also discussed in their study. According to Ozkaya's 2018 survey [50], the viewpoints supported by the largest number of languages are also the viewpoints most often modelled by practitioners according to the 2020 survey [34].

Two studies designed their survey according to phases in the development lifecycle. While they did not directly refer to the Rational Unified Process (RUP) framework, this framework was used in this meta-review to unify the results of the two studies because it matches the phases used by the authors. The RUP framework [53] includes six engineering disciplines (business modelling, requirements engineering (RE), analysis and design, implementation, testing, and deployment) and three supporting disciplines (configuration and change management, project management, and environment). Ho-Quang et al. [14] conducted a survey of open source software developers. In 68% of the projects that use UML for design, the UML models were implemented completely or with minor changes. Akdur et al. [43] conducted a survey in the embedded systems industry. Their findings reveal that modelling was most often used in analysis and design (89.5%), implementation (74.4%), and RE (64.1%) disciplines.

Finally, some surveys asked questions that were not based on a framework. To be able to compare the answers from this group, the topics from surveys [13], [14], [39], [43], [45] were grouped according to the three core activities of the RE framework [54], as shown in Table 2.3, where the topics with high ($\geq$70%), medium (<70% and $\geq$40%) and low (<40%) frequencies of use are listed separately. RE is mainly conducted at the start of a development project but continues to be relevant throughout the development cycle [54]: it is the process of consolidating a set of different, informal, biased, and opaque inputs into a complete specification of the system that is represented in a formal model and that all stakeholders agree on [55]. To achieve this, the three types of activities indicated by the RE framework are required. Elicitation leads to a complete specification; documentation leads to a formal representation; negotiation leads to stakeholder agreement. Liebel et al. [39], [43] and Akdur et al. [43] focused on software engineering for embedded systems and reported that the main purposes are code generation and documentation. The activities for which more than 70% of participants indicated that models are frequently used led to the conclusion that the main purposes are documentation and elicitation of requirements, with use for negotiation occurring to a lesser extent. The van der Linden et al. survey [8] is discussed separately since it is the only survey in which participants chose, on average, only one purpose for their models. Therefore, the percentages reported in this publication [8] cannot be compared to the other surveys. Van der Linden et al. [8] coded the activities into six purposes. The first five were mapped in this meta-review onto the core activities of the RE framework. The sixth coded purpose was "Requirements Engineering" in general. Similar to the other surveys, most participants chose an elicitation activity: 42.6% of the participants selected an elicitation activity, 28.7% of participants selected a documentation activity, 26.9% selected a negotiation activity, and 11.1% of participants selected an activity that the authors classified under the general category "Requirements Engineering".

Kocbek et al. [51] conducted a systematic literature review of BPMN and concluded that documentation is the main activity for which BPMN is used.

A final observation is that the purposes that fall outside the three core activities of the RE framework score low (code generation, creating a domain-specific language (DSL), prototyping design, reconstructing knowledge from source code...).

2.4.2   RQ2 - Which other modelling languages are in use next to BPMN and UML, and how often are they used?

For this research question, only general publications were considered, which do not focus on a specific language: surveys [8], [13], [38], [39], [40], [43], [45]. In 6 of the 7 publications, UML was reported as the most used modelling language, with at least 41.6% of the survey participants using it. The study by Badreddin et al. [13] showed slightly different results. Here ERD was the most popular modelling language, with 40% of participants using it very often, followed by structured design models used very often by 38%. The use of UML was split into three categories in this survey. 34% of the participants used UML 2.* very often, 33% used any version of UML very often, and 27% used UML 1.* very often. The survey by Badreddin et al. [13] was the only study with American authors, and it reported that 70% of the participants were either from the USA or Canada, as shown in Table 2.2.

In surveys [34], [38], [43], [46], participants were also asked about the UML diagram types they use the most. Across all studies alike, class diagrams were among the top two most used diagram types.

According to studies [13], [38], [39], [43], [45] the secondary group of languages are DSLs. The percentage of use varied from 8% [39] to 36% [38].

BPMN is highlighted in two studies that reported contradicting results. Van der Linden et al. [8] reported that 34.6% of the 108 participants used BPMN, and Störrle [45] reported that only 12 of the 96 participants (12.5%) used BPMN. A notable difference is that Störrle [45] reported that 40% of the respondents are from Germany, while the population surveyed by van der Linden et al. [8] is more diverse. This could partially explain the differences since BPMN is discussed more in European research than in North American research [56]. Another difference is that Störrle [45] specifically targeted industrial software development. In five surveys [8], [38], [39], [43], [45], 5% to 21.2% of the participants used SysML and in two surveys [38], [43], 16.9% to 19% of the participants used UML profiles.

Table 2.3 Software development activities grouped by the core activities of the RE framework

RE activity	paper	What are models used for?	fraction using models frequently for this activity
		HIGH frequency of use	
negotiation	[45]	discuss with colleagues	0,790
documentation	[43]	documentation generation	0,768
	[45]	visualize an idea or concept	0,750
	[14]	documentation (e.g., reverse engineered)	0,712
elicitation	[14]	design/architecture for (existing/new) systems parts	0,705
	[45]	help me think, sketch a thought	0,700
	[43]	understanding a problem	0,670
-	[43]	code generation	0,762
	[39]	simulation	0,681
	[39]	code generation	0,664
		MEDIUM frequency of use	
negotiation	[45]	communicate with clients	0,440
	[43]	communication	0,405
documentation	[43]	documenting designs	0,578
	[39]	information/documentation	0,531
	[13]	transcribing a design into digital format	0,517
	[45]	document a system or code	0,450
elicitation	[45]	capture domain knowledge	0,570
	[13]	developing a design	0,551
	[45]	design systems or code	0,550
	[45]	capture technical requirements	0,430
	[45]	capture client requirements	0,470
	[13]	brainstorming possible designs	0,448

(continued)

2.4.3 RQ3 - Which problems/difficulties/requirements do practitioners have with MDE?

Of the 21 selected publications, 15 discussed practitioners' problems/difficulties/requirements. Eleven of these are surveys that asked about the requirements practitioners have for modelling languages, shortcomings in MDE, disadvantages of modelling languages, and tools and inhibitors for successful adoption of MDE. Six surveys [8], [13], [39], [42], [43], [44] asked their participants to answer using a 5-point Likert scale. The approach described in RQ1 was applied to merge their results. For example,[39] regarding the problem of "difficulties with model-level debugging," Akdur et al. [43] reported that 6% of participants indicated "strongly agree" and 68% of the participants indicated "agree." Therefore, this is summarized as 74% of participants considering "difficulties with model-level debugging" a problem of MDE environments or tools.

Table 2.3 (*continued*)

LOW frequency of use			
negotiation	[45]	negotiate consensus	0,260
	[45]	define contract (model is part of contract)	0,180
documentation	[45]	reconstruct knowledge from source code etc.	0,200
-	[39]	test case generation	0,398
	[43]	test-case generation	0,384
	[39]	structural consistency checks	0,381
	[43]	model-to-model (M2M) transformation	0,373
	[45]	generate prototype code	0,350
	[13]	generating code (code editable)	0,344
	[39]	traceability	0,336
	[39]	behavioural consistency checks	0,336
	[13]	prototyping a design	0,322
	[13]	generating all code	0,310
	[39]	timing analysis	0,283
	[45]	generate production code	0,280
	[45]	create a DSL	0,260
	[39]	safety compliance checks	0,230
	[39]	formal verification	0,221
	[45]	look up product details	0,200
	[14]	verification	0,178
	[43]	model simulation	0,151
	[39]	reliability analysis	0,142
	[14]	refactoring	0,141
	[14]	code generation	0,129
	[14]	models are test data	0,060

These percentages can now be compared to the results of the surveys that did not use
Likert scale data ([35], [38], [40], [41], [47]). For these eleven surveys, the problems
identified by more than 60% of the participants were consolidated. The next step is to
code the different responses to summarize them (see Table 2.4). Van der Linden et al.
[8] performed a survey to determine what practitioners found important in a visual notation for conceptual modelling. They interviewed their participants about the importance
of the principles from PoN when modelling with modelling experts and non-experts.
Overall, more than 60% of participants agreed that all principles are important, except
for cognitive fit when modelling with experts. Only 50% of the participants found it
important. Perceptual discriminability and dual coding are considered among the most
important principles for modelling in general. Semiotic clarity and complexity management are the other important principles for modelling with experts. When modelling
with non-experts, graphic economy and semantic transparency are more important.

Badreddin et al. [13] conducted a survey on trends in the field of software design
and modelling. This survey was first conducted in 2007 and updated in 2017. One of
the questions in their survey asked whether the participants considered a given issue a
"slight problem" or a "bad problem." It can be assumed that participants were asked to

leave the question blank if they did not consider the proposed issue a problem. Almost every proposed issue was considered at least a slight problem by 60% of the participants ("models become out of date and inconsistent with code," "modelling tools are 'heavyweight' (install, learn, configure, use)," "code generated from modelling tool not to the kind I would like," "cannot model in enough detail - must write code," "creating and editing model is slow," "modelling tools change, models become obsolete," "modelling tools lack features I need or want," "modelling tools hide too many detail (fully visible in source)," "modelling tools cannot be analysed as intended," "semantics of models different from prog. Languages", "modelling languages are not expressive enough," "modelling languages are hard to understand" and "have had bad experience with modelling"). Notably, none of these issues were considered a "bad problem" by more than 40% of the participants.

The Badreddin et al. [35] study is an extension of Badreddin et al. [13], where the same participants were asked to fill in a post-survey questionnaire. Additional issues identified by more than 60% of the participants in this study are concerns about the continuity of support for the modelling tools and programming languages that the participants use.

Ozkaya [38] conducted a survey on practitioners' satisfaction with formal and informal modelling languages. One of their questions was about practitioners' concerns regarding formal modelling languages. A large group of participants (30%) indicated that they did not have any concerns. The concerns that were selected most frequently were "high learning curve" (47%), "nobody knows formal specification languages" (37%), and "not popular in industry" (37%). However, since none of the concerns were selected by more than 60% of the participants, the concerns from this study were excluded from the meta-review analysis.

Liebel et al. [39] conducted a survey with professionals in the embedded systems domain on model-based engineering. More than 60% of the participants found the following aspects to be the shortcomings of MBE: "difficulties with interfaces to interoperate with other tools," "difficulties with variability management support," "many usability issues with the tools," "benefits require high efforts," "high effort for training of developers," "difficulties of syntactic integration with other tools," "difficulties with version management support," "difficulties of semantic interoperability with other tools," "difficulties of integration with legacy code," "difficulties for distributed development," "difficulties with integration into development process," and "high overhead involved."

Ozkaya [40] conducted a survey on software architectures with practitioners from industry and academia. When asked what the disadvantages and missing features of software architecture modelling languages and tools are, more than 60% answered "lack of support for analysis." Other answers included "difficult to use and learn" (45%) and "lack of support for automatic code generation" (45%).

Saleh et al. [41] developed a new notation for misuse case diagrams, complying with the principles of PoN [31]. Then, they conducted a survey that investigated the participants' preference for the old and new notations. Most participants preferred the new notation, concluding that practitioners require compliance with the PoN framework to improve the understandability of misuse case diagrams.

Huldt et al. [42] conducted a survey that investigated the state of practice of model-based systems engineering. One of their questions measured to what extent participants believe a given factor is an inhibitor for adopting MBSE. The factors that are believed to be at least somewhat an inhibitor by more than 60% of the participants were "cultural and general lack of perceived value of MBSE," "availability of skills," "lack of management support," "MBSE learning curve," "method maturity," "MBSE training," and "risk associated with the adoption of MBSE."

Akdur et al. [43] conducted a survey on the practice of modelling and MDE in the embedded software industry. At least 60% of the participants agreed that problems with MDE platforms and tools include "difficulties with model-level debugging," "many usability issues in [the tool's] editor," "lack of model checking capabilities," and "difficulties in taking technical support from the tool supplier." Another question measured the level of agreement with several positive and negative statements regarding model-driven code generation, model-based/driven testing, and complexity. The only statement for which more than 60% of participants indicated a potential issue is "for the user of MDE tool, the goal should be 'visualization of models' without concerning about the strict/formal notations of modelling languages." This issue may be related to the cognitive fit principle in PoN [31].

Farias et al. [44] conducted a survey on the use of UML in the Brazilian industry. They suggested four possible improvements to UML tools: "collaborative modelling tool," "function-oriented diagrams," "big picture," and "round-trip engineering." More than 60% of the participants at least partially agreed that these factors would improve the UML modelling tools.

Monsalve et al. [47] conducted a survey with experienced practitioners on the use of business process models with levels of abstraction. They developed five propositions, of which the survey data statistically support three. These three propositions are included in this meta-review analysis: "A business process model at the strategic level of abstraction eases the communication to customers, non-IT employees, and new employees involved in the business processes represented," "Qualigram notation is preferred over BPMN notation by practitioners to model business processes when the target user is a customer, a non-IT employee, a new employee or a management-oriented stakeholder," and "modelling business processes at the strategic, tactical and operational levels of abstraction contributes to generating consistent business process models that can be shared by the various groups of stakeholders."

To summarize the findings of these surveys, each identified problem was placed into one of the following categories: "missing tool functionalities," "high effort in using tool," "high effort in acquiring MBSE skills," "continuity of technology," "lack of method maturity," "modelling practices and tools come with a high cost," "previous negative experiences with modelling can inhibit the adoption," and "the organization's culture inhibits the adoption of modelling practices." The category "visual notations should follow the principles of PoN" was added to reflect that many practitioners list this as a requirement (Table 2.4). The categories that were most often mentioned (and by the largest number of papers) are "missing tool functionalities" and "visual notations should follow the principles of PoN." In the studies that mentioned missing tool functionalities, the type of features that participants miss are often mentioned. The types of features mentioned in the two different studies are "automated quality analysis," "collaboration," "overview," and "integration with other tools and applications." The other types of missing features encountered were mentioned only in one study ("code generation," "customer support," "function-oriented diagrams," "round-trip engineering," "synchronization between model and code," and "versioning support").

Finally, four papers addressing this research question didn't include a survey [48], [49], [50], [51]. Ozkaya [30] provided a list of requirements for tools that practitioners find important and evaluated a set of tools against these requirements. The requirements used in this study were inspired by Lago's framework [57], which is based on practitioners' opinions. Awadid et al. [49] performed a systematic literature review that listed quality criteria used in primary studies and their frequency of appearance. The most discussed quality criterion was expressiveness, a principle of the PoN framework. Ozkaya [50] listed the requirements for architectural languages based on the framework developed by Lago [57] and evaluated a set of architectural languages against these requirements. Kocbek [51] performed a systematic literature review on BPMN that reported two common disadvantages of BPMN: "less than 20% of the BPMN vocabulary is common used" and "utilization in specific domain can be difficult."

Table 2.4 Results of RQ3

Papers	Categories	Number of issues mentioned	Number of papers
[35]	continuity of technology	2	1
[13], [39], [42]	high effort in acquiring MBSE skills	5	3
[13], [39], [43]	high effort in using tool	5	3
[42]	lack of method maturity	1	1
[13], [39], [40], [43], [44]	missing tool functionalities	24	5
[39]	modelling (tools) comes with a high cost	1	1
[13]	negative previous experiences with modelling can inhibit adoption	1	1
[42]	the organization's culture inhibits the adoption of modelling practices	4	1
[8], [13], [41], [43], [47]	visual notations should follow the principles of PoN	23	5

2.4.4   RQ4 - What are the benefits of MDE according to the practitioners?

Nine of the 21 selected publications discussed this topic, out of which 8 are surveys: [13], [14], [38], [39], [40], [42], [43], [45]. Again, the data collection approaches are quite varied. The benefits confirmed by at least 60% of the participants were selected from each survey. The same approach was used for surveys using a Likert scale as in RQ3. Table 2.5 shows the results of this research question.

Table 2.5 Results for RQ4

Papers	Categories	Number of issues mentioned	Number of papers
[14], [36], [38], [45]	modelling is useful and beneficial for several stakeholders	9	4
[39], [43]	cost savings	2	2
[36], [38]	modelling is easy to use	2	2
[13], [37], [39], [42], [43], [45]	improved productivity	26	6
[13], [39], [42], [43], [45]	improved quality	15	5
[13], [14], [37], [38], [42]	improved understanding of the system	13	5
[13], [14], [39], [43]	provides support for software development activities	13	4

Badreddin et al. [13] questioned what modelling tools are good for. More than 60% of the 2017 participants indicated that modelling tools are good for "transcribing a design into digital format," "generating code (code is editable)," "prototyping a design," and "brainstorming possible designs." Although this is not included in Table 2.5 because less than 60% of the participants agreed, it is still interesting to note that the percentage of participants who believe that modelling tools are good for "generating all code (no manual coding)" has increased from 8.7% in 2007 to 42.9% in 2017. Another aspect that Badreddin et al. [3] investigated was which tasks were better performed in a model-centric and code-centric approach. Most participants in 2017 preferred a model-centric approach for "creating a prototype," "creating a usable system for end users," "modifying a system when requirements change," "creating a system that most accurately meets requirements," "creating a re-usable system," "creating a new system overall," "comprehending a system's behaviour," and "explaining a system to others." All activities were included in the meta-review analysis for which a larger group of participants explicitly preferred a model-centric approach to a code-centric one. Especially for the last three activities ("creating a new system overall," "comprehending a system's behaviour," and "explaining a system to others"), most participants ($>60\%$) preferred a model-centric approach.

According to Ho-Quang et al. [14], the subgroup of participants who are non-UML contributors agreed that they find UML diagrams helpful for understanding the system and communicating with other contributors. Most participants ($>60\%$) agreed that UML models are helpful for a new contributor when joining a project, mostly for comprehension and implementation. They also found that most participants believed that the use of UML diagrams has an overall positive impact on their open source projects.

Ozkaya [38] measured how satisfied the practitioners were with formal and informal modelling languages. According to the participants, the three main benefits of informal modelling languages were "easy to learn and use," "general-purpose scope," and "visual."

Liebel et al. [39] reported that the majority (60% or more) of their participants agreed that the reasons for introducing MBSE were "the need to improve reusability," "the need for shorter development time," "the need for quality improvements," "the need to improve maintainability," "the need to improve reliability," "the need for cost savings," "the need for traceability," "the need to improve safety," "the need to improve integrity," and "the need for formal methods."

Ozkaya [40] asked their participants which software architecture languages and tools they used and what their advantages were. The benefits mentioned were "easy to learn and use" (57%), "visual notations" (28%), "automatic analysis for quality properties, such as reliability and performance" (28%), "automatic analysis for design errors" (22%), and "automatic implementation code generation" (20%). Since none of the benefits mentioned attained the threshold of 60%, they were excluded from the analysis.

Huldt et al. [42] found that, according to their participants, following a model-based systems approach increases the quality of "architecting and design," "requirement analysis," "architectural view," and "traceability between systems requirements and the realization." Most participants also agreed that the MBSE approach increases the efficiency of performing "architecting and design," "requirements analysis," and "traceability between systems requirements and the realization."

Akdur et al. [43] reported that the benefits of MDE identified by most of their participants are "cost savings," "shorter development time," "test effectiveness," "productivity," "ensuring source code and design compatibility," "reliability," "quality improvement," "reusability," "maintainability," "traceability," and "portability". Most of their participants also agreed with the following statements: "[when using model-driven code generation,] the developer does not worry about implementation details with the appropriate level of abstraction," "[about model-driven code generation:] if code generation is synchronized with other artefacts (i.e., document and test driver), MDE benefits are maximized," "[about model-based/driven testing:] it makes it easier to develop and execute test cases," "[about model-based/driven testing:] it supports test automation by generating test scripts," "[about model-based/driven testing:] it helps to start test and its design earlier" and "[about complexity:] modelling reduces the design complexities."

Störrle [45] conducted a survey on the use of conceptual models in industry. Most participants believed that modelling benefits the following groups: software architects, developers and testers, domain experts, and requirement analysts. Most participants also agreed with the following statements: "modelling helps me deliver software with higher quality", "modelling was important when it was applied," "modelling should be used in more projects," "modelling helps me deliver software with less effort," "modelling helps me deliver software faster," and "modelling helps me react faster to client or market demands or changed requirements."

To summarize the findings of these surveys, each identified benefit was placed into one of the following categories: "modelling is useful and beneficial for several stake-holders," "cost savings," "(some) modelling languages are easy to use," "improved productivity," "improved quality," "improved understanding of the system," and "provides support for software development activities" (Table 2.5). The categories most often mentioned (and by the largest number of studies) are "improved productivity," "improved quality," and "improved understanding of the system."

Kocbek et al. [51] is the only study without a survey. This study identified the following benefits of BPMN: "[BPMN] enables transformations," "[BPMN has the] ability to define real world domains," "[BPMN has a] good composition of notation," "[BPMN is] easy to understand," "[BPMN is] used in combination with other technologies," and "[BPMN is] used by academics and business personnel."

2.5 Discussion

Generally, there is a lack of unified terminology used in the publications to describe the issues practitioners face when using modelling languages. Many publications also do not provide enough details about the demographics of the survey's sample or do not provide the details about the questionnaire used. These elements make it hard to compare and summarize the results across different surveys.

For RQ1, we noticed that the modelling purpose "documentation (e.g., reverse engineered)" scored high in the work of Ho-Quang et al. [14], but the similar purpose "reconstruct knowledge from source code, etc." in Störrle's work [45] scored low. This could be due to differences in the populations of the surveys. The survey by Ho-Quang et al. [14] has 485 respondents across 91 different countries, while Störrle's survey [45] has 96 participants, of which 40% are from Germany. Similarly, for RQ2, the reported results in the studies varied. Also, these differences in results could be due to differences in the population or a different focus/domain of expertise of the respondents.

When contrasting the results of RQ1 and RQ4, we see that in RQ1, it can be concluded that modelling is mostly used for the "analysis and design," "implementation," and "RE" disciplines of the RUP framework [53]. The main benefits in RQ4 are "improved productivity," "improved quality," and "improved understanding of the system." Although these benefits are mostly related to the creation of a new system (RE, analysis and design, and implementation), they also contribute to maintaining the developed software and adapting it to new or changing requirements [13], [39], [43], [45].

When contrasting the results of RQ1 and RQ3, the results for RQ1 reveal that besides the information and functional viewpoint, modelling is frequently used for the other viewpoints as well, and—considering the lifecycle phases—not only for the early phases of analysis & design and RE but also for implementation. These phases, especially the implementation phase, require satisfactory tool support. This explains why missing tool functionalities are such an important category in RQ3. Given the high frequency of goals in the range of communication, it is not surprising that compliance with the principles of PoN is often mentioned as a requirement for visual notations.

Figure 2.2 shows a mapping between the categories of issues and benefits identified in the results of RQ3 and RQ4, respectively. The benefits are pictured on the left in oval shapes, while the problems are pictured on the right in square shapes. The issue of "visual notations should follow the principles of PoN" is a strong recommendation for improvement rather than a problem. Therefore, we included it as a parallelogram in the figure. The colours indicate the number of times benefits/problems have been mentioned: darker green/red when mentioned often, lighter green/red when less often mentioned, and blue/orange when mentioned just once. Due to the different levels of granularity in the studies, we realize that the categories that we created are related. For example, it can be assumed that the benefits in the category "provides support for software development activities" result in increased productivity. On the side of the problem categories, missing tool functionalities will increase the effort required to use the tool. To visualize the relations between the categories in Figure 2.2, we included 'impacts' arrows showing how one category is likely impacted by other categories.

When contrasting the results of RQ3 and RQ4, we see that while "improved under-standing of the system" is one of the main benefits of modelling according to the results of RQ4, RQ3 indicates that there are still many practitioners that believe that understand-ability of modelling notations can be improved by complying better with the principles of the PoN framework. Two other contradictions between the results of RQ3 and RQ4 can be deduced. The first is between the benefit of "cost savings" versus the problem of "modelling practices and tools come with a high cost," and the second is between the benefit of "increased productivity" and the problems of "high effort in acquiring MBSE skills" and "high effort in using tool." These contradictions are visualized with a bold red line between the categories. These contradictions could be due to the varying levels of experience and fields of expertise of the survey participants. Therefore, it is important to keep improving the understandability of modelling languages to account for users' diversity.

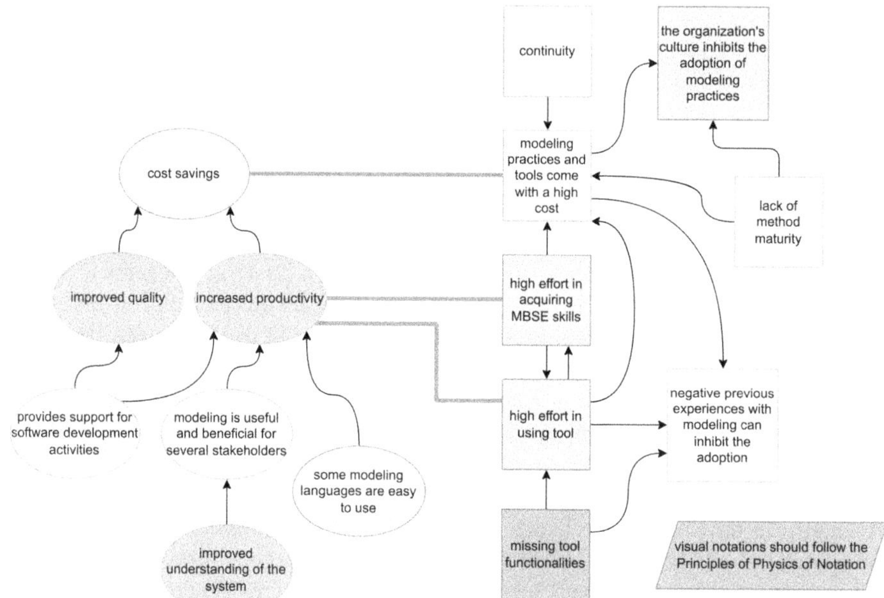

Figure 2.2 Mapping of benefits (left) and problems (right). More frequent benefits/problems are colored darker, arrows show how one benefit/problem likely impacts another, and the red lines indicate contradictions

Due to the diversity in scope, perspective, and reporting in the studies selected for this review, it is impossible to draw conclusions about the evolution of MDE in the last five years. However, the three most recent surveys added in the latest round of publication search do not contain any conclusions contradicting the initial findings reported in [11]: they confirm the results of RQ3 and RQ4.

2.5.1 Related Research versus Results

We can contrast the conclusions from the related research with the results from this meta-review. According to the related research, modelling languages are mostly informal or semi-formal (e.g., communication with stakeholders or brainstorming with colleagues). The results of RQ1 confirm this; however, documentation is also a frequent purpose of modelling languages according to the results of RQ1.

The related research contains many surveys that specifically focus on UML. The results of RQ2 confirm that UML is the most used modelling language. According to the related research, the most used UML diagram types are the class and sequence diagrams. The popularity of class diagrams is confirmed in the results of RQ2.

The first practitioners' challenge that is most often mentioned in the related research is balancing the two contrasting purposes of models: detailed and formal versus abstraction for human understanding and communication. This challenge is reflected in the results of RQ3, where we see problems related to the need for formal models as well as knowledge representation problems (focus on human understanding). The two most prominent issues according to RQ3 are missing tool functionalities and compliance with the principles of PoN. Many requested tool functionalities require formal models (e.g., automatic quality analysis, code generation, and integration with other tools). On the other hand, compliance with the principles of PoN is a knowledge representation issue. Finding a way to embed sufficient formal information in the models for efficient MDE will typically lead to more complex models that are more difficult to learn. This will likely hamper modelling language adoption. Finding a way to reconcile the need for formality and sufficient levels of details with the principles of PoN a necessary step to increase the adoption of MDE and modelling practices in general. The second challenge most often mentioned in the related research is having organizational support for adopting modelling practices. It is mentioned only by Huldt & Stenius [42].

The benefits of conceptual modelling found in RQ4 are reflected in the main benefits of ontologies listed in the work of Dermeval et al. [29], which are improvements in quality and requirements management.

2.5.2 Addressing the challenges

Providing a full analysis of possible solutions to the problems presented in Section 2.4.3 is out of the scope of this review. However, in the following, an illustrative selection of publications that address the issues mentioned by more than one publication is provided (see Table 2.4). This selection should not be regarded as a complete overview.

Tool integration is mentioned as a missing tool functionality in two different studies. This issue depends on the tools that an organization uses. Often, a customized approach is required for a given organization. Therefore, not much general research can be found about this issue. However, one of the surveys included in this review provides an overview of the UML tools and their features [48].

Regarding the issue of high effort in using tools, Naranjo et al. [58] conducted a study on enterprise architecture modelling tools and how they support visual analysis and understanding of the created models. Pourali and Atlee [59] conducted an empirical study that identified the barriers to adopting modelling tools. The main barriers that the authors found were keeping track of the context of the modelling problem, which is case specific, and debugging. After that, the authors created a prototype of a tool that implements improvements to these problems. They describe these improvements in [60], [61].

The issue of understandability of visual notations was addressed by Moody in [31], where he provided a framework for evaluating the understandability of a visual notation. According to this review's results, the two principles that practitioners have the most issues with are visual expressiveness and cognitive fit. Visual expressiveness is the number of visual variables a notation uses (e.g., colour and shape). Increasing the visual expressiveness implies that more information can be encoded in the notation symbols. The principle of cognitive fit is the use of "different visual dialects for different tasks and audiences" [31]. Moody [31] identified interactions between certain principles. For example, providing different dialects of a notation for expert and novice modelers allows adapting the level of visual expressiveness to the type of modeler. An expert modeler can benefit from more visual expressiveness, while the same level of visual expressiveness might overwhelm a novice user. In response to Moody's work, the issue of understandability has already been frequently addressed in research. A few examples are the following. Bork et al. [62] performed a systematic analysis of eleven standardized modelling notations, including UML and BPMN. They presented a framework for evaluating the visual notation of a modelling language based on Moody's PoNs. They used this framework to evaluate the modelling notations and provided recommendations to improve them. Liaskos et al. [63] proposed "a framework for empirically evaluating the vocabulary appropriateness of modelling languages." They demonstrated how the framework can be used for evaluating a modelling language. Bork et al. [64] presented a technique that modelling language designers can use to evaluate and improve the semantic transparency of their language. They illustrated the technique by applying it to the process–goal alignment modelling language notation and analysing the results.

The issue of high effort in acquiring MBSE skills can be addressed by improving how modelling and MDE are taught. Previous research has demonstrated that prototyping has a positive impact on learning conceptual modelling [65], [66], and the same goes for error-based exercises [67]. Generally, modelling pedagogy should be grounded in educational science to improve instructional design and ensure better scaffolding of the learning process [68].

2.5.3 Threats to Validity

The results presented in this meta-review are also subject to validity threats. In terms of the *reliability* of the research, this meta-review attempted to report sufficient details to make the research reproducible. On the downside, the limitations of the search needed to be considered. While this meta-review followed Kitchenham's guidelines [32] and used two databases containing millions of publications, it is nevertheless possible that the query missed some publications.

The *construct validity* of the research obviously depends on the reliability of the results of the analysed publications and the conclusions formulated in these publications. Assuming that the authors of the publications reported on in this meta-review ensured the construct validity of their results, the results reported in this chapter are equally valid. A threat to construct validity is that the surveys were based on different frameworks and often incomplete in reporting the demographic information and explaining their questions and answer options. As aggregation may already affect the construct validity of the measured concepts, this review tried to choose the best possible methods for aggregating results across publications. Nevertheless, while this review attempted to be as careful as possible when matching results, it was sometimes required to make certain interpretations to summarize the results.

The *internal* validity of the relationships established in Figure 2.2 cannot be formally assessed: they are established by argumentation and not through experimentation. Regarding *external* validity, the current set of publications is sufficiently large was considered to allow for an acceptable level of confidence in the results. Assuming that all surveys have been issued to disjoint populations, a population of around 2500 practitioners is reported in this meta-survey. This provides a sufficient level of confidence in the generalizability of the findings. On the downside, the publication lag had to be accounted for. The most recent survey dates from 2018, but often the surveys are older, or the period where the survey was conducted is not reported. While this meta-review reviewed the period of 2015–2020, in practice, the data relates to 2013–2018. As the modelling domain is evolving quickly, some of the results of this meta-review report may already be outdated.

2.6 Conclusion

This meta-review surveyed and reviewed publications published in the last six years and provides an overview of how practitioners use modelling languages and what they perceive to be the benefits and issues of MDE. It was found that modelling is highly used for the functional and information viewpoint, during the design phase of the software development lifecycle, and for documentation and elicitation of requirements. The most frequently used modelling language is UML, and the most frequently used UML diagram types are class diagrams. While practitioners experience the benefits of MDE (modelling is beneficial for several stakeholders, cost savings, easy to use, improves productivity, quality, and understanding of the system, and provides support for software development activities), they still struggle with several significant issues. In particular, the most commonly reported problems are missing tool functionalities. Many studies also confirmed that compliance with the PoN principles would improve modelling languages.

Interestingly, there are some contradictions between the problems and benefits. The high cost of modelling and modelling tools is a problem, while cost savings are considered a benefit for MDE. Also, the problems related to the high effort required for acquiring MBSE skills and using the tools contrast with the benefit of increased productivity. In conclusion, the varying levels of experience and expertise of the stakeholders influence their perception of the benefits and problems of MDE.

2.7 Future Work

The issues identified in this review may serve to identify a research agenda based on the issues and interactions that were summarized in Figure 2.2. The first proposed path for future research is investigating how an organisation's culture affects the adoption of modelling practices. As reported in this meta-review, many researchers already investigated the adoption of modelling practices in the industry. However, companies are constantly evolving, and academia continues to develop new modelling languages, practices and tools at a rapid pace. Therefore, it is still important to continue learning about the factors that influence adoption of these new artefacts in industry practice.

The second research path relates to the contradiction between the reported benefit of cost savings and the issue that modelling practices and tools come with a high cost (see Figure 2.2). To understand this contradiction, more in-depth research needs to be conducted on the cause of the perceived high cost: is it company-specific, related to the tools used, the profile of the stakeholder, or some other factor?

The third proposed research path is investigating how the format and quality of practitioners' modelling education can affect their perceived usefulness and ease of use of modelling languages. This could inform instructors both for in higher education software engineering curricula and in-company training of employees. Similarly, the fourth suggested research path is investigating how the format and quality of a practitioners modelling education can affect their perceived usefulness and ease of use of modelling tools. This would not only inform tool vendors and developers, but also instructors in the selection of an appropriate tool for their course. Apart from the provided education, the stakeholder's profile can also affect the perceived usefulness and ease of use, both for modelling languages and modelling tools. Although this could be seen as a separate research path, it would be interesting to investigate if there is an interaction effect between the stakeholder's profile and the perceived usefulness and ease of use resulting from training and education. The answer to these research questions could explain the contradiction between the benefit of increased productivity and the issues that a high effort is needed to acquire MBSE skills and tool use (see Figure 2.2).

As stated in Section 2.5.2, the issues related to tool integration often depend on the specific tools that are used. Therefore, there is not much general research on this topic. The sixth proposed research path is therefore to investigate whether the individual challenges that practitioners face, can be generalized. If so, this may open the avenue to developing tool-independent solutions.

Chapter 3
Case studies with students on their understanding of multi-perspective modelling

3.1 Introduction

Both UML and BPMN are frequently used in education to teach students the methodology and the principles behind information systems development. UML Class diagrams are often used for teaching database or software structure while BPMN provides the business process perspective. These languages are typically taught in different courses or course sections, and are illustrated with cases and exercises tailored to illustrate specific features of the language [69]. In practice, however, the UML Class diagram and the BPMN process model provide different perspectives of the same information system. It is therefore important that students learn to differentiate between the perspectives (i.e. know what to capture in what perspective) while maintaining consistency between these two perspectives. In other words, learning the individual languages is not enough: a skilled modeler needs to integrate the knowledge of both languages so as to be able to co-model the data and process perspective of a given process-aware information system. Although there are many courses on UML Class diagrams and BPMN process models and these languages may be taught in a single course addressing enterprise modelling (e.g. teaching ARIS, 4EM, MEMO), devoting specific attention to teaching the integration of both can instil important insights in students on the overall design of a process-aware information system.

This section is structured as follows. In section 3.2, we provide an overview of related work. Section 3.3 describes the pilot experiment and Section 3.4 reports the follow-up experiment.

3.2 Related Work

When querying Google Scholar and Web of Science, we searched on the keywords (multi-modelling OR "integrated modelling" OR "integrated modelling") AND (teaching OR education OR learning OR instruction). In Web of Science, we looked in all relevant categories for software and information systems modelling, and in Google Scholar, we filtered on articles published in the SoSyM journal. We found zero publications in in Software and Information Systems Modelling conference proceedings or journals that focus on the topic of teaching multi-perspective modelling. Although a lot of research exists on teaching modelling techniques, most papers report on the teaching of an individual modelling language or perspective, not on teaching an integrated approach with multiple perspectives.

Rosenthal et al. [70] provide a literature review on conceptual modelling in education. Their selection consists of 121 published papers from 1986 until 2017. The majority of papers where published after 2004. They classified the publications in distinct groups based on the modelling purpose they focus on. Object-oriented modelling is the biggest topic, with 51% of the papers focusing on this topic. The other categories identified by Rosenthal et al. are data modelling (27%), conceptual modelling in general (11%), business process modelling (8%) enterprise modelling (2%) and goal modelling with i* (1%). While Object-oriented modelling and enterprise modelling can capture multi-perspective modelling approaches, this was not discussed as an emerging research theme. The literature review provides an overview of the learning paradigms, learning approaches, learning theories and teaching methods mentioned in these publications. It is notable that not many publications discuss these aspects. However, the publications that discuss a learning paradigm mostly mention the constructivism paradigm, where "the learner is viewed as independently constructing her own subjective representations and understandings of reality through critical reflection" [70]. The publications mentioning a learning approach focus on collaborative learning. Finally, Rosenthal et al. identify four emerging research themes. The most important research theme is "Learning tool support", especially learning support built into object-oriented modelling tools and data modelling tools. The second research theme is "Feedback", with 22 publications reporting on process-oriented feedback and 10 publications reporting on outcome feedback. The other two research themes are "Learning Analytics" and "Gamification/Serious games". Regarding learning analytics, Rosenthal et al. [70] observe that learning analytics in conceptual modelling education is mostly focused on data mining of logging data from modelling tools. They identify the limitation that this approach neglects other aspects of the learning process, such as "learner motivation and willingness-to-learn or the use of additional tools outside of the modelling tool, e.g., paper-based modelling". They suggest thinking-out-loud experiments to fill this gap. The creation of multi-perspective models by students is not mentioned in the paper as a prevalent research theme.

While teaching conceptual data modelling is the topic of many studies, there is still a lack of understanding what makes modelling a difficult task, and how the learning of conceptual modelling can be supported. In 2019, Rosenthal et al. [71] conducted a study with a mixed-modal approach analysing the data modelling process of novice modelers and the difficulties they face. In 2020, Rosenthal et al. [72] further investigated modelling difficulties in data modelling. They investigated the modelers' experience using a mixed-method approach, including recording the modelers while they think aloud. They contrast this with the experiences of novice modelers. This paper was followed by another iteration of the experiment [73] that confirms the findings from the previous iterations that most difficulties for both novice and more experienced participants are related to relationships between entities. Bogdanova and Snoeck [68] present a framework for the education of conceptual data modelling based on Bloom's taxonomy. The aim of this framework is to link the assessment of students to the related learning outcomes of the course, and to provide appropriate feedback as a means to support leaning. The framework can be used to automate the process of providing personalized feedback, as demonstrated in [74], [75]. Besides feedback, also prototyping can be a useful tool for helping the learning to understand the meaning of a model better [66], [76], [77]. Amongst the most frequently occurring difficulties mentioned in [72] and [67] is the modelling of relationships. Nevertheless, when a case description is intentionally cluttered with information relating to other aspects, the research in [67] demonstrates that (unless specific training is provided) up to 30% of the solutions contain superfluous classes, part of which are due to attempts to capture too many aspects in a single perspective. A sequel research mapping errors to learning objectives [74], reveals that out the four errors appearing in more than 60% of the tasks, three are related to the learning objective of distinguishing that requirements may address a different viewpoint than the one addressed by the model under construction.

The publications mentioned above focus on the perspective of data modelling. Other publications investigate the cognitive process of creating process models. For example, Figl et al. [78] analysed the influence of notational aspects on the comprehension of process models. In a different study, Figl and Laue [79] looked at the comprehensive complexity of relationships between elements in a process model. In [80], Figl et al. investigate how the layout of a process model affects the cognitive load via eye tracking. They conclude that the visibility of control flow patterns is essential. Burattin et al. [81] developed a machine learning approach to automatically identify the different phases a modeler goes through when creating a process model. Sorg et al. [82] apply eye tracking to investigate which parts of the source code of programs requires a high cognitive load during development.

Other research addresses students' thinking about modelling but not the cognitive process of modelling itself. Chakraborty and Liebel [83] investigate the perception students have of software modelling and its usefulness via interviews with students and instructors. They conclude that students often don't see the merit of software modelling. This can be explained by two issues mentioned by their participants. On one hand, students often lack knowledge of the problem domain of a given exercise. On the other hand, modelling tools used by the participants lack automated feedback, and manual feedback from the instructors is often limited to syntax issues. Panach and Pastor [84] conducted a study on teaching model-driven development (MDD) to manual programming students. They observed that these students do not perceive MDD to be useful, confirming the findings of [83]. They introduce a project-based teaching methodology where students have to develop two systems, one with a traditional software development approach, and one employing MDD. After applying the proposed teaching methodology, the students' perception of the usefulness of MDD improved. A similar study was conducted by Manjunath et al. [85] where robotics students were taught software engineering in two groups. One group was taught using traditional software engineering approaches, while the other group was taught using a conceptual modelling approach. They also found that students' perception of the usefulness of conceptual modelling improves as the course progresses.

When considering research on students' understanding of modelling languages or on recurring difficulties in teaching modelling, all of the afore-mentioned research papers address only one modelling language (e.g., BPMN, UML Class diagrams, ER, etc.). To the authors' best knowledge, research that addresses the learning or teaching of a multi-modelling approach is inexistent. The goal of the research presented here is to study to what extent the co-modelling of different perspectives of a single case study can shed light on the problems faced by students, in view of creating better support for learning multi-modelling.

3.3 Pilot experiment on students' understanding of multi-perspective modelling

This section describes the pilot experiment that was conducted at KU Leuven in 2022 and was previously published in [86]. We first describe the context in which the experiment was conducted.

3.3.1 Context

The course "Architecture and Modelling of Management Information Systems" at KU Leuven addresses the need of teaching multi-modelling by teaching the MERODE approach, where multi-modelling is the most important learning objective. The approach is structured in three layers, each encapsulating one or more perspectives. The first layer is the enterprise layer (EL) which contains two sub-layers: the domain layer (DL) and the event handling layer (EHL). The DL consists of a UML Class diagram where each association must express existence dependency. Each Business Object in the DL is further completed with an Object Life Cycle (OLC). The events that trigger transitions in the OLCs of the Business Objects, are captured in the EHL. The EHL contains an Object Event Table (OET) that maps each business event to the Business Objects it affects. The second layer is the Information System Services Layer (ISL). This layer captures the input and output services that provide access to the EL. Finally, the third layer is the Business Process Layer (BPL) where the input and output services from the ISL can be invoked. A complete explanation of the Merode approach can be found in section 4.4.1.

Currently, the learning goals of the course include "Upon completion of this course, the student is capable of organizing requirements in a layered architecture", "Upon completion of this course, the student is capable of performing a requirements analysis to create an enterprise model" and "Upon completion of this course, the student is able to relate the enterprise model and the information system services to a business process model." In other words, students have to identify which requirements belong to the business process model, but they don't have to create this model. The course thus sets a step towards the integration of domain modelling and BP modelling, but there is still a significant gap towards a true integrated multi-modelling approach.

3.3.2   Methodology

The methodology used in this study is inspired by [72] and aims to capture the cognitive process of novice modelers by means of a thinking-out-loud experiment. The aim of the experiment is to determine whether modelling the business process in combination with the domain model, improves the understanding of the layered structure of MERODE, compared to just modelling the enterprise layer.

In the experiment, a number of students are given a case description (see Appendix A) and asked to model the enterprise layer as a UML class diagram and the business process layer as a BPMN process model (see Appendix A for model solutions). The selected case description for this exercise is adapted from [87], as that case lends itself to multi-perspective modelling: it contains ingredients for both a process model and a data model and the ingredients are not separated. So, the students have to filter out themselves what is relevant for the process model and what is relevant for the data model. Bogdanova and Snoeck have demonstrated that this is a task students often struggle with [67], [74].

The participants are all students in the course "Architecture and Modelling of Management Information Systems". At the time of the experiment, the participants have just finished week 3 of the course, meaning they were introduced to the layered approach of MERODE and had seen Chapter 1 to 3 of the handbook "Enterprise Information Systems Engineering" [88]. The students following this course also have had a prior course on database management, and most followed at least one course where the BPMN notation is taught. The call for participation included the prerequisite that participants should have some experience with UML class diagrams and BPMN process models. Before starting the experiment, the participants were sent a short demo of the tool Signavio.

Experiment Setup

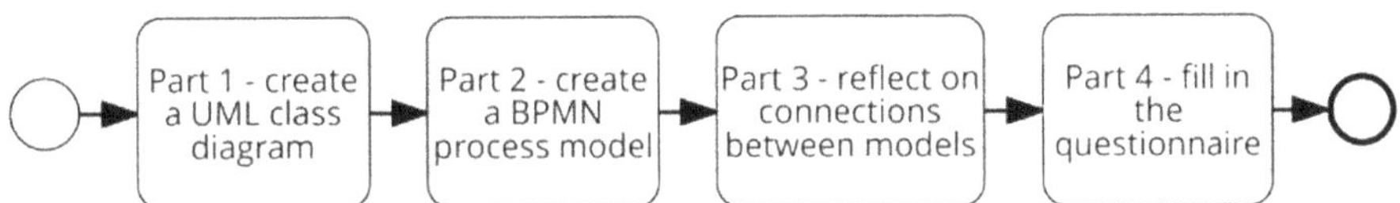

Figure 3.1 Experiment process

Based on the recommendation by Rosenthal et al. [72], we use a multi-modal approach, combining several methods of data collection. The cognitive processes of the participants are recorded in various ways in order to capture as much information as possible. Participants are asked to think out loud which is audio-recorded, their modelling actions are captured via screen recording, and an over-the-shoulder video-recording captures the annotations they make to the case description provided on paper. The experiment consists of 4 parts, as shown in Figure 3.1. In the first part, the participants create a domain model for the given case by means of a UML class diagram. Then, they model the process for the same case in a BPMN process model. In the third part, they indicate at which places in the BPMN model it is necessary to access the information from the UML class diagram. Finally, they are asked to fill a questionnaire on their experience during the experiment.

3.3.3 Results

Measured performance

In first instance, we analysed the models created by the participants by listing the mistakes found in the models. Each mistake is grouped into a mistake type (e.g. "missing task"). These mistake types are then categorized again into one of four mistake groups: "BPMN model", "UML class diagram", "layer allocation", and "notation". The "layer allocation" category consists of mistakes where a certain requirement was accounted for in the wrong model. For example, when "HR Department" was modelled as a class in the UML class diagram, while it is the user of the system, and thus needs (only) to appear as actor in the BPMN diagram. The category of "notation" deals with notational issues (i.e. syntactical issues), either for BPMN models or for UML class diagrams, for example, an exclusive-or gateway in the BPMN model that has only one incoming flow and only one outgoing flow.

In total, the models contain 125 mistakes, both syntactic and semantic (see Table 3.1). More than half of the mistakes were found in the BPMN models. The UML class diagrams account for 16% of the mistakes, and 18.4% of the mistakes are related to notation. The smallest group are "layer allocation" mistakes, accounting for 10.4% of the mistakes. However, they might have repercussions on the quality of the model that represent the distinct perspectives. Therefore, we discuss them in more detail below.

The most frequently occurring error in the UML class diagram is the missing class. Of the four classes that were expected (Job Vacancy – Candidate/Application – Review – Interview), Candidate was the only class present in all solutions. Job Vacancy was part of three solutions. Review and Interview each appeared only once in a different solution, even though we made sure to include sentences in the case description that suggest modelling these as classes: "All reviews [...] should be filed within four weeks of being requested" and "[...] interviews are registered in the system".

The most frequently occurring errors in the BPMN model are the missing task and the missing path. Often this is due to an incomplete model, see the discussion section.

The group of "layer allocation" mistakes consists of four types of mistakes. The mistake type that occurs most often is **"actor as UML class"**, meaning that, in the scope of a small application, an actor such as "HR Department", "Professor" or "International Office" is unnecessarily modelled as a class in the UML class diagram. This mistake is made by three out of six participants and each of those participants makes this mistake multiple times. It is notable that in seven out of eight cases where this mistake is made, the actor is modelled both as a class in the UML class diagram and as a pool in the BPMN model. In the other case, the participant ran out of time. The second mistake type is **"class as task"**, meaning that the BPMN model contains tasks like "review the candidate" and "register interview", while the corresponding classes where the information is stored are missing from the UML class diagram. This mistake occurs once in three different solutions. The other two mistake types occur only once each: **"attribute as task"** and **"input form as class"**. On average, participants made two layer allocation mistakes and only one participant did not make any layer allocation mistakes.

Our sample of six participants is too small to make a statistical analysis, but overall, the ratio of layer allocation mistakes to total mistakes seems fairly consistent around 13% (not counting the participant that didn't make any layer allocation mistakes).

Table 3.1 Overview of mistakes made by the 6 participants

	Participant						Total	Total %
	1	2	3	4	5	6		
BPMN model	12	10	8	7	16	16	69	**55,2%**
missing path	4	1	1	1	5	3	15	
missing task	4	2	2	2	6	7	23	
missing timer	2	2		1	2		7	
multiplicity of task	1	1			1	1	4	
Universe of discourse as pool		1					1	
overspecification of task	1	1	1	1	1	1	6	
task in wrong pool		2	2			1	5	
missing pool			2	1	1	1	5	
unneeded subprocess				1		1	2	
unneeded pool						1	1	
layer allocation	3	4	2	1	0	3	13	**10,4%**
attribute as task		1					1	
actor as class	2	3				3	8	
class as task	1		1	1			3	
input form as class		1					1	
notation	5	5	3	5	1	4	23	**18,4%**
BPMN - event is not atomic	1	2					3	
BPMN - loose task	1					1	2	
BPMN - missing end event	2	1				1	4	
UML - association as attribute			1	1			2	
BPMN - missing message flows		1		1		1	3	
BPMN - pool name missing						1	1	
BPMN - unneeded gateway				1	1		2	
UML - missing multiplicity			2	2			4	
UML - unconnected diagram	1	1					2	
UML class diagram	3	6	1	3	3	4	20	**16,0%**
wrong attributes		1					1	
association multiplicity		2				2	4	
missing association		1					1	
missing class	2	1	1	1	2	2	9	
unneeded class	1			1	1		3	
Universe of discourse as class		1					1	
class as attribute				1			1	
Total	23	25	14	16	20	27	125	**100,0%**

Recordings

We can inspect the time spent on each part of the exercise. Each participant was given a timeslot of one hour to work on the exercise and fill in the survey. However, four of the six participants were unable to finish the exercise in the allocated time. This explains that 58% of the mistakes are related to missing elements. Noticeably, the two participants that did not run out of time, spent about 30% of their time on the UML class diagram, while the other four participants spent 50%-60% on the UML class diagram (see Table 3.2). Those two 'faster' participants have a low number of layer allocation mistakes. They also have the lowest ratio of total mistakes to total number of elements and they spent noticeably more time explaining the connection between the models. They are the only two students that made changes to their models in the third part of the exercise.

Table 3.2 Division of time over models

Participant	1	2	3	4	5	6
% time UML	52%	50%	29%	34%	52%	59%
% time BPMN	42%	49%	57%	55%	44%	35%
% time explaining connections	6%	1%	15%	12%	5%	6%

By analysing the video recordings, we can conclude that the three participants that have the least amount of layer allocation mistakes (0, 1 or 2) were able to connect their models to each other to some extent. The other three participants made more mistakes (3 or 4) and did not understand how to connect their models.

Finally, we look at the type of notes participants make on the case description. Participants were given a pen and a set of markers. All participants highlighted words (this includes underlining or circling in pen) while reading the case for the first time. Only three participants continued making notes, highlights or sketches while they were modelling. We did not find any meaningful correlations between note taking and the understanding of multi-perspective modelling.

Questionnaire

The first two questions of the questionnaire are about previous experience with UML class diagrams and BPMN models. Half of the participants (1, 2, 3) indicate that they have some experience with UML class diagrams, and half indicate that they have a reasonable amount of experience (e.g. active participation in a course). For BPMN, participant 2 has some experience, the others indicate having a reasonable amount.

The questionnaire also investigates their perceived understanding of the layers during the creation of the UML model, and how this evolved over the next parts of the exercise. Half of the participants (3, 4, 6) indicate that they have some issues allocating requirements to layers during the creation of the UML class diagram. The only participant experiencing no layer allocation problems (5) indeed did not include superfluous classes in the UML diagram. However, the process model was highly incomplete. Half of the participants (1, 3, 4) also agree that creating the BPMN model helped them to identify to which layer each requirement belongs. Two of these (3, 4) are the faster modelers, who also made the lowest number of errors overall. In a follow-up question, the participants can clarify how creating the BPMN model helped or didn't help. Of the three participants that don't agree that the BPMN model is helpful, two explain that they didn't think about the layers while solving the exercise, and one only discusses the BPMN model instead of the connections between both models. Those three participants (2, 5 and 6) have the highest numbers of errors overall. All participants who agree that the creation of the BPMN model was helpful for layer allocation also agree that the third part of the exercise (thinking about the connections between the models) is helpful to understand the interaction between the layers. In a follow-up question, the others indicate that they either didn't see the relation, didn't think of the layers while modelling, or have a lack of experience. All six participants agree that they have a better understanding of the case after finishing part 2 and part 3 of the exercise, and four out of six (1, 3, 4, 5) indicate that they have a better understanding of the layers in general.

The final two questions of the questionnaire investigate whether students think additional similar exercises and code generation for the business process layer would be helpful when studying the course "Architecture and Modelling of Management Information Systems". The same group of participants that indicate that part 2 and part 3 of the exercise were helpful (1, 3, 4), agree that including this type of exercise in the course would be beneficial. Five out of six participants (all but 4) believe that code generation for the business process layer would help them.

3.3.4 Discussion

This exploratory study is a first step in investigating the use of multi-perspective modelling in computer science education. Although the experiment is small-scale, the results already indicate that more research in this domain could lead to some interesting insights. In this study, the data was gathered at the start of the course "Architecture and Modelling of Management Information Systems". As the students progress through the course, we will gather more data and perform a more in-depth analysis.

Analysis of mistakes
The type of mistakes that occurs the most (23 times in total) is a missing task in the BPMN model. In each solution, at least two tasks were missing, but generally speaking many more were missing, leading also to missing paths (15), etc. The third type of mistake is a missing class in the UML class diagram. This occurred at least once in each solution and nine times in total. The high number of missing tasks can be explained by the fact that four out of six participants spent quite some time on creating the UML class diagram and then ran out of time for modelling the business process. However, while the participants were instructed to start with the UML class diagram, they were free to decide themselves when the diagram was finished. Therefore, the time constraint does not explain the missing classes. The participants' inability to identify review and interview as potential classes, and not even including these as attributes could be explained by the participants' limited experience with data modelling.

The fourth type of mistake that occurred often, was a layer allocation mistake: "actor as class". Three participants (3, 4, 5) did not make this mistake, the other three made the mistake multiple times. We can make two observations concerning this mistake. First, the three participants that made this mistake were also unable to reflect on the connections between both models in part 3. Two of these participants said that they didn't know what the connections were and one participant only talked about the BPMN process model. This could indicate that the interaction between the layers is a complex concept to grasp for students. Second, two out of the three students that did not make this mistake (3, 4), made fewer mistakes overall. Even when we discard the layer allocation mistakes, these two students made the least number of mistakes. This could indicate that once students understand the interactions between layers, the overall quality of their models improves. Participant 5 also didn't make this mistake, however, the process model was highly incomplete, thus leading to a large number of mistakes overall. The other layer allocation mistakes were less frequent, showing that, at least in this case, the modelling of actors in a system is one of the main challenges of layer allocation. For another case this could turn out to be different.

In this analysis, we did not consider the amount of correctly modelled aspects of the case. This also influences the quality of a solution. For example, participant 2 made the most mistakes, however, their models were more complete than for example the models of participant 5. The ratio of mistakes to total number of elements in the models could account for this discrepancy. As shown in Table 3.3, this ratio suggests that the solution of participant 2 is better than the solutions of participants 1, 5 and 6, despite having the highest number of mistakes.

Table 3.3 Total mistakes vs Total number of elements

Participant	1	2	3	4	5	6	Total
total mistakes	23	25	14	16	20	27	125
total number of elements	20	50	36	37	21	21	185
Total mistakes / Total number of elements	1,15	0,50	0,39	0,43	0,95	1,29	0,68

Analysis of recordings

As indicated in the results, there seems to be a correlation between the number of layer allocation mistakes and the time spent on the UML class diagram, at least for the better performing participants 3 and 4. It would be interesting to study whether there is a causal relation between the understanding of the interaction between layers and ease of identifying classes for the UML class diagram, reducing the time spent on this task. Alternatively, spending more time on the business process layer could improve the understanding of the interaction between layers, resulting in fewer mistakes.

Another interesting observation from the recordings is that one of the participants who understands the interaction between the layers well, explicitly mentioned that they would prefer to switch between the models and not follow the instructed order. This was the only participant who explicitly modelled the connections between the models by including in the BPMN model datastores representing the classes of the UML class diagram. Repeating the experiment where students are allowed to determine the order themselves, could provide more insight into the cognitive process of novice modelers.

Analysis of survey results

A first observation regarding the questionnaire, is that the level of experience in UML class diagrams was lower than expected. Since the participants were all students of the program "Master of Information Management" or "Master of Business and Information Systems Engineering", we assume they have all taken the courses "Business Information Systems" and "Principles of Database Management", as these courses are mandatory in both programs that are planned before the "Architecture and Modelling of Management Information Systems" course. Both courses include UML class diagrams. However, three participants indicated they only have some experience with UML class diagrams, instead of choosing the option "*I have a reasonable amount of experience (e.g. active participation in a course about UML class diagrams)*".

The second observation is that there is a slight discrepancy between the answers to some questions. More specifically, only half of the participants indicated that Part 2 and 3 where helpful for understanding the interaction between the layers, but all participants agreed that Part 2 and Part 3 contributed to their overall understanding of the case. Apparently, understanding the case is different from understanding the different layers and perspectives present in the case description. This could indicate a mismatch between the actual issues novice modelers have (understanding to which perspective a requirement relates), and their perception of the issues that they face (understanding a requirement).

Finally, our third observation is related to the last two questions, which measure the perceived usefulness of these types of exercises and prototyping of the business process layer. While not all participants agreed that these would be useful additions to the course material, no participant showed disagreement, instead choosing for the option "Neutral". So overall, we can expect a positive response to these additions.

Reflection on methodology

In this study, we used a multi-modal data collection method in order to capture as much information as possible. Out of the different modes that were used for the collection of data, the correction of the participants' solutions, the screen and voice recordings and the questionnaire yielded interesting information. However, the recordings of the notation did not bring any additional insights. To simplify the experiment, we might consider leaving this out. In view of repeating the experiment with larger groups, and considering the amount of time needed for processing all the data, in future repetitions of this study we will consider focusing on correcting mistakes, data gathering while observing and a well-designed survey. Data gathering while observing would significantly reduce the time spent on transcribing recordings, since the recordings would serve mostly verification for the gathered data and not as a primary source.

Limitations

The exploratory nature of this study comes with a number of limitations. The first limitation is the small number of participants. With only six participants, the results of this study are only an indication of the understanding that novice modelers have of multi-perspective modelling. Nevertheless, the insights gathered in terms of timing, order of tasks, etc., provides useful insights in how to set up experiments with larger groups of participants to obtain more significant results.

As the participants come from an international group of students, none of them were native English speakers, and they had differing levels of fluency in the English language. Also, not all participants were accustomed to thinking-out-loud exercises. This likely led to a loss of information about their cognitive process. Despite this loss of information, some interesting insights could already be captured from this observational study.

A third limitation, as indicated in the previous section of the discussion, is that some participants had limited experience with UML class diagrams. Also, some participants seemed to have limited experience with Signavio, despite receiving a demo beforehand and using this tool in a previous course. This probably led to the fact that most participants needed more time than we anticipated, resulting in incomplete BPMN diagrams. For future experiments, we can consider providing tool training beforehand.

A fourth limitation is that the students were only given one case. It would be interesting to investigate if the results of this experiment persist when students are given different cases. That way, we could eliminate the wording and specific aspects of a given case as cause for issues.

A fifth limitation of the study is that there is always room for interpretation when creating a model based on a case description. This was taken into account when correcting and comparing the solutions in the following way: we didn't penalize for sub-optimal naming of model elements, missing conditions on gateway paths or missing attributes. To further mitigate for this problem, we use a case from another researcher, for which we created an own solution that turned out to be almost identical to the original solution. Both the original solution [87] and our own variant [89] were published in the context of papers that underwent a review process. In this sense, we can consider the case and its solution as validated by several experts.

3.3.5 Conclusion

This exploratory study is a first step in the investigation of novice modelers' understanding of multi-perspective modelling. The study uses a combination of participant's solutions to the exercise, recordings and a survey to gather data. The inclusion of the recordings and the survey added meaning to the overview of mistakes made. The study shows promising results including a potential correlation between the understanding of multi-perspective modelling and overall model quality, and between the understanding of multi-perspective modelling and the time distribution over the two models. Further research is needed to confirm these findings and to investigate if there is a causal relation. Another result is that the modelling of actors in the system can be a challenge for novice modelers. The study highlights points of consideration for future studies, such as time constraints and modelling experience of the participants, and prompts new research questions for further research.

3.4 Follow-up Study: Evaluation of Students' Understanding of Modelling in a Multi-Perspective Context

In the previous section, we investigated whether students that have participated in separate courses on different modelling languages are able to create several models each addressing different perspectives for a case description where elements from these perspectives are intertwined in a pilot experiment with six participants. In this section, we focus on the perspectives of data and process modelling, as these perspectives make up the core aspects of a business information system. This section continuous the pilot experiment from section 3.3 by improving the experimental setup based on the findings of the pilot experiment and conducting a new experiment with 22 participants.

This section is structured as follows: Section 3.4.1 presents the methodology design. This includes the lessons learned from the pilot experiment, the improved experimental setup and the design of the error typology. Section 3.4.2 presents the results and section 3.4.3 provides a discussion. Section 3.4.4 concludes the section.

The main research question of this section is the following: *How well can students, that have participated in separate courses on data and process modelling, create both a data and a process model for a case description where elements from both perspectives are intertwined?*

3.4.1 Methodology

This section describes the methodology applied for the experiment. First, the central research question is divided in sub questions. The next part of this section describes the lessons learned from the pilot experiment, followed by the improved experimental setup. Finally, the construction of the error typology used to evaluate the models created by the participants and the data analysis are described.

Detailed research questions

To investigate the process of creating two models capturing distinct perspectives of the same case description, we will answer the following research questions:

1. Model Quality: How well can students create a UML class diagram and a BPMN process model for a joint case description?
   a. Which types of mistakes occur most often in each model?
   b. Is there a correlation between the quality of the UML class diagram and the quality of the BPMN process model?
   c. Did the participants make annotations on the case description and is there a correlation with the results of RQ1?
2. Do the demographic characteristics (English proficiency, previous experience) of the participants affect their result?
3. How do students rate the ease of use of the selected modelling languages, and does this correspond their result?
4. How do the participants experience the task of creating both models for a joint case description?
   a. How difficult did the participants find the exercise, and does this correspond to the results of RQ1?
   b. While working on one model, do the participants also consider the other model, and does this affect the results of RQ1?
   c. Did the participant make any changes to their first model while working on the second model, and is there a correlation with the results of RQ1?
   d. Do the participants prefer the execution order they were given or would their have preferred the inverted execution order, and does this affect the result of RQ1?
5. For which of RQ1-7 is there a noticeable difference between group A and group B?

Lessons learned from the pilot experiment

To the best of our knowledge, there has been no research on the learning or teaching of a multi-modelling approach before the pilot experiment. Therefore, the methodology of the pilot experiment was not yet ideal as some limitations came to our attention during its execution. The overall methodology of the pilot experiments is illustrated in Figure 3.1 in section 3.3.1. For the experiment in this section, the methodology was adapted based on the limitations and unexpected results of the pilot experiment in the following ways:

1. The main limitation of the pilot experiment is the limited number of participants, as
   only six students participated. To address this limitation the experiment was repeated with 22 students from the Polytechnic University of Valencia. Using a larger group of participants from a slightly different background allows us to verify the external validity of the results.

2. In the pilot experiment, none of the participants were native English speakers and thus their level of fluency in English varied. Some participants were also not accustomed to thinking-out-loud exercises. Thus, asking them to think out loud might have interrupted their cognitive process when modelling, and there was likely a loss of information when capturing this cognitive process. Therefore, we decided to leave out the thinking-out-loud aspect of the experiment. Instead, the portion of the questionnaire that deals with the creation of the UML class diagram and the BPMN Process Model was extended. The questions that were added are inspired by the questionnaire of the Method Evaluation Model by Moody, more specifically the section that deals with ease of use.

3. The participants in the pilot experiment had limited knowledge of UML class diagrams, despite having received prior training in two university courses in previous academic years, and experienced issues when using the modelling tool. The issue of limited knowledge of UML class diagrams is addressed by the selection of the participants. All participants are students of a modelling course. In this course UML class diagrams are discussed in the weeks prior to the experiment. The course uses weekly tasks for permanent evaluation, enforcing active participation by the students. In addition, the students of this program follow a second course where BPMN is taught. These lessons also occurred before the experiment. Finally, at the start of the experiment, the participants were given a brief recapitulation of both modelling languages to ensure that they all had a good understanding of the basic concepts. As BPMN has much more different constructs that can be used than in UML class diagrams, we provided a list of the core constructs that participants were allowed to use, making the potential for errors between the UML class diagram and the BPMN process model more balanced. To eliminate tool usability issues affecting the results of the experiment, the exercises where done on paper.

4. Part 3 of the pilot experiment, where participants were asked to list the connections between their models, was replaced by a question in the questionnaire. This is a consequence of running the experiment with all participants simultaneously, making it impossible to interview each participant.

5. During the pilot experiment, participants typically needed much more time than initially planned to finish the exercise. To ensure that the experiment could be concluded with the time constraints of the class, the case description was slightly adapted to reduce the complexity of the BPMN process model.

6. The result of the pilot experiment suggest that the order of execution might impact the difficulty of the exercise, as several participants expressed the wish to choose their own order of creating the models. In this experiment, we decided to split the group of participants in two, where one group would start with the UML class diagram, and the other group would start with the BPMN process model. Afterwards, they filled in the same questionnaire. This way, the order is still restricted, but we can compare results from both groups.

7. A final limitation of the methodology used in the pilot methodology, is that error types were determined ad hoc based on the errors made by the participants. This way, potential error types that were never made by the participants are not included in the analysis. For the current experiment, we created an error typology for combined modelling of UML class diagrams and BPMN process models before the experiment

was conducted. Note that we did not adapt the case description to ensure that it provides equal opportunity for each error type to be made, as this is rarely the case in a real-world setting. However, the error typology ensures the completeness of the potential errors discussed.

Experimental setup

The follow-up experiment was conducted during a 2-hour session with all 22 participants. Participants were rewarded for their participation as their result for the experiment contributed to their overall grade for the course. The aim of the experiment is to measure how well students are able to create both a UML class diagram and a BPMN Process Model for one given case description that combines the requirements for both models. Figure 3.2 summarizes the process followed in the experiment. The experiment started with a brief training of UML class diagrams and BPMN Process Models. Each training included a short exercise and lasted 20 minutes. Students were also given a legend of symbols for both modelling languages, to avoid mistakes due to misremembering the notation. For BPMN, this legend was restricted to some core symbols that were sufficient for this specific case. Then, the participants where given the case description of the main exercise. After reading the case description, the participants were split in two groups. Group A started with the UML class diagram and switched to the BPMN Process model after 25 minutes. Group B started with the BPMN process model and switched to the UML class diagram after 25 minutes. Afterwards, all participants filled in the questionnaire and the session was concluded. The created models were evaluated to measure the objective quality. This serves as an estimation of the capabilities of the participants to create both model types when the requirements are combined in a single case description. The questionnaire gathers information about the cognitive process and opinions of the participants.

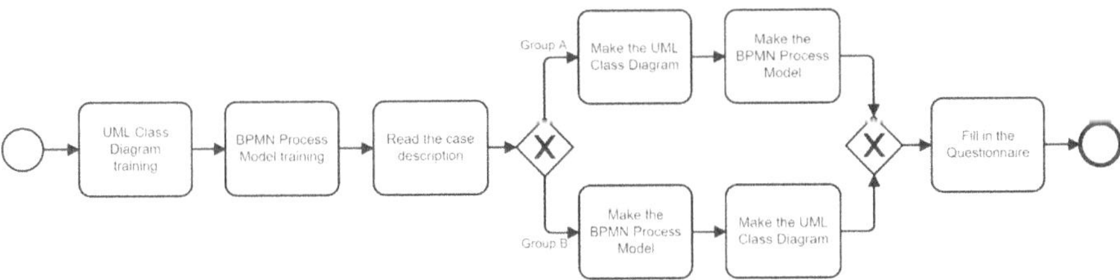

Figure 3.2 Experiment setup

Defining an error typology

We developed an error typology to facilitate a formal and systematic evaluation of the quality of the models created by the participants, based on the work of Bogdanova and Snoeck [90]. In order to obtain this typology, we followed four steps. First, the error typology for conceptual data models proposed by Bogdanova and Snoeck [90] was slightly adapted to fit the context of this experiment. Second, this typology was 'translated' for BPMN process models. Finally, the resulting typology was validated by mapping the errors found in the pilot experiment to the complete error typology.

Step 1 – An error typology for UML class diagrams.
Bogdanova and Snoeck [90] propose to classify the errors according to the modelling quality framework by Lindland et al. [91], and to further divide the categories according to the constructs of the modelling language. They provide an example error typology for conceptual data models. The modelling quality framework distinguishes between Syntactic quality, Semantic quality and Pragmatic quality. The framework also identifies five error types, independent of the modelling language used. The definitions of the three types of modelling quality, and the types of errors that are associated with them are summarized in the first two columns of Table . The error typology of Bogdanova and Snoeck [90], does not include syntactic errors because the models were created with modelling tools that automatically verify their syntactic quality. In our experiment, the models are drawn on paper, leaving room for syntactic errors. The UML class diagram training also specifically discussed attributes of classes. Therefore, we extend the error typology of Bogdanova and Snoeck [90] with errors related to syntax and errors related to attributes. The final error typology for the UML class diagram is shown in the last two columns of Table 3.4. Most errors have straightforward names, but name-concept mismatch, unnecessary reification and role inversion/degree problem errors require some clarification:

- *Name-concept mismatch* errors are defined as "problems where an association has been reified to an association class, and the name of the association class does not convey the meaning of the association" [67].
- *Unnecessary reification* is defined as "and association that has been reified to an association class, and whereby one of the resulting new associations has been reified again" [67]. In this section, we will define this more generally as unnecessarily reifying an association as a class or an association class.
- The definition of the *role inversion* error is slightly adjusted as the experiment by Bogdanova and Snoeck [67] required participants to identify the "strong" and the "weak" entity in all associations. Since this is not required for this experiment, we define inverted roles simply as wrongly assigning the role belonging to one entity of the association to the other entity of the association. Bogdanova and Snoeck [67] combine role inversion errors with degree errors (pertaining to the correct use of recursive association) in a single category. While the definition of degree errors is compatible with the UML class diagram, recursive associations are not present in the case used for this experiment, and are therefore not relevant for this section.

Step 2 – An error typology for BPMN process models.
The error typology for UML class diagrams can now be mapped onto BPMN process models. During the BPMN process modelling training, three guidelines on modelling gateways were provided: "avoid implicit gateways", "avoid combining split and merge in a single gateway" and "gateways should come in split-merge pairs of equal types". Violations against these guidelines are also included in the error typology. Event errors are not included (apart from "Missing start/end event"), since students were not expected to include intermediate events in the solution and they were not part of the training. The resulting error typology for BPMN process modelling is shown in Table 3.5. The complete error typology can be found in Appendix B.

Table 3.4 summary of the quality definitions, error type definitions, and the errors for UML class diagrams (based on the typology of Bogdanova and Snoeck [17])

CONCEPT	ERRORS	CLASS ERRORS	ASSOCIATION ERRORS
Syntactic quality is how well the model corresponds to the language.	**Morphological errors** (model expresses statements with symbols that are not defined in the language's alphabet)	morphological error	
	Syntactic incompleteness (the model lacks constructs or information to obey the language's grammar)	missing class name	missing association name
		missing attribute name	missing multiplicities
		missing attribute data type	
Semantic quality is how well the model corresponds to the domain	**Invalidity** (the model is not valid, meaning that not all statements made by the model are correct and/or relevant to the problem)	superfluous class	superfluous association
		superfluous(/duplicate) attribute	wrong multiplicity
		attribute in wrong class	
		wrong attribute data type	
		name-concept mismatch	
		unnecessary association reification	
			role inversion
			wrongly linked association
	Incompleteness (the model is not complete, meaning that the model does not contain all the statements about the domain that are correct and relevant)	missing class	missing association
		missing attribute	
Pragmatic quality is how well the model corresponds to its audience diaterpretation	**Incomprehension** (not all model projections have been understood by their relevant audience)	no meaningful name for class	no meaningful name for association
		no meaningful name for attribute	

Table 3.5 errors for BPMN process models

CONCEPT	ERRORS	TASK ERRORS	FLOW ERRORS
Syntactic quality	**Morphological errors**	Morphological error	
	Syntactic incompleteness	Missing task name	Missing start/end event
			Missing gateway conditions
Semantic quality	**Invalidity**	Superfluous task	Superfluous sequence flow
			Superfluous gateway
			Wrong gateway / gateways do not come in split-merge pairs of equal types
			Wrongly linked sequence flow
			Wrong gateway conditions
	Incompleteness	Missing task	Missing sequence flow
			Missing gateway
Pragmatic quality	**Incomprehension**	No meaningful name for task	Implicit gateways
			Split and merge in a single gateway
			Assign task to a different actor

Step 3 – Validation of the complete error typology.
We validated the complete error typology by mapping the errors found in the pilot experiment to the errors listed in the typology in Table 3.6. However, not all errors found in the pilot experiment are relevant for the current experiment, due to the changes made to the case description to reduce the complexity of the BPMN process model: pools, message flows, timers and multiplicity of tasks are no longer part of the case description. Therefore, the errors against these model elements are not included in the error typology. Apart from these errors, all errors found in the pilot experiment can be mapped directly to an error – or a combination of errors – in the typology. More specifically, the errors from the pilot experiment map to 13 of the 38 errors from the typology. These 13 errors are mostly semantic errors, except for "missing start/end event" (syntax error), "no meaningful name for task" (pragmatic error) and "assign task to different actor" (pragmatic error). The error typology thus contains 25 errors that did not occur during the pilot experiment. Eight of these errors are syntax errors. In the pilot experiment, participants used a modelling tool that enforces syntactic quality, so syntax

errors did indeed occur rarely. In the current experiment setup, participants draw their models on paper, which does allow for syntactic errors. Twelve errors from the typology that do not occur in the pilot experiment are semantic errors, and five are pragmatic errors. In conclusion, the error typology contains all relevant errors found in the pilot experiment and is more complete than the list of errors reported in the pilot experiment.

Table 3.6 Mapping of errors from the pilot experiment onto the error typology

Pilot experiment	Error typology
UML class diagram	
wrong attribute	superfluous attribute
association multiplicity	wrong multiplicity
missing association	missing association
missing class, class as attribute	missing class
unneeded class, universe of discourse as class	superfluous class
BPMN model	
missing path	missing sequence flow
missing task	missing task
over-specification of task	no meaningful name for task
task in wrong pool	assign task to different actor
unneeded subprocess	superfluous task
missing timer, multiplicity of task, universe of discourse as pool, missing pool, unneeded pool	N.A.
layer allocation	
attribute as task	superfluous task / missing attribute
class as task	superfluous task / missing class
actor as class, input form as class	superfluous class
Notation	
BPMN - event is not atomic	no meaningful name for task
BPMN - loose task	missing sequence flow
BPMN - missing end event	missing start/end event
BPMN - missing message flows, pool name missing, missing multiplicity	N.A.
BPMN - unneeded gateway	superfluous gateway
UML - association as attribute	missing association / superfluous attribute
UML - unconnected diagram	missing association

Methodology for the data analysis

The first step in the data analysis is to correct the solutions for both model types. We do this by counting the errors that occur as well as providing an overall grade. The grade does not only depend on the number of mistakes, but also on the severity and weight of the mistake. For example, semantic errors usually have a higher weight than notation errors. The severity of the mistakes for example plays a role in 'superfluous class' errors: Having a superfluous class "International Office" is considered a more severe mistake than having a superfluous class "Professor", given that there is usually only one international office per university, and thus it is not a good class. On the other hand, adding a class Professor makes sense if the modeller wants to keep track of which professor wrote each review. To ensure grading was done in a systematic manner, we used the criteria presented in Table 3.7.

Table 3.7 grading criteria

Grade	UML class diagram	BPMN process model
D (major flaws)	Several superfluous/ missing classes, as well as wrongly linked association(s) and/or many wrong multiplicities	Order of tasks is incorrect
C (satisfactory)	Several of the following mistakes: missing elements, some wrong multiplicities and/or wrongly linked associations, but the core data structure (vacancy, application, review, interview) is correct.	Several of the following mistakes: missing model element, missing conditions, task name is not meaningful and/or wrong gateway, but the sequence of tasks is correct.
B (good)	Core data structure is correct, most mistakes are related to attributes.	Sequence of tasks is correct, most mistakes are related to missing tasks, implicit gateways, superfluous sequence flows, superfluous tasks, morphological issues, etc.
A (very good)	Core data structure is correct, only a few mistakes, "International Office" and/or "HR Department" are not included	Sequence of tasks is correct, only a few mistakes, no severe mistakes
A+ (excellent)	Model solution	Model solution

The second step is to process the answers to the post-experiment questionnaire. The questions on the questionnaire were labelled as D1-2 (descriptive characteristics), EXP1-5 (previous experience of the participant), MEM1-11 (questions adapted from the MEM questionnaire to measure ease of use of UML class diagrams and BPMN process models), DIF (what is most difficult part of the exercise) and INT1-6 (interaction between UML class diagram modelling and BPMN process modelling). Table 3.8 summarizes which data points are used to answer each research question.

Table 3.8 Data points analysed for each research question

Research Question	Data point	Research Question	Data point
RQ1	Correction of models	RQ6	MEM4,6,10 and DIF
RQ2	Correction of models	RQ7a	INT1
RQ3	Correction of models	RQ7b	INT2,5-6
RQ4	D2 and EXP1-5	RQ7c	Correction of models
RQ5	MEM1-3,5,7-9,11	RQ7d	INT3-4

3.4.2 Results

RQ1 - Model Quality

The first research question investigates how well students can create a UML class diagram and a BPMN process model for a joint case description. We will answer this question by analysing the number and types of mistakes made in each diagram and the grades that the students received for their solution. The errors were counted based on the model solution in Appendix C. Model elements that diverge from this model solution were only counted as an error if they result in a requirement from the case description not being met or if they add unnecessary restrictions that were not part of the case description. Therefore, some alternative solutions were allowed, for example, including a class Professor in the class diagram.

Table 3.9 provides an overview of the errors in the UML class diagrams and Table 3.10 provides an overview of the errors in the BPMN process models. In total, students made about the same number of errors in both diagrams (189 in the UML class diagram and 182 in the BPMN process model). On average, participants made 8.59 errors in the UML class diagram and 8.27 errors in the BPMN process model.

Table 3.9 overview of UML class diagram errors

		# errors	# participants	Avg. # errors
Error types	Notation errors	8	6	0.36
	Association errors	91	21	4.14
	Class errors	35	14	1.59
	Attribute errors	55	18	2.5
Model quality	Syntax errors	48	14	2.18
	Semantic validity errors	105	22	4.77
	Semantic completeness errors	35	19	1.59
	Pragmatic errors	1	1	0.05

Table 3.10 overview of BPMN process model errors

		# errors	# participants	Avg. # errors
Error types	Notation errors	9	8	0.41
	Task errors	88	22	4
	Flow errors	85	21	3.86
Model quality	Syntax errors	17	11	0.77
	Semantic validity errors	79	19	3.59
	Semantic completeness errors	43	19	1.95
	Pragmatic errors	43	21	1.95

Regarding the UML class diagram error types, participants made on average the most association errors, followed by attribute errors, class errors and notation errors. Regarding UML model quality, participants made the most errors related to semantic validity, followed by syntax, semantic completeness and pragmatic quality. Looking at the BPMN process model error types, participants made on average the most task errors, followed by flow errors and notation errors. Regarding the quality dimension, while the same number of participants made semantic validity and semantic completeness errors, participants made on average more semantic validity errors than semantic completeness errors. It is interesting to note the difference in pragmatic quality between the UML diagram (1 error by 1 participant) and the BPMN process model (43 errors by 21 of the 22 participants). This could be explained by the fact that there were more potential errors to be made in the BPMN process model ('no meaningful name for a task', 'implicit gateways', 'split and merge in a single gateway' and 'assigning a task to a different actor') than in the UML class diagram ('no meaningful name for a class', 'no meaningful name for an attribute', 'no meaningful name for an attribute').

Some errors are specifically related to the interaction between the UML class diagram and the BPMN process model. These errors can be categorized in two groups. The first group of errors consists of business process elements that are unnecessarily included in the UML class diagram. These errors are mostly actors that are included as a class in the class diagram, but one participant also modelled the two outgoing flows of a gateway as two separate associations in the class diagram. This is type of error was made 17 times by a total of 10 participants. The second group of errors consists of data elements that are used by the BPMN process model but that are not represented in the UML class diagram, in this case, missing classes for review or interview. These errors were only made by 6 participants, and never more than once by the same participant.

Regarding the grades, the overall grade distribution for the UML class diagram is more evenly spread than the grade distribution for the BPMN process model (see Figure 3.3). There is some correlation between the grades of the UML class diagram and the BPMN process model (Spearman rank correlation coefficient = 0.534). Taking a closer look at the data, there is a clear relationship between both variables: apart from one participant, the grades of all participants is equal or differs by only one level.

In summary, for the UML class diagram the most frequent error type are Association errors, and for the BPMN process model the majority of the errors are against the Task and Flow dimensions. For both models, the majority of errors fall under semantic validity. The data also indicate a potential positive correlation between the overall grades of both models.

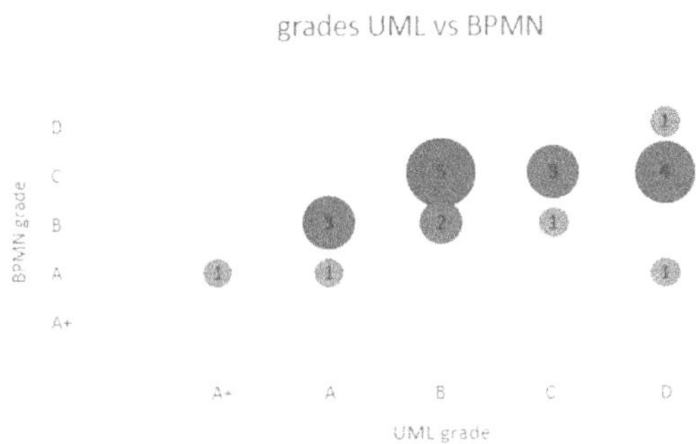

Figure 3.3 grades

Annotations

In general, there was a fairly even split between participants who made annotations (10/22) and participants that didn't make annotations (12/22). Regarding UML error types, there is no clear difference between both groups. However, it is interesting to note that in the group that did not make annotations, all participants made association and attribute errors, while in the group that did make annotations, a slightly lower proportion of participants made these errors (9/10 and 6/10 respectively). Regarding UML quality error types, the group that did make annotations had a higher proportion of participants making syntax errors (8/10 vs 6/12 for the group with annotations), and made on average slightly more syntax errors per person . Regarding BPMN error types on the other hand, the group that did make annotations performed slightly better overall compared to the group that did not make annotations, although the difference is not very noticeable. The group without annotations performs slightly better on semantic completeness, while the group with annotations performs slightly better on syntax, semantic validity and pragmatic quality.

While the difference between both groups is not very noticeable regarding the error types, the difference between both groups regarding grades is more interesting. For the UML class diagram, the grades seem normally distributed for the group without annotations, while for the group with annotations, grades tend to be more extreme (see Figure 3.4). For the BPMN process model, grades without annotations also seem to follow a normal distribution, although skewed to the right. On the other hand, grades for the group with annotation are distributed more uniformly (see Figure 3.5).

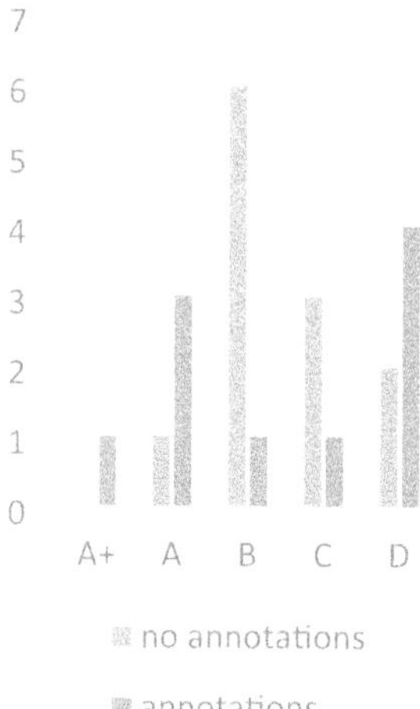

Figure 3.4 grades for the UML class diagram for the groups with and without annotations

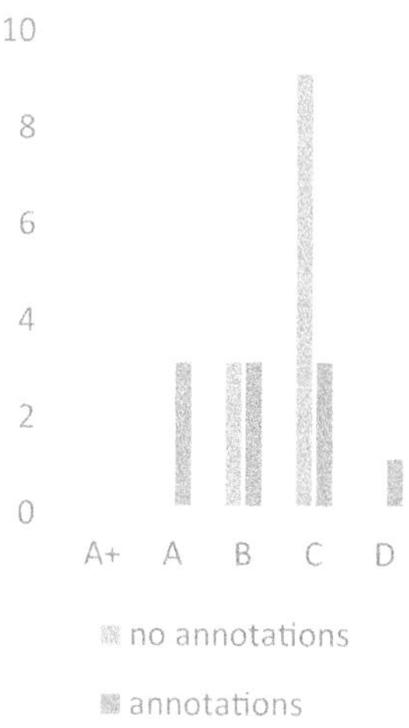

Figure 3.5 grades for the BPMN process model for the groups with and without annotations

RQ2 – Demographic Characteristics

English

In general, the majority of participants estimates their English proficiency level to be intermediate (7/22) or advanced (12/22). One participant estimates their English proficiency level to be basic and two participants estimate their level to be expert or native speaker. Due to the very small number of participants with English proficiency level

'Basic' or 'Expert/Native speaker', we grouped them with the categories 'Intermediate' and 'Expert/Native speaker' respectively in Table 3.11.

Table 3.11 grades for the UML class diagram and the BPMN process model for the groups with English proficiency level 'Basic + Intermediate' and 'Advanced + Expert/Native speaker'

	UML		BPMN	
grade	Basic + Intermediate	Advanced + Expert/Native speaker	Basic + Intermediate	Advanced + Expert/Native speaker
A+	0	1	0	0
A	1	3	0	3
B	0	7	1	5
C	3	1	7	5
D	4	2	0	1

Regarding the UML error types, there is no major difference between the group with English proficiency level 'Intermediate' and the group with English proficiency level 'Advanced'. Regarding UML model quality, the group with English proficiency level 'Advanced + Expert/Native speaker' clearly performs better on semantic validity than the group with English proficiency level 'Basic + Intermediate'. Also, for syntax and semantic completeness, this group performs slightly better. Regarding the BPMN error types, the proportion of participants that make notation errors and the average number of notation errors per participant decreases as the English proficiency level increases. The group with English proficiency level 'Advanced + Expert/Native speaker' makes on average fewer task and flow errors than the group with English proficiency level 'Basic + Intermediate'. Regarding BPMN model quality, the group with English proficiency level 'Advanced + Expert/Native speaker' performs better on semantic validity and pragmatic quality than the group with English proficiency level 'Basic + Intermediate', while the group with English proficiency level 'Basic + Intermediate' performs on average better on syntax and semantic completeness.

Regarding the grades for both models, the group with English proficiency level 'Advanced + Expert/Native speaker' scores better than the group with English level 'Basic + Intermediate'. In summary, the group with English level 'Advanced scores better overall than the group with English level 'Intermediate', except for syntax and semantic completeness of the BPMN process model.

UML Class Diagram experience
In general, there were no participants without any experience of UML class diagrams. Two participants had heard of UML class diagrams and seven participants had some previous experience with UML class diagrams. Half of the participants had a reasonable amount of experience, which corresponds to active participation in a course, and two

participants had a lot of experience, which corresponds to several courses or practical use. Since the large majority of participants have some or a reasonable amount of experience (18/22 combined), we will exclude the other groups from this summary.

Regarding UML error types, the group with a reasonable amount of experience in UML class diagrams performs better than the group with only some experience in UML class diagrams. The difference is the least noticeable for attribute errors. The two participants with a lot of experience did not make any notation errors. Overall, the group with a reasonable amount of experience in UML class diagrams performs better than the group with only some experience in UML class diagrams regarding model quality as well, except for semantic completeness where they make slightly more errors on average. Regarding the grades for the UML class diagram (see Figure 3.6), the group with a reasonable amount of experience in UML class diagrams scores better than the group with only some experience in UML class diagrams.

In summary, in line with expectations, the group with a reasonable amount of experience in UML class diagrams performs better for the UML class diagram compared to the group with only some experience in UML class diagrams.

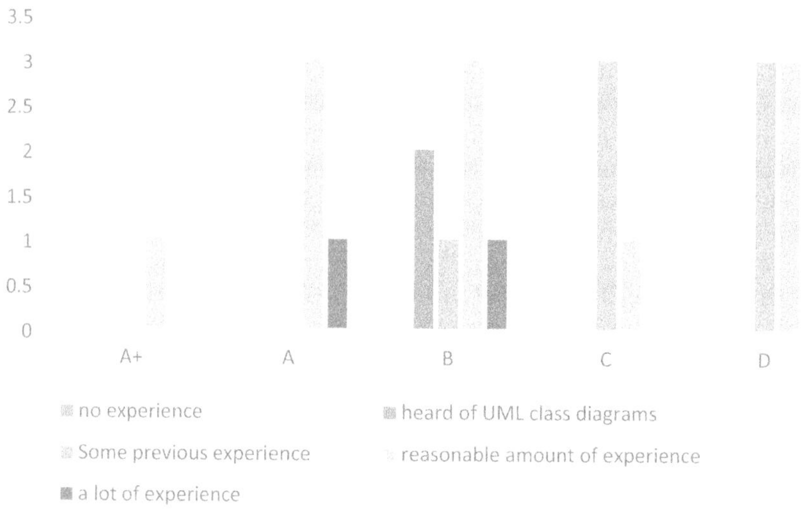

Figure 3.6 grades for the UML class diagram for the groups with different levels of UML class diagram experience

BPMN process model experience
In terms of BPMN process model experience, three participants had no experience, 7 participants had heard of BPMN process models and 12 participants had some previous experience with BPMN process models. There were no participants with a reasonable

amount of experience (e.g., active participation in a course) or a lot of experience (e.g., several courses or practical use).

Regarding the BPMN process model, in line with expectations, the percentage of participants making notation errors and the average number of notation errors per participant decreases as the level of experience with BPMN process models increases. While every participant made task errors, the average number of task errors per participants decreases as the level of experience with BPMN process models increases. The group that has no experience in BPMN process models makes on average more flow errors than the other two groups (5.67 for the group without experience, versus 3.29 for the group that has heard of BPMN process models and 3.75 for the group with some experience). The percentage of participants making syntax, semantic validity and pragmatic errors decreases as the level of experience with BPMN process models increase. Only for semantic completeness, the group that had heard of BPMN process models has a lower percentage of participants making errors compared to the group with some experience. The average number of semantic validity, semantic completeness and pragmatic quality errors decreases as the level of experience with BPMN process models increases. Only for syntax errors, the group that had heard of BPMN process models makes slightly fewer errors on average than the group with some experience.

Regarding the grades (see Figure 3.7), the grades for the BPMN process model seem to increase as the level of experience in BPMN process models increases.

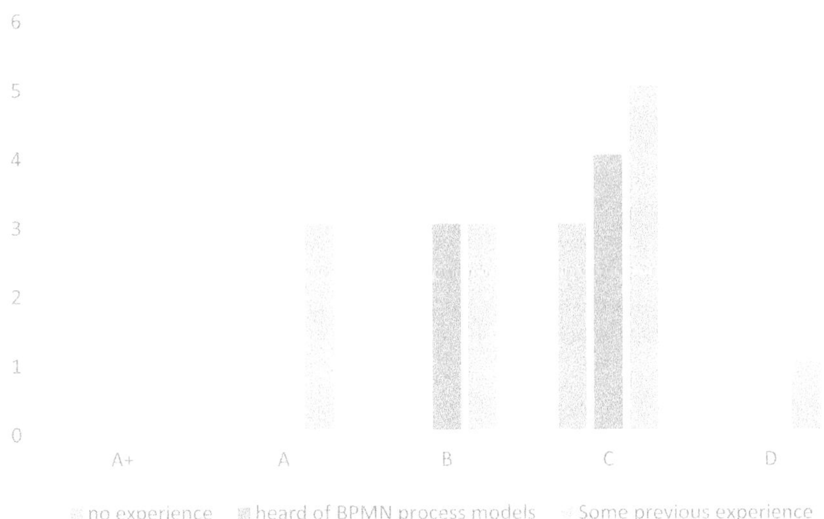

Figure 3.7 grades for the BPMN process model for the groups with different levels of BPMN process model experience

Other modelling language experience

The majority of the participants did not mention any other experience with modelling languages (12/22). Four participants had previous experience with at least one other data modelling language, three participants had previous experience with at least one other behaviour modelling language, and three participants had previous experience with both data and behaviour modelling languages.

Regarding the UML class diagram, the participants with no other experience in modelling languages performs better on associations and attributes than the other groups. However, it is interesting to see that the group with only experience in other behaviour modelling languages performs the best regarding notation (as they didn't make a single notation error) and classes. Regarding syntax and semantic completeness, the group that has only experience with other data modelling languages and the group that has only experience with only other behaviour modelling languages, perform worse than the groups that have either no other experience or a combination of other experience in both data and behaviour modelling languages. For semantic validity on the other hand, the participants with only one type of 'other modelling language experience' make on average fewer errors.

Regarding the BPMN process model, the group with only experience in other behaviour modelling languages also performs better regarding notation and tasks, whereas the group with only experience in other data modelling languages performs best regarding flow. Regarding the quality of the BPMN process model, the results are varied: the group with no other experience made the least semantic completeness errors on average, the group with only other experience in data modelling languages made the least pragmatic errors on average, the group with only other experience in behaviour modelling languages made the least semantic validity errors on average and the group with other experience in both data and behaviour modelling languages made the least syntax errors.

Regarding the grades for both the UML class diagram and the BPMN process model see Figure 3.8 and Figure 3.9 respectively), participants with no other experience and participants with other experience in both data and behaviour modelling seem to score worse than the other two groups. Interestingly, participants with only other experience in behaviour modelling score slightly better than participants with only other experience in data modelling for both models.

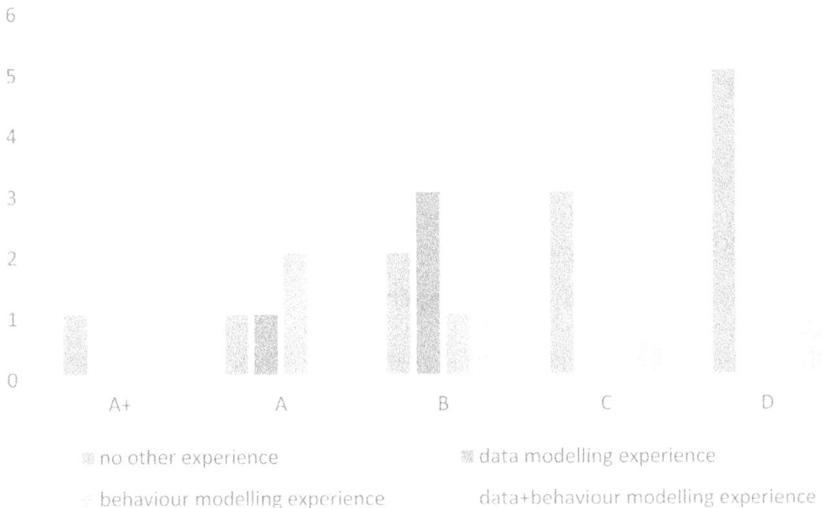

Figure 3.8 grades for the UML class diagram for the groups with different levels of other modelling experience

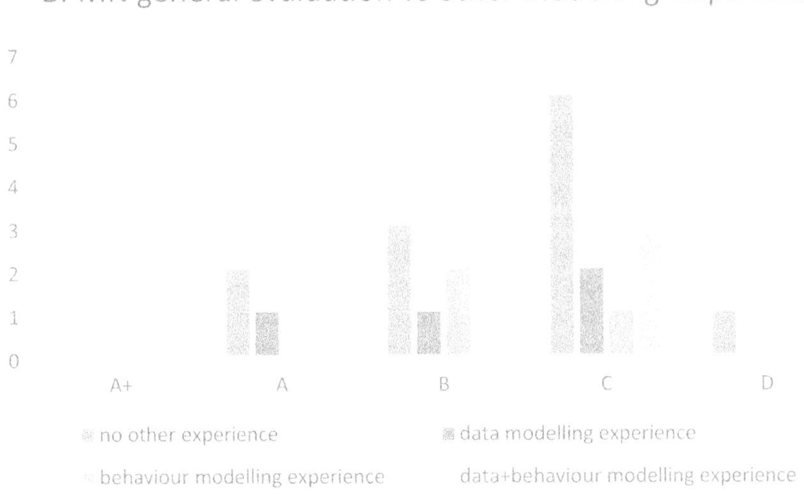

Figure 3.9 grades for the BPMN process model for the groups with different levels of other modelling experience

RQ3 – Ease of Use of Modelling Languages

The ease of use for UML class diagrams and BPMN process models is a calculated average of scores ranging from –2 to 2. Overall, both UML and BPMN receive a positive average ease of use score (UML: 0.86; BPMN: 0.53). The majority of participants gave a positive score. UML class diagrams score slightly better than BPMN process models. There does not seem to be a strong correlation between the perceived ease of use of a modelling language and the obtained score (the correlation coefficient between UML grade and UML ease of use is –0.126, and the correlation coefficient between the BPMN grade and the BPMN ease of use is –0.192).

RQ4 – Participants Perspective on the Experiment

Model Difficulty

The difficulty of the given exercise is measured in two different ways. On one hand, the questionnaire contains three Likert-scale questions (on a scale of –2 to 2) inspired by the MEM questionnaire [92] on the difficulty of creating the UML class diagram, creating the BPMN process model, and assigning a given requirement to the correct model. These questions can be considered individually, and additionally, an overall difficulty score per participant can be calculated. On the other hand, the questionnaire contains a question where participants have to indicate which of both models was the most difficult to create. Additionally, the questionnaire includes an open question where participants can name the most difficult aspect of the entire exercise.

Regarding the difficulty of the exercise, the result of the three Likert scale questions and the calculated overall score is positive, meaning that creating the UML class diagram (average score of 0.27), creating the BPMN process model (0.59) and allocating the requirements to the correct model (0.50) is on average not considered difficult by the participants. Creating the UML class diagram is considered more difficult than creating the BPMN process model or allocating the requirements to the correct model. For each participant, we derived which model they considered the easiest based on which model received the highest score on these Likert scale questions. This results in 8 participants finding creating the UML class diagram the easiest and 11 participants finding creating the BPMN process model the easiest (for 3 participants, both models receive the same score). There is a slight inconsistency between these results and the results of the direct question "Which model was the easiest to make?" (see Table 3.12). To the direct question, 7 participants answer that the UML class diagram is the easiest to create, while 15 participants answer that the BPMN process model is the easiest to create. This inconsistency cannot be explained by the three students that give both models the same difficulty score: there are 7 participants for whom the easiest model according to the Likert scale questions contradicts their answer to the direct question. We conclude that these participants had difficulties with comparing the difficulty level of both models. The answers to the open question on the most difficult aspect of the entire exercise were coded with one or two labels, and overall, the majority of participants mentioned identifying correct classes as the most difficult issue (see Table 3.13). One participant explained: *"I found difficult the UML part because in the exercise the process where more explicit than the data type [...]"*. There does not seem to be a clear correlation between the difficulty of the models and the obtained grade.

Table 3.12 Easiest model according to the MEM questions vs easiest model according to participants

		MEM quest. easiest model		
		UML	-	BPMN
Easiest model	UML	3	2	2
	BPMN	5	1	9

Table 3.13 Codes for the most difficult aspects of the exercise according to the participants, and how often they were mentioned

Difficult aspect	**Count**
Classes	12
Associations	4
Tasks	3
Gateways	2
Requirement allocation	2
Actor as class	1
BPMN in general	1
Gateway pairs	1

Simultaneous Modelling

This research question aims to investigate whether participants consider both models simultaneously while working on their solution. Theoretically, this would help them achieve better alignment between both models, which should result in better models. When considering the entire group, the average score per participant for iterative modelling is close to zero (−0.12), which is represented by the boxplot in Figure 3.10 showing a more or less equal spread of positive and negative scores. More importantly, there does not seem to be a correlation between whether or not the participant considers both models simultaneously, and their grade (the correlation coefficient between iterative modelling and the UML grade is 0.021 and the correlation coefficient between iterative modelling and the BPMN grade is 0.047).

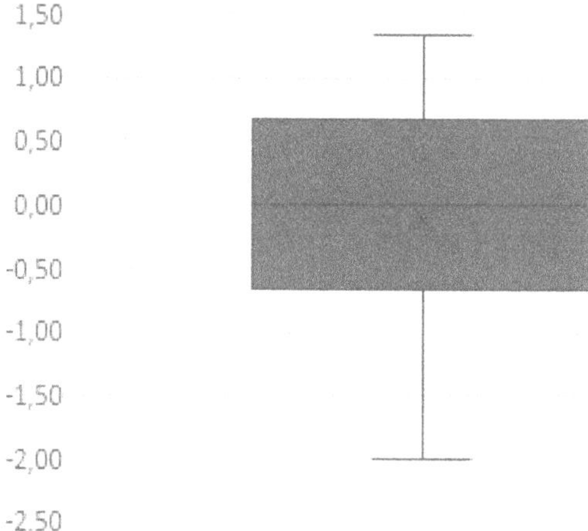

Figure 3.10 Average score for iterative modelling per participant

Editing
Only 5 participants made changes to the first model while working on the second. These participants obtained a good or average score compared to their peers, however, the group is too small to draw any conclusions.

Execution Order

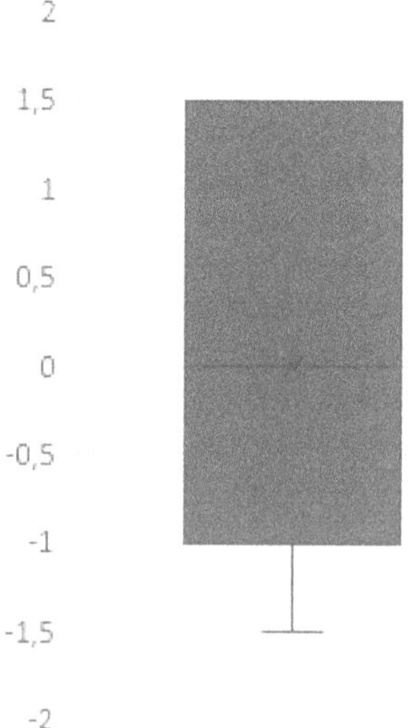

Figure 3.11 Average score per participant for the preference to execute the exercise in the different order.

When considering the entire group, the average score per participant for their order preference is zero, while the boxplot in Figure 3.11 shows that the results are mostly spread between –1 and 1.5 (for a range of –2 to 2). There seems to be a negative correlation between participants agreeing that they would prefer to solve the exercise in the different order, and their grade (–0.273 for UML and –0.389 for BPMN).

RQ5 - For which of RQ1-4 is there a noticeable difference between group A and group B?

First, we discuss the independent characteristics of both groups. Group A estimated their English level slightly higher than group B, although in both groups, the majority of participants estimate their English level to be 'intermediate' or 'advanced'. The level of experience in UML is very similar in both groups, however, in group B, most participants estimate their experience level in BPMN to be level 2, while in group A, this is more spread over level 1 and 2. Regarding experience with other ML, only 1 participant from group A mentions experience with behavioural modelling, whereas 5 participants from group B mention behavioural modelling.

Generally speaking, students make fewer mistakes in the models that they start with. Group A started whit the UML class diagram and made a total of 77 mistakes in the UML Diagram (7 per student on average), and 99 mistakes in the BPMN process model (9 per student on average). On the other hand, group B started with the BPMN process model and made a total of 112 mistakes in the UML class diagram (10.2 per student on average) and only 83 mistakes in the BPMN process model (7.5 per student on average).

For the UML class diagram, students in group A make on average slightly fewer association errors (3.55 for group A and 4.73 for group B). Group A also made on average slightly fewer attribute errors (1.73 for group A and 3.27 for group B). Also, the number of students making attribute errors was lower in group A (8/11) than in group B (10/11). Interestingly, for the class errors we observed that more participants in group A made class errors (8/11 vs 6/11 for group B), while the average number of class errors per participant is slightly lower for group A (1.36 vs 1.82 for group B). More students from group B made syntax errors (A: 5p, B:9p), while all participants made errors on semantic validity, students from group B made on average more errors of this type (A: 3.91/p, B: 5.64). Similarly, the number of participants making errors on semantic completeness is comparable between groups (A: 9p, B: 10p), but participants from group B made on average more errors of this type (A: 1.0/p, B: 2.18/p). finally, only one student in group A made an error on pragmatic quality, and no participants in group B made an error of this type.

Regarding the BPMN process model, the main difference between the groups regarding error types is in notation errors. In group A, 7 participants made notation errors, while in group B only 1 participant made notation errors. For the task errors, there is no notable difference between the groups. For the flow errors, the participants from group A make on average 4.36 errors, while participants from group B make on average 3.36 errors. More students from group A made syntax errors (A: 7p, B: 4p), and on average students from group A also made more syntax errors per person (A: 1.18, B: 0.36). in group B 8 participants made errors on semantic validity, while all participants from group A made these types of errors. However, students from group B still made on average more errors of this type (A: 3.45/p, B: 3.73). The number of participants making errors on semantic completeness is comparable between groups (A: 10p, B: 9p). Finally, the number of participants making errors on pragmatic quality is comparable between groups (A: 11p, B: 10p). participants of group A made on average more errors of this type than participants of group B (A: 2.27, B: 1.64).

Dividing group A and group B along the independent characteristics leads to very small groups of participants, making it not very useful to perform a further analysis. Therefore, we cannot answer whether there is an interaction between execution order and demographic characteristics or the perceived ease of use of modelling languages.

The variable recording whether or not students made annotations on their case description is not an independent characteristic because the order in which they performed the tasks might have affected their behaviour. The majority of group A did not make annotations (only 3/11 made annotations), while the majority of group B did make annotations (7/11). We do not notice a major difference between both groups, or between the groups and the results of the combined group discussed at the beginning of this section.

Regarding the difficulty of the exercise, Table 3.14 shows a deviation in how group A and group B score the difficulty of the individual models: group A seems to find the BPMN process model easier than the UML class diagram, while for group B, both models are equally difficult. We also see that for both groups, the grades of the model they started with seem to be positively correlated with how easy the participants find that model to create (0.434 for group A; 0.400 for group B), while the grades of the second model show a slight negative correlation with how easy they found this model (−0.327 for group A; −0.258 for group B).

Table 3.14 average scores of group A and group B for the difficulty of the exercise

	Average score for group A	Average score for group B
Creating the UML class diagram is easy	0.18	0.36
Creating the BPMN process model is easy	0.82	0.36
Allocating the requirements to the correct model is easy	0.45	0.55
Overall the exercise is easy *(average of the other three scores)*	0.48	0.41

Regarding the most difficult aspect of the entire exercise, there is no clear difference between groups, and in both groups identifying classes is the most frequently mentioned aspect as shown in Table 3.15.

Table 3.15 Codes for the most difficult aspects of the exercise according to the participants, and how often they were mentioned in each group

Difficult aspect	Count in group A	Count in group B
Classes	5	7
Associations	2	2
Tasks	1	2
Gateways	1	1
Requirement allocation	0	2
Actor as class	1	0
BPMN in general	1	0
Gateway pairs	1	0

Regarding iterative modelling, the average score per participant stays close to zero in both groups (0.06 for group A and –0.3 for group B, see Figure 3.12), although the score for group B leans more negative. The boxplot also shows that the scores in group A are more varied than the scores in group B, which is represented by the boxplot showing a more or less equal spread of positive and negative scores. More importantly, while still close to zero, the correlation coefficients between whether or not the participant considers both models simultaneously, and their grade, diverges when considering the groups separately: the correlation coefficient between iterative modelling and the UML grades is 0.164 for group A and –0.321 for group B, and the correlation coefficient between iterative modelling and the BPMN grades is 0.236 for group A and –0.192 for group B.

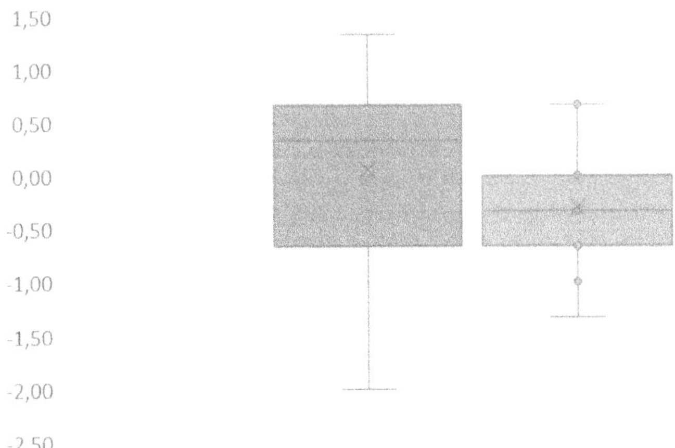

Figure 3.12 Average score for iterative modelling per participant in group A (left) and group B (right)

Due to the small sample of participants editing their models, we do not analyse the difference between both groups in this regard.

Finally, we analyse the difference between both groups with regard to their preferred execution order. Here we see that group A leans towards agreeing that they would prefer a different order, while group B leans towards disagreeing that they want a different order. Again, the boxplots in Figure 3.13 show that the scores are spread wider in group A. The suspected negative correlation between participants agreeing that they would prefer to solve the exercise in the different order, and their grade, remains.

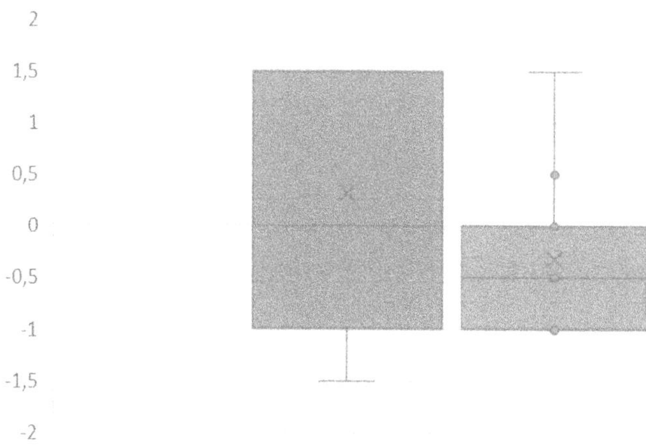

Figure 3.13 Average score per participant for the preference to execute the exercise in the different order for group A (left) and group B(right)

3.4.3 Discussion

Generally speaking, most results are in line with what can be expected. For example, participants that estimate their level of English to be higher perform slightly better. Similarly, the performance on the UML class diagrams improves as the level of experience with UML class diagrams increases and the performance on the BPMN process models improves as the level of experience with BPMN process models increases. One interesting finding from this study is that there seems to be a positive correlation between the grades of the UML class diagram and the grades of the BPMN process model. There could be several explanations for this correlation. One explanation is that participants need the same skill for both modelling tasks: abstraction. Thus, it could be that the grade is mostly explained by how well the participant can make abstractions. On the other hand, the interaction between both models could also be a factor: If the participant is good at identifying which requirement should be included in which model, and how the models can interact, in theory, the overall quality of both models increases because the models contain the correct elements.

Another interesting finding is the relationship between making annotations on the case description and the result of the UML class diagram. Participants who made annotations tend to score either on the high end of the spectrum or on the low end of the spectrum, while participants who did not make annotations had grades that were distributed normally. However, further research is required to investigate whether a causal relationship is actually present here.

A third finding we want to highlight is the observed relationship between previous experience of the participants and the overall model quality. Previous experience with data modelling languages other than UML class diagrams and behaviour modelling languages other than BPMN process models could play a role: participants that report experience in only one type of modelling language (either data or behaviour) tend to score slightly better than participants that report no experience other than UML class diagrams and BPMN process models, and also tend to score slightly better than participants that report experience in both types of modelling languages. While it could be interesting to further investigate whether there is a causal relationship between these observations, it is important to keep in mind that the previous experience with modelling languages other than UML class diagrams and BPMN process models is one of the few open questions on the questionnaire, making it more susceptible to bias in self-reporting. Further research is required to investigate the impact of previous knowledge and experience on the quality of created models.

A fourth observation is that there seems to be a potential relationship between solving the exercise in the individual participant's order preference and the overall grade. Participants that indicated they would have preferred to start with the other model than the one assigned to them, tend to have lower grades. We also want to highlight the observations made when comparting the group starting with the UML class diagram and the group starting with the BPMN process model. In both groups, participants made fewer mistakes in the first model they made. Also, there seems to be a positive correlation between how easy the participants find the first model and the quality of their first model, which is to be expected, but this relationship is reversed for their second model. This relationship is difficult to explain and should be investigated further in the future. Additionally, we see the majority of the participants across both groups would prefer to start with the BPMN process model. This could be because it is easier to pick up on terminology of business processes in a joint case description than it is to pick up on the terminology of the database structure. However, this could also be specific to the given case and should be further investigated by repeating similar experiments with different cases.

A final observation from correcting the models that did not come forward when reporting the results, is that 20/22 participants correctly model the task "contact professor for review", which is mentioned explicitly, while only 1 participant correctly identified the task "contact IO for review" which is not mentioned explicitly but should be deduced from the provided context. This was surprising given that both tasks are extremely similar and could be indicative for a lack of inference capabilities. Therefore, investigating how the use of different wording for the same case description yields different results could also lead to interesting insights in future work.

We can also compare the results from this experiment to the results from the pilot experiment. In this experiment, the participants as a group made more or less the same number of mistakes in both models. In the pilot experiment, participants made more mistakes in the BPMN process model than in the UML class diagram: in the pilot experiment, 70,4% of mistakes can be allocated to the BPMN model. This could be explained by the fact that the BPMN model for this experiment was simplified based on the findings of the pilot experiment. In this experiment, the most frequent error types for the UML class diagram were association errors, while in the pilot experiment, class errors are more frequent. While the case description was edited with regard to the process, the information that should be captured by the UML class diagram remained mostly unchanged. Therefore, this disparity is more likely due to the different backgrounds of the participants in both settings. In both experimental settings, the most frequent error types of the BPMN model were task errors.

Finally, we can compare the results from both experiments with the related work. Table 3.16 provides an overview of the main findings from the related work on difficulties students face in data modelling, as well as the corresponding findings in from both experiments.

Table 3.16 Comparison between related work and both experiments

Modelling difficulty according to related work	Pilot experiment	Follow-up experiment
Most difficulties for both novice and more experienced participants are related to relationships between entities [67], [72], [73]	There were relatively few mistakes on identifying relationships between entities, although one of the most frequent mistake in the UML class diagram was missing classes, which automatically results in missing relationships. These missing relationships were not counted separately as mistakes.	The largest group of error types in the UML class diagram are association errors (91/189). The largest group of error types in the UML class diagram are association errors (91/189).
The majority of errors are association errors. The largest error type are associations with wrong multiplicities [67]	The majority of errors are class errors, with missing classes and superfluous classes being the most frequent error types. (after combining layer allocation errors with UML class diagram errors)	
Most cognitive breakdowns occur when participants try to determine cardinalities, followed by deciding on a label for their relationship types and deciding between entity type and relationship types [72], [73]	After missing classes and superfluous classes the most frequent occurring error type in the UML class diagram were issues with cardinalities.	

(*continued*)

Table 3.16 (*continued*)

Modelling difficulty according to related work	Pilot experiment	Follow-up experiment
Up to 30% of solutions contain superfluous classes when case description contains aspects not relevant for data model [67]	Superfluous classes are the most occurring error type in the UML class diagram, together with missing classes	Almost half of the participants included process elements in their data model
Out of the four most occurring errors (in more than 60% of solutions), three relate to distinguishing between layers [74]	Most of the superfluous classes represent concepts that belong in a different layer.	

As stated in the introduction, this study aims to identify potential factors impacting the quality of models created by students. Including a wide variety of factors could impact the internal validity as there could be interaction effects present. wide scope of this study comes with a number of limitations. However, the potential relationships reported in this study highlight new potential research avenues for future work, given that not much research on education of multi-modelling exists yet. Regarding external validity there are also a few limitations to keep in mind. First, the questionnaire relies partially on self-reported data, which could introduce a certain bias in the results. Second, the correction of the models was done by only one evaluator, however, the use of an error typology resulted in a very systematic approach, reducing the bias.

3.4.4 Conclusion

This section presents an experiment on combined data and process modelling by students. To the best of our knowledge, there has been no prior research on this topic apart from our pilot experiment. Therefore, the study is set up to be exploratory and covers several different factors. We investigate model quality (RQ1), as well as the potential influence of the following factors: whether or not participants made annotations, self-reported level of English (RQ2.1), level of experience with UML class diagrams (RQ2.2), level of experience with BPMN process models (RQ2.3), experience with other modelling languages (RQ2.4), perceived ease of use of UML class diagrams and BPMN process models (RQ3), The difficulty of the given case (RQ4.1), whether or not participants report they consider both models simultaneously (RQ4.2), whether participants edited their first model while working on their second model (RQ4.3), the preferred order in which students want to create the models (RQ4.4), and the actual order in which models were created (RQ5). Generally speaking, most results are in line with expectations. For example, the performance on the UML class diagrams improves as the level of experience with UML class diagrams increases. An interesting finding from this study is that there seems to be a positive correlation between the grades of the UML class diagram and the grades of the BPMN process model. This could be explained by the fact that participants need abstraction skills for both modelling tasks and/or by the interaction between both models. Another observation is that there seems to be a potential relationship between solving the exercise in the individual participant's preferred order and the overall grade. When considering the group two groups that each started the exercise with a different model, participants made fewer mistakes in the first model they made. Additionally, we see the majority of the participants across both groups would prefer to start with the BPMN process model.

Part III
Design and Demonstration of the Integration of MERODE and BPMN

This part consists of five chapters on the design and demonstration of the integration of Merode and BPMN. The fourth chapter starts with addressing the need for an abstract syntax and basic semantics for the integration of Merode and BPMN through the construction of a meta-model. In the fifth chapter, we address the additional semantics required for the integration and present the development of a prototype modelling tool. Finally, the sixth chapter demonstrates the use of the MERODExBPMN integration by using the meta-model as a basis for defining a common terminology for object-centric event logging and data-centric process modelling.

Chapter 4
MERODExBPMN - A Meta-model for Integrated Domain and Process Modelling

4.1 Introduction

While data-aware process modelling has recently gained some traction, these approaches address the data aspect in a variety of ways, but rarely according to state-of-the art conceptual domain modelling approaches [93]. There is therefore, as indicated in [89], a need for more research on data-aware processes based on a full-fledged domain model. Meaning, a domain model that represents a full overview of the business concepts and that can support *all* business processes of an organization. Such a full-fledged domain model should therefore also be aware of the processes it supports, in order to be able to provide all the necessary data. Assuming that a full-fledged domain model exists, as well as a set of business process models referring to this data model, implementing the connection between these data-aware processes and the (applications based on the) domain model can obviously be done ad hoc, on a case by case basis. However, ideally, it should be possible to deploy data-aware process models to a process engine, without the need for hand-crafting connections between the process models and the data and application services that need to be invoked. In order to achieve a true multi-modelling approach, process and data models should be deployable together, and the integration of the process models and the data models should be based on a conceptualization of the connection between the respective meta-models. This would allow for the model-driven deployment of data-aware process models, without the need for handcrafted code, thus realizing immediate utility of modelling efforts. Achieving such model-driven deployment for software in a production environment, is quite ambitious and challenging. As a more modest step towards this ambitious goal, our research targets the generation of a throw-way prototype instead, thus enabling the simultaneous fast prototyping of a process-aware data model and its data-aware process models. Fast prototyping has many different benefits. It can be used in education to help students evaluating the quality of their models. This has been demonstrated by the research presented in [66] and [76]. Prototyping is also used in agile development, as described in [94].

The goal of this chapter is twofold. The first research goal (RG1) is developing a conceptual model that captures the connection between a process model and a domain model. The second research goal (RG2) is creating a proof of concept implementation (PoC) based on the connected meta-models, such that this PoC provides the necessary knowledge to develop model-to-code transformations at a later stage. Besides the benefits of demonstrating the achievability of fast prototyping capabilities, the result of the second goal will also be used to validate the results obtained for the first goal (RG3).

© The Author(s), under exclusive license to Springer Nature Switzerland AG 2026
C. Verbruggen, *Advancing Multi-modelling in MDE for Integrated Domain and Business Process Modelling*, Lecture Notes in Business Information Processing 576,
https://doi.org/10.1007/978-3-032-13876-7_4

The development of this approach and the corresponding tool support, follows the design science research methodology described by Hevner in [10].

In the next section, we briefly discuss the related research. Then, section 4.3 provides an overview of the design science research methodology that we followed. Section 4.4 reviews the existing meta-models for MERODE and BPMN that are reused from the knowledge base. Section 4.5 describes the developed artefacts: the combined meta-model as an answer to RG1, the implementation of a proof of concept to satisfy RG2 and the validation of the meta-model (RG3). In section 4.6, we reflect on the proposed MERODExBPMN meta-model and how it supports the proof of concept. Finally, section 4.7 contains the conclusion and a discussion of the future work.

4.2 Related Work

In the field of application development, many low-code or no-code approaches rely on model-driven engineering principles. However, as demonstrated in a recent review of such approaches these tools rely on a classical data modelling language or a proprietary language [95]. Due to their focus on either data management, or workflow management or Graphical User Interface design, they fail in offering a multi-modelling approach. Moreover, while modelling is at the core of such platforms, their approach to modelling is rather simplistic and lags behind the state of the art of conceptual modelling. In [93] the authors conducted a systematic literature review of data-centric process modelling approaches in order to develop an evaluation framework for such approaches. In this review, 17 different approaches were found. Several papers were based on the artefact-centric approach (13). Steinau et al. define an artefact-centric process model as folows: *"An artefact-centric process model encapsulates data and process logic into artifacts. Artifacts consists of an information model holding the data and a lifecycle model describing the changes to the information model."* [93]. Other papers included in the literature review were based on case management, data-centric dynamic systems, object-aware approaches, object-centric approach and the stateless approach (2 − 4 each), plus eleven other approaches discussed in only one paper. Many of these approaches define the data on a process or process instance level, disregarding the overall data structure of the system. Other approaches, such as the artefact-centric approach, model the data structure of an IS, but capture all the process logic within the lifecycles of data constructs. None of the approaches seem to provide integration between a full-fledged data/business artefact model and a full-fledged process model, as they do not include a data-model.

In [89], the authors discuss the importance of using a full-fledged domain modelling approach for the development of data-aware processes, as this would provide enterprise-wide definitions of business concepts and their relations that can be used by all business processes. The authors propose how this can be achieved by the integration of Merode and BPMN. In [89] the authors provide a conceptual proof of concept based on a running case describing how these models can be conceptually integrated by making use of the Merode tools and the Camunda BPM platform and Modeler, and how such integration would satisfy the majority of the requirements for data-aware process modelling identified in [87]. The present work extends the work of [89] by developing a meta-model and the running code for the same case.

An important aspect of an effective and useful modelling approach is whether or not it can rely on adequate tool support. A well-known tool in the research community is Adoxx [96], developed by OmiLab and the University of Vienna. This tool focusses on the development of meta-models and modelling tools for domain-specific languages. Using Adoxx, OmiLab created the Bee-Up tool, which combines UML, BPMN, EPC, ER and Petri Nets. The tool is very flexible in the connections that are allowed between the different model types. Bee-Up provides extensive support for the simulation and analysis of process models. However, it does not seem to provide fully automated code generation for a working application, whereby the generated code for process models and data models is fully integrated without any manual intervention. Similarly, a tool like Signavio offers tool support for BPMN and for the drawing of UML class diagrams, but does not allow generating integrated code from these models.

4.3 Design Science Research Methodology

Hevner et al. [10] provide a framework for IS Research that characterizes the interactions between the Environment, the IS Research and the Knowledge Base. The applicable knowledge from the knowledge base and the business needs of the environment inform the IS research. In turn, the artefact that is the result of the IS research leads to new knowledge in the knowledge base and/or a new application in the environment.

In this chapter, the existing Merode and BPMN meta-models are part of the knowledge base. The business need we identified is an integrated meta-model that formalizes the connections between an artefact-centric domain model and BPMN. The artefact we develop in this chapter is the MERODExBPMN meta-model (RG1) and the implementation of a prototype (RG2). The result of RG2 is then used for evaluating the proposed meta-model (RG3). The artefact is added to the knowledge base for next iterations.

Hevner et al. [10] provide seven guidelines for effective design science research, described in Table 4.1. The first guideline is addressed by producing a meta-model (RG1) and an instantiation of the meta-model (RG2). The importance and relevance of the business problem was discussed in the previous sections, which satisfies guideline 2. The quality and efficacy of the meta-model is demonstrated with the prototype. The utility will be further evaluated in future work. Guideline 3 is thus already partially satisfied. The research contribution required by Guideline 4 is the ability to formally model the connections between a full-fledged domain model and a process model. The construction of the artefact was done in a rigorous manner as we examined the existing meta-models carefully before identifying the most appropriate connections. The evaluation of the artefact by means of a proof of concept was performed in a rigorous manner as the developed meta-model was implemented 'as-is', and shortcomings were systematically identified and addressed in a next iteration. Guideline 5 is thus satisfied. Future evaluations (see Guideline 3) will follow a rigorous method as well. Guideline 6 requires a search process to come to a final solution. Our overall goal is to develop a model-driven approach for integrated data and process modelling with the corresponding tool support. The research presented in this chapter are the first two steps in that direction. The next steps in our search strategy for the overall solution are further explained in section 4.7. Finally, the seventh guideline is satisfied since our research

Table 4.1 Design Science Research Guidelines [10]

Guideline	Description
Guideline 1: Design as an Artefact	Design-science research must produce a viable artefact in the form of a construct, a model, a method or an instantiation.
Guideline 2: Problem Relevance	The objective of design-science research is to develop technology-based solutions to important and relevant business problems.
Guideline 3: Design Evaluation	The utility, quality, and efficacy of a design artefact must be rigorously demonstrated via well-executed evaluation methods.
Guideline 4: Research Contributions	Effective design-science research must provide clear and verifiable contributions in the areas of the design artefact, design foundations, and/or design methodologies.
Guideline 5: Research Rigor	Design-science research relies upon the application of rigorous methods in both the construction and evaluation of the design artefact.
Guideline 6: Design as a Search Process	The search for an effective artefact requires utilizing available means to reach desired ends while satisfying laws in the problem environment.
Guideline 7: Communication of Research	Design-science research must be presented effectively both to technology-oriented as well as management-oriented audiences.

is presented to an audience of researchers in this chapter. Additionally, on the Merode website both technology-oriented and management-oriented audiences can find a demo of the prototype presented in this chapter [97]. In conclusion, our research complies with all guidelines except for guideline 3, which is partially satisfied.

4.4 Knowledge Base: Merode and BPMN Meta-models & Tools

This section presents the knowledge base on Merode and BPMN. Section 4.4.1 presents the Merode approach in detail, as well as its existing meta-model. As BPMN is a well-known process modelling language, section 4.4.2 only provides the core aspects of the BPMN meta-model that are relevant for this dissertation. Finally, section 4.4.3 discusses the modelling tools used.

4.4.1 Merode Approach and Meta-model

Merode is a modelling approach for Information Systems Engineering that is based on a layered architecture and that provides guidelines to build an artefact-centric domain model – consisting of a UML class diagram and state charts – at its core. The Merode set of layers includes a layer for business processes, however, a formal specification defining how such a process is modelled and how a process model is integrated with the models in the other layers is not yet defined. Additionally, the Merode approach is supported by a modelling tool and a code generation tool. This code generation tool allows the modeler to generate a prototype of the (artefact-centric) domain model of an application with a single click of a button. The Merode approach is thus a model-driven approach for (artefact-centric) Information Systems engineering.

The Merode approach consists of three layers, where each layer can only access information from the layer below it. The bottom layer is the Enterprise Layer (EL), which consists of two sublayers itself: the Domain Layer (DL) and the Event Handling Layer (EHL). The middle layer is the Information System Service Layer (ISSL) and the top layer is the Business Process Layer (BP).

The DL consists of an Existence Dependency Graph (EDG) which defines the object types. Instances of object types are called objects. The EDG is very similar to a UML Class Diagram, with the added constraint that each relation between two object types should either express existence dependency or it should express inheritance. Existence dependency implies a hierarchical relationship so that each instance of the dependent object type can only exist within the lifecycle of one and always the same instance of the master object type. Therefore, the multiplicity on the side of the master is a read-only 1..1 (a dependent object is linked to one and always the same master object, which corresponds to a {readOnly} 1..1 multiplicity in UML). On the side of the dependent object type, the minimum multiplicity can be 0 or 1 (in Merode, this is called an optional or a mandatory dependency, respectively). The maximum multiplicity is 1 or many (*). Merode adapts the Backman notation for multiplicities, as illustrated in Figure 4.1. Apart from existence dependency relations between object types, the EDG can also contain Inheritance. Object types can have attributes, however, attributes should never be references to other object types as this should be captured with dependencies between object types. Each object type also has a Finite State Machine (FSM) that models its lifecycle. Finally, the DL also contains an Object-Event Table. This table lists all event types that can affect the objects and specifies which object types participate in each event type. If a given object type participates in a given event type, the cell of the OET that corresponds to that event type (row) and that object type (column) is filled. A cell in the OET can be filled in six ways. On the one hand, an event type can be owned (indicated with 'O/?') or acquired (indicated with 'A/?') by a given object type. The propagation rule states that "a master object type by definition participates in all event types in which one of its dependent object types participates" [98]. In other words, master object types always acquire a participation in all event types that are owned or acquired by their dependent object types. On the other hand, event types can create (indicated with '?/C'), modify (indicated with '?/M') or end (indicated with '?/E') instances of object types. This results in six possible combinations: O/C, O/M, O/E, A/C, A/M and A/E. The implementation of the participation of an object type in an event type results in the definition of an operation, which is called a Method in Merode (and a "behavioural feature" in UML). Each Transition in an FSM corresponds to a Method in the OET. Finally, the DL also contains constraints. The Merode Approach defines six types of constraints. Referential integrity constraints are constraints that follow from the EDG due to existence dependency. For example, in order to end the lifecycle of a master object, all its dependent objects should be in a final state (=ended). And in order to create an object, its master objects should exist first. Referential integrity constraints are preconditions for the creating and ending events. Sequence constraints are preconditions for methods based on the state the object is in. All sequence constraints are captured by the FSMs. The other three constraint types cover aspects that cannot be captured by the EDG, OET or FSMs. Uniqueness constraints allow the modeller to identify the attribute or combination of attributes that can be used to uniquely identify an object. A uniqueness constraint can also be expressed making use of a reference to a master object of the constraint object, instead of its attributes. Attribute constraints restrict the possible values of attributes. A method constraint can be used to add constraints to methods that do not follow from the referential integrity constraints and/or the sequence constraints, e.g. preconditions to methods. The final type of constraints are multiple propagation constraints. These constraints can only be applied in a specific circumstance, namely, if a master object type acquires an event owned by one of its dependents via two (or more) different dependency paths. In that case, the master object type will participate twice (or more) in the event. This is called multiple propagation. On instance level, this means that a dependent object could be dependent of two (or more) different instances of the same master object type. For example, an order in a web shop is dependent both on the customer that placed the order and on the product that is ordered. Multiple propagation constraints can express that, if multiple propagation occurs, the two (or more) instances of the master object type that the dependent object type is dependent on, should always be different instances. Alternatively, multiple propagation constraints can express that these instances of the master object type should be one and the same instance. For example, the customer of an order could be the same as or different from the customer of the invoice for that order. If no multiple propagation constraint is added, the EDG allows both scenarios. The formal definitions and rules of the DL in Merode are briefly mentioned at the end of each chapter in the Merode handbook [88]. For a more detailed explanation of the formal definitions and rules of the EDG, OET and FSMs, the reader is referred to [99], [100].

The EHL does not contain any models, but deals with the execution of events (instances of event types). If the execution of an event is requested (triggered), the EHL will first check whether all relevant instances of the object types participating in that event are able to execute the method/transition related to the triggered event. If so, all methods are triggered. However, if one of the objects is unable to execute the

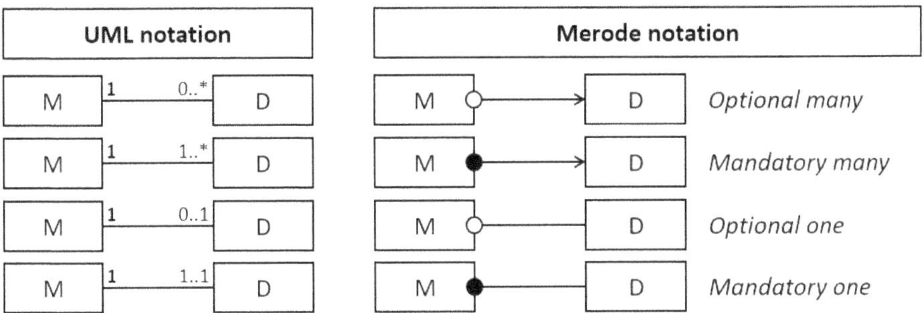

Figure 4.1 The four possible combinations of multiplicities in Merode, adapted from [101]

method (due to any of the constraints of the DL), the EHL will make sure that none of the methods are executed and an error is returned to the component that requested the event execution. In other words, the EHL will ensure that all events can be considered as atomic events.

The ISSL consist of input services and output services. A trivial input service triggers a single event for a single object. As stated above, the EHL will then make sure that the corresponding methods/transitions are executed for that object and its masters. Output services query information from the EL and present it to the user. There are three types of trivial output services: showing a list of all objects of a given object type, searching a specific object of an object type based on search criteria, and showing/selecting the attribute values and state of a specific object of an object type. Finally, complex services can be defined by combining trivial input and/or output services. A complex service that only consists of trivial input services is called a complex input service, and a complex service that only consists of trivial output services is called a complex output service.

Finally, the BPL consist of one or more business process models. In contrast to the EL and ISSL, Merode does not specify which business process modelling language should be used. The business process model should capture the order in which tasks need to be executed, which actor should execute which task, and time constraints of the process. The Merode approach also makes a distinction between business event types (the event types listed in the OET and considered as part of the DL) and process event types (events relevant to the business process, but not to the EL and ISSL, for example, a deadline or timer). The interaction between the BPL and the ISSL can be modelled by means of a mapping table with a row for each process task. In the second column of the mapping table, the input/output service that is triggered by that task is specified.

In Merode, the coordination between layers is ensured through the events. Events are handled in several layers at different granularity levels [102]. The EHL contains both consistent and inconsistent atomic business events. Inconsistent atomic business events are events that put the database in a state that is inconsistent with the model. For example, when the EDG contains a mandatory dependency, creating an instance of the master object type will put the database in an inconsistent state until an instance of the dependent object type has been created too. An inconsistent atomic business event can therefore be replaced by a consistent composed event that combines the inconsistent atomic event with one or more other atomic events that are needed to ensure the database remains consistent with the model. So, in the example of a mandatory dependency, creating instances of the master and the dependent object type can be combined in a consistent composed event. A third granularity level of event handling in Merode occurs in the ISSL, where consistent atomic business events and consistent composed events can be combined in a single input service for the sake of user friendliness.

The Merode meta-model can be found in [88] where each chapter ends with the corresponding fragment of the meta-model. Figure 4.2 combines all these fragments into the complete Merode meta-model.

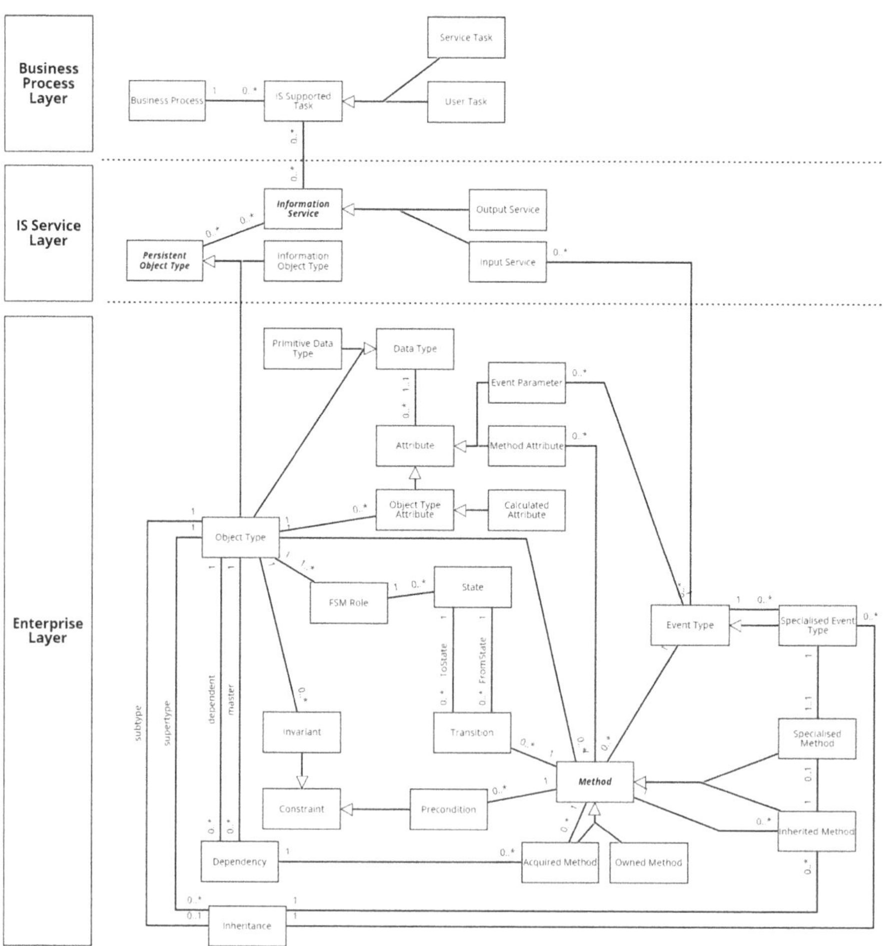

Figure 4.2 The full MERODE meta-model, adapted from [88]

Figure 4.3 shows the parts of the Merode meta-model that are relevant for this chapter. The domain layer part is indicated in blue. The domain object types (BusinessObjectType) are related by binary Associations expressing existence dependency. The BusinessObjectTypes also contain Methods that are triggered by Business Events (BusinessEventType). This is managed by the EHL, since one BusinessEventType can trigger Methods in several BusinessObjectTypes. The part relevant for the ISL is shown in the yellow box and its connection to the EL in the dashed yellow box. An InputService from the ISL will issue one or several EventTriggers in the EHL. Each EventTrigger triggers one BusinessEventType in the Domain layer, which each triggers one or several Methods. Both Input and Output Services can inspect BusinessObjectTypes by means of an ObjectTypeInspection. Finally, the relevant aspects of Merode's BPL are indicated by a green box, and the connection between the BPL and the ISL is indicated by a dashed green box. The activities in the BPL can be supported by an IS by invoking Information Services in the ISL through one or several ISServiceInvocations.

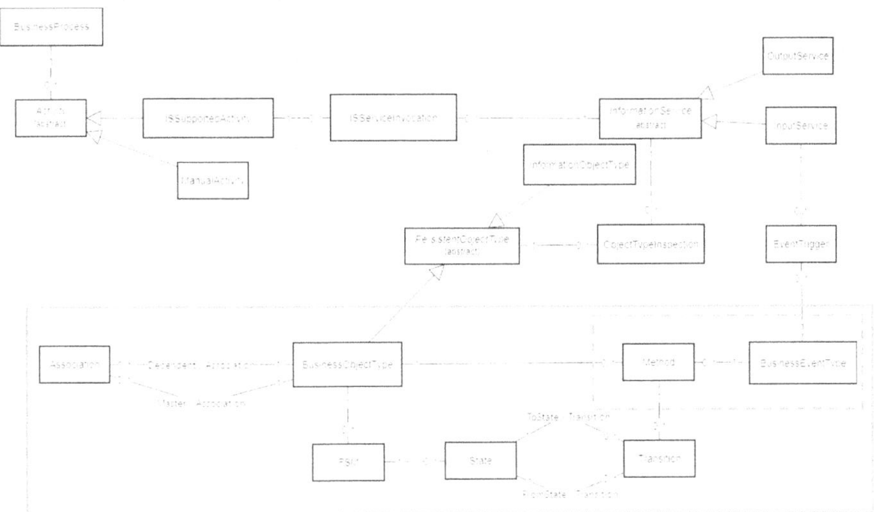

Figure 4.3 The Merode meta-model - adapted from [88]

To demonstrate the different layers, we will make use of the case developed in [89], which is a variant of the recruitment process from [87], slightly adapted for the hiring of PhD candidates at a university.

The UML Class diagram is given in Figure 4.4. The OET in Figure 4.5 provides an overview of the business events and their relation to the business objects. Each class has an FSM. The FSM of Interview is a default FSM. The FSMs of Job, Application and Review are shown in Figure 4.6. The reader is referred to [89] for an in-depth explanation.

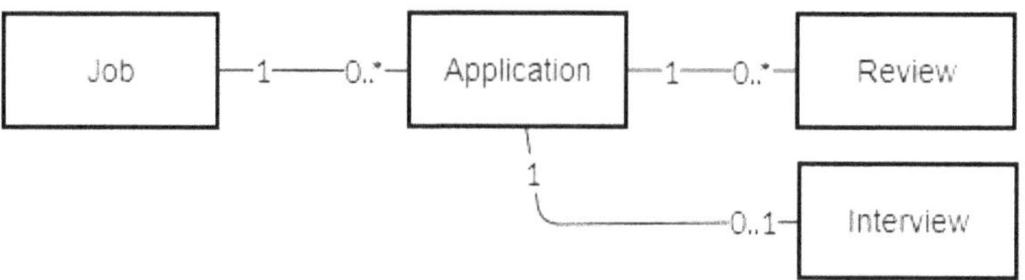

Figure 4.4 EDG [89]

The process used in [89] is shown in Figure 4.7. In this process, an applicant can apply for a job. Then, the HR department determines if the applicant is eligible or not. If the applicant is eligible, the application needs to be reviewed. An international application is first reviewed by the International Office of the university. Then, all applications need to be reviewed by three professors. To obtain these reviews, the HR department sends a request to a professor, who can accept or reject the request. This step is repeated until three professors have committed to writing a review.

	Job	Application	Review	Interview
EVcrJob	O/C			
EVendJob	O/E			
EVcrApplication	A/M	O/C		
EVendApplication	A/M	O/E		
EVcrReview	A/M	A/M	O/C	
EVendReview	A/M	A/M	O/E	
EVcrInterview	A/M	A/M		O/C
EVendInterview	A/M	A/M		O/E
EVsetIneligible	A/M	O/E		
EVsetEligible	A/M	O/M		
EVsubmitApplication	A/M	O/M		
EVmodApplication	A/M	O/M		
FVupdateMotivation	A/M	A/M	O/M	
EVsubmitReview	A/M	A/M	O/M	
EVdecideToHire	A/M	O/M		
EVdecideNotToHire	A/M	O/M		

Figure 4.5 OET [89]

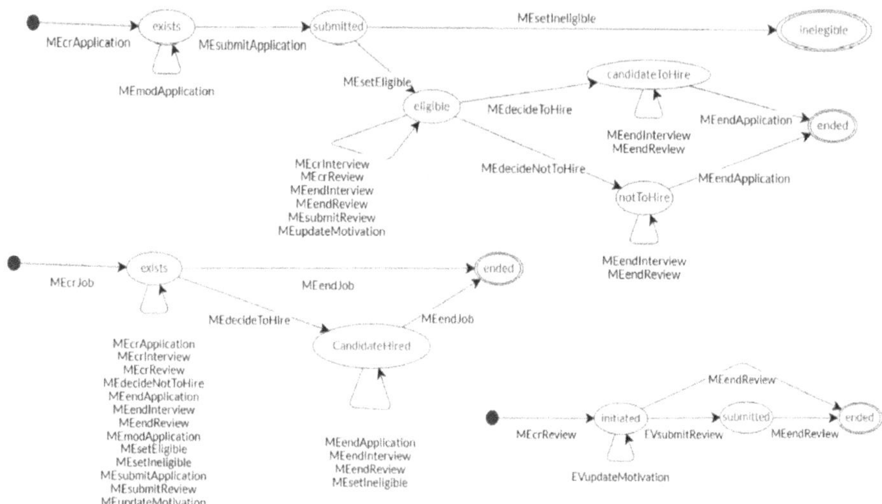

Figure 4.6 FSMs of Application, Job and Review [89]

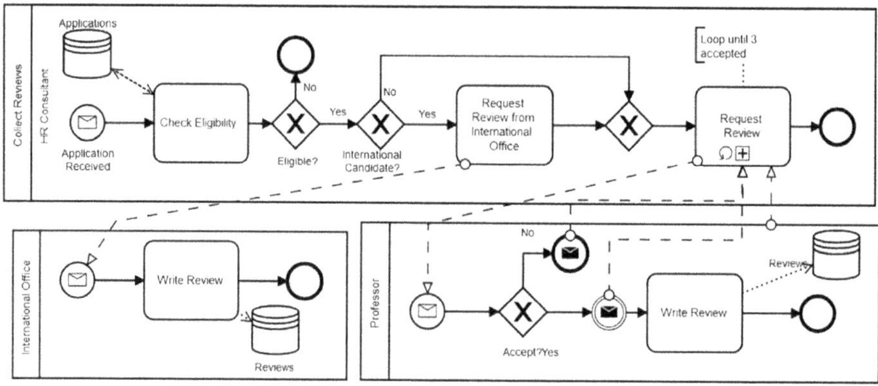

Figure 4.7 Business Process Model [89]

4.4.2 The BPMN Meta-model

According to the BPMN specification [7], the different types of tasks (send tasks, receive tasks, service tasks, user tasks, manual tasks, script tasks and business rule tasks) inherit from the class Task, which inherits from the class Activity. Most of these types of tasks have their own meta-model fragment in the BPMN manual. We have combined these class diagrams fragments into one class diagram (Figure 4.8) showing the combined meta-model fragment related to tasks.

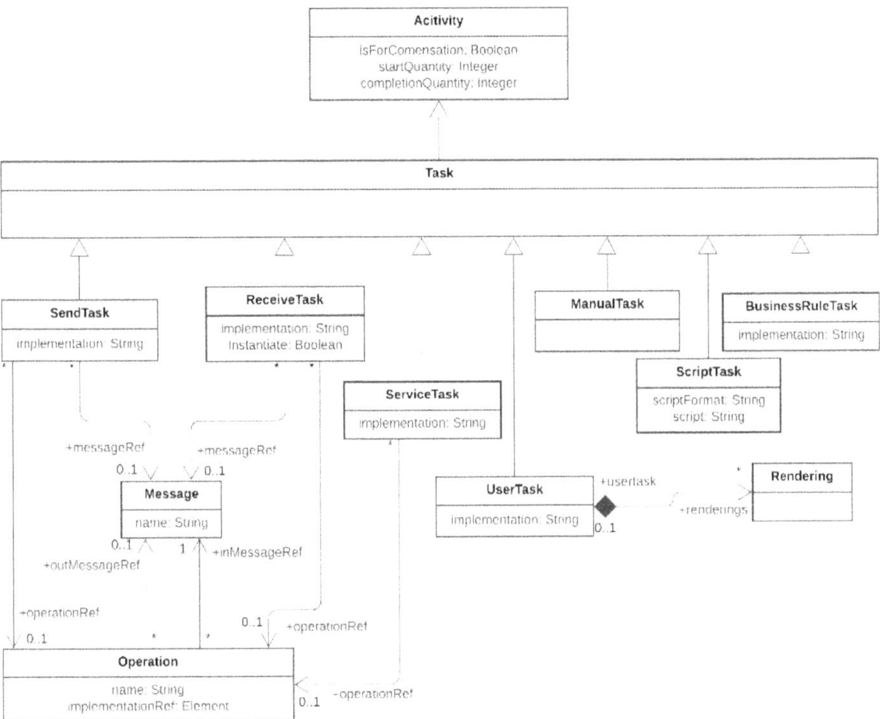

Figure 4.8 Tasks in the BPMN meta-model - adapted from [7]

4.4.3   Existing Tools

The Merode Approach is supported by two tools: Merlin and the Merode Code Generator. The modelling tool is called Merlin and fully supports the EL. Modellers can create EDGs, FSMs and OETs, including data attributes, inheritance and multiple propagation constraints. The other types of constraints that are not captured by the EDG or FSMs can be added to object types and methods as text. Merlin has several additional features, such as model versioning, model checking, the generation of a textual description of the model into a learning report, an alternative visualization of the EDG as a UML Class Diagram, automatic layout of the EDG, automatic propagation of events, and model export as an mxp file (an xml file with a specified structure) or as images. The ISSL and BPL are not supported by Merlin.

The second tool is the Merode Code Generator (MCG). This tool takes an mxp file as input and automatically generates a prototype application based on the Merode model. The MCG implements the full DL, except for the constraints that were specified as text. The MCG also implements the EHL as this does not require any additional models. Finally, the MCG implements all trivial input services and some trivial output services. The user can choose to generate the prototype as a stand-alone desktop application, or as a web application that allows the user to invoke input & output services as REST webservices. This allows accessing the prototype application via a business process engine as will be discussed in this chapter. Complex services triggering several business events or combining input and output services are not yet supported by the tools. In case of a stand-alone desktop application, the MCG also generates a default user interface so that the user can interact with the input and output services.

The Camunda tool suite is used for modelling and deploying processes, for the reasons explained in [1]: Camunda is open source and provides a modelling tool and a platform for the execution of the process model. The Camunda Modeler allows the model to be extended with implementations for the tasks. This makes it possible to invoke the input and output services. The Camunda BPM platform consists of three different viewpoints. The first viewpoint is the Camunda Tasklist which allows users to start a new process and to interact with the active tasks of a running process. The second viewpoint is the Camunda Cockpit, where the deployed processes can be managed. It also provides a view on the running instances of the process deployments. Finally, Camunda Admin provides a view on the users and their authorizations.

4.5   Results: Meta-model integration and proof of concept

While the Merode code generator allows generating a working Java application from a model, this application is not "process-aware". It can obviously be used for manual execution of a business process, but does not provide readily support for simulating processes in a "process-aware" way by making use of a process engine. Reversely, while the Camunda process engine can be used to execute the process represented in Figure 4.6, making such process execution "data-aware" requires quite some extra coding. The conceptual integration of a process model and a Merode model in order to obtain a data-aware process model was described in [89]. The challenge addressed in this chapter is how to integrate the process engine with the generated application so as to make the application "process-aware" and the process "data-aware". The goal is to realize the integration in a model-driven way so as to avoid the need for handcrafting code for each set of models individually. The challenge is thus to identify the concepts needed for such integration, as well as outlining the relationships between the concepts that will set the basis for an automated transformation. In the next two sections, we will discuss how we approached the conceptualization and the implementation of the PoC.

4.5.1   RG1 – Conceptualization: MERODExBPMN meta-model

To integrate the process with the application, we consider that certain types of tasks need to be able to invoke IS Services. As a starting point, we provide support for the User tasks and Service tasks as they cover the most common cases where IS services need to be invoked: User tasks allow users of the system to interact with system, and Service tasks specify automated tasks in a process. In both cases, this constitues of invoking IS services in Merode. A Manual task cannot invoke IS Service as it describes manual operations and thus no interaction with the system. According to the specification, Business Rule tasks need to access a business rule engine, which is not part of the Merode meta-model and thus not supported by Merode (yet). Send tasks, Receive tasks and Script Tasks could potentially be supported in the future. For now, their functionalities can by captured by using messages, User tasks and Service tasks. The Merode meta-model can be integrated with BPMN by removing the overlap (green box in Figure 4.3) and adjusting the connection to the ISL (dashed green box in Figure 4.3), namely by linking the concepts of the task sub-model of BPMN to the Information System Service concept from the Merode meta-model. Figure 4.9 shows a fragment of the combined MERODExBPMN meta-model as a UML Class diagram, focusing on the interface between the supported types of tasks and IS Services (the tasks types that are not supported and the other BPMN constructs are not shown).

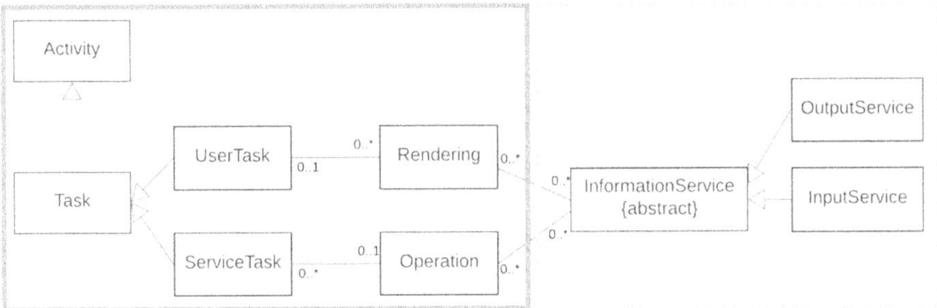

Figure 4.9 A fragment of the MERODExBPMN meta-model, as a UML Class Diagram

4.5.2   RG2 – PoC Implementation

For the implementation of the proof of concept, we use a running case adapted from [89] that is also described in 4.4.1. The non-executable business process model of [89] was elaborated to an executable business process, taking into account what features are supported by Camunda. More specifically, in the 'Collect Reviews' process, the start event is a catching message event. In order to start an instance of this process in Camunda, we also need to throw the corresponding message in another process. Therefore, the process of the 'Applicant' was added. Furthermore, we need to consider that Camunda does not readily support implementing the conditions for a loop task for 'Request Review' in the 'Collect Reviews' process. Therefore, this task was replaced with a multi-instance subprocess. This way, we are able to indicate that the subprocess should reach its end event three times. Both Applications and Reviews need to be submitted according to the OLC defined in the EL. Therefore, we added service tasks to automate this step. The adapted and now executable business process model is shown in Figure 4.10.

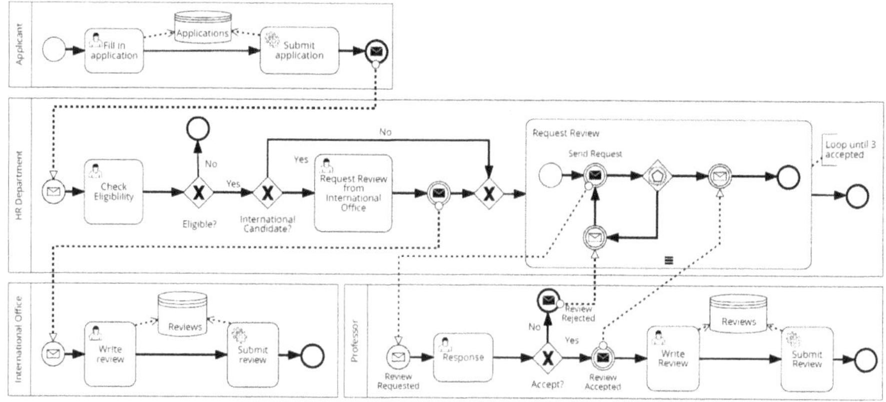

Figure 4.10 Business Process adapted from [89]

Enterprise Layer and Information System Services Layer. As discussed in section 4.4.3, the Merode Code Generator generates code for the full Enterprise layer, the default input and output services of the Information System Services Layer, a Graphical User Interface and REST web-services for each of the generated input and output services. The latter will allow accessing the services from the Camunda platform, which will be discussed in the next section.

As the default services may not always provide for all desired functionality to achieve a good user experience, we investigated if non-default output services can be implemented in Camunda as well. In particular, we defined a REST service allowing the process modeler to select a subset of objects using a query. For example, a rule of the EL is that an Application can only be created for a Job that is in the state 'exists'. So, when the Applicant fills in an application in the BPL, we want them to be able to select a Job vacancy from a list of Jobs in the state 'exists'. This list is retrieved with the added output service, ensuring that the task can always be executed.

Business Process Layer. The Business Process Layer is implemented using the Community edition of the Camunda Platform. Following the instruction video by Camunda [104], we set up a Maven project in Eclipse with a Camunda archetype. The project contains a default business process model that we can adapt to our own model (Figure 4.10) using the Camunda Modeler tool. The next step is to implement the tasks and automate the message events and the gateways.

Although the BPMN meta-model allows a UserTask to have multiple Renderings, Camunda only allows one reference to an HTML form. Therefore, for each user task, a "Rendering" is created as an HTML form and included in the Eclipse project. We include a reference to this form in the user task. Camunda provides a cam-script tag that can be included in the HTML file. With this tag we can interact with the process variables and we can call predefined functions. These functions are used to invoke the REST web-services described in the previous sections. Any interaction with the database that is supported by a REST web-service can be implemented in the form. An HTML form is therefore quite flexible as it allows to define user input, to invoke input and output services of the ISL and interact with the process variables. For each service task, an Operation is implemented as a Java Class with a function that invokes the necessary REST-webservice(s). If the HTML form contains invalid input, the function will not be executed and the REST-webservice will not be invoked.

For the throwing message events, a global message name is defined in the Camunda Modeler tool, a java Class file is created in the Eclipse project to define the contents of the message, and a reference to this java Class file is included in the message event. For the catching message events, we only need to define the global message name of the message that the event should catch.

To automate the gateways, we use process variables that were set in previous tasks or retrieved from the database. The Camunda Modeler tool allows us to use an expression that evaluates the value of a process variable to indicate which path should be taken after a gateway. The Eclipse project is now finished and can be deployed into the Camunda BPM platform. This step is also explained in [104].

Using the prototype. In order to run the prototype, the web application that was generated by the Merode Code Generator needs to be started. Although all relevant input and output services are invoked by the business process, it is also possible to invoke the services from a browser or an API platform such as Postman to consult the business objects. For example, creating the job vacancies that applicants can apply for are part of processes that are not yet implemented with Camunda. We therefore create these objects using Postman before testing the implemented process.

To test the process, the user needs to login to the Camunda Platform and start an instance of the process that we deployed in the Camunda Tasklist. Now, the tasks will be presented to the users who can execute them. A visual demonstration of the user experience can be found on the MERODExBPMN website [97].

4.5.3 RG3 – Evaluation of the meta-model

Overall, the PoC demonstrates that the MERODExBPMN meta-model is a good representation of the concepts needed to bridge Merode and BPMN. For the service tasks, the Java Class implementing the task is an instance of the Operation object type. The REST service invoking the EvsubmitApplication event is an instance of the InputService object type. The instance of the ISServiceInvocationST links that REST-service to the "Submit application" service tasks. The lines of code where the REST-service is called in the Java Class can be seen as an instance of the ISServiceInvocationST. This will be very helpful when we define the transformation from the MERODExBPMN meta-model to code.

The process model provides several examples of user tasks. As described in the BPMN specification [7], the HTML forms for these user tasks are instances of the Rendering object type. The lines of code where an Information Service is called in the Java Class can be seen as an instance of the ISServiceInvocationUT. This shows that the proposed meta-model supports the needed connections between both types of models.

The PoC does not comply with the BPMN specification regarding the association between UserTask and Rendering. According to BPMN, a UserTask is an aggregate that can have zero, one or many Renderings, and a Rendering belongs to zero or one UserTask. In Camunda, a user tasks can be connected to at most one HTML form. Although this is specific to the Camunda modeler tool, we believe that assigning at most one HTML form is a good practice to avoid ambiguity. Instead of linking the user task directly to different HTML forms (renderings), the HTML form linked to the user task could contain references to other forms. A user task is then still connected to multiple renderings indirectly. Additionally, the specification dictates that a given Rendering can only be connected to one UserTask. In our example, both the International Office and the professors need to fill in the same form to write a review. According to the specification, we should create two separate forms with exactly the same content. Although this is possible, it can create redundancy in large scale projects, increasing the maintenance cost. There is also a loss of information since we can no longer know which tasks use the same forms. Therefore, we allow a Rendering to be connected to multiple UserTasks in the MERODExBPMN meta-model. As the association no longer indicates existence dependency, it needs to be reified with a RenderingRef object type. Figure 4.11 presents the adaptions to the corresponding fragment in the final meta-model.

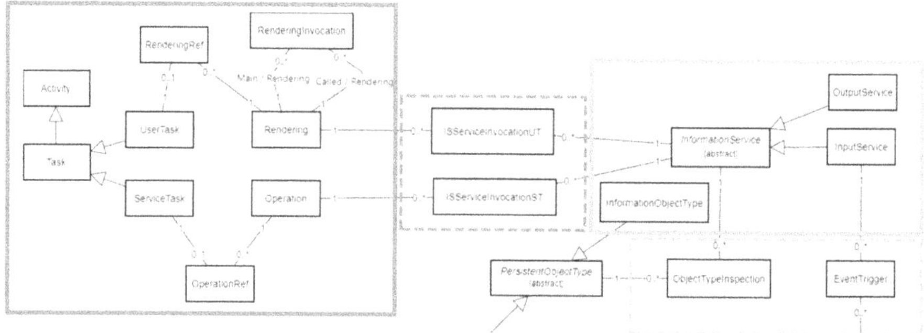

Figure 4.11 Adapted fragment of the MERODExBPMN meta-model, adaptions are shown in the two green boxes

4.6 Discussion

The implementation of the PoC demonstrates that the proposed meta-model supports the required connection between BPMN models and Merode models. While implementing the PoC, care was taken not to include elements in the code that are not present in the MERODExBPMN model, so as to ensure that all required code can be generated from the models only.

A first limitation of the PoC is that it is based on a Merode model with only default services. However, the definition of an additional GET service allowing to select objects by means of a query demonstrates that the proposed meta-model interface also supports user-defined ISServices. Modelling of such user-defined services will however require extending the Merode modelling tools. The feasibility of modelling such user-defined output services has already been demonstrated in [77].

A second limitation is that for now, only User Tasks and Service Tasks have been implemented. Business Rules tasks will require interfacing with DMN. However, in essence, such tasks will rely on user-defined output services, which we have demonstrated to be feasible to support. We do not expect other types of tasks to generate fundamental problems.

A third limitation has to do with the association between a Rendering and a UserTask. We could argue to maintain that a Rendering can only be linked to at most one UserTask as described in the BPMN specification. Any two user tasks that use the same rendering could be assumed to be identical. Therefore, we could enforce the modeller to embed this task in a call activity so that the rendering only needs to be invoked by this one call activity. For a call activity that consists of more than just one task, this makes sense. However, if the call activity is a wrapper for a single task, this adds to the steps that the modeller needs to take and to the overall model size. Therefore, we allow a Rendering to be linked to more than one UserTask for the sake of usability and maintainability.

A fourth limitation is that the approach relies on Merode instead of UML. However, As Merode relies on a simplified version of UML, its meta-model is much simpler than the UML meta-model. It is however not in conflict with the UML meta-model: a MERODE-model can be stored as an instantiation of a UML meta-model, be it with some loss of information about BusinessEventTypes. Therefore, to a certain extent, this approach can used for the integration of UML and BPMN.

A final limitation of the integrated MERODExBPMN approach is that it does not provide support for automated consistency checking between the rules of the BPL and the other layers. As illustrated by our PoC, a modeler can implement a domain layer consistency rule in the process (showing only 'open' jobs to the user), but verifying that such rules implemented in the BPL do not violate the rules defined in the EL is not yet possible. Theoretical work has already been done in this direction [105], [106], but needs to be further elaborated to provide for verification algorithms in the modelling environment.

4.7 Conclusion and Future Work

This chapter is a step in achieving a true multi-modelling approach, where process and data models are deployable together, and the integration of the process models and the data models is be based on a conceptualization of the connection between the respective meta-models, rather than on application and process-specific hand crafting of code. To achieve the realisation of domain-model aware processes, we combined the Merode domain modelling meta-model and tools with the BPMN-meta-model and Camunda tools. The multi-modelling approach was realized by conceptualizing the connection between the two meta-models by connecting the BPMN task meta-model to MERODE's Information System Layer meta-model (RG1). The viability of the resulting MERODExBPMN meta-model was tested by implementation a proof of concept (RG2). After some final adjustments, we found that the MERODExBPMN meta-model fully supports the proof of concept, and provides the necessary ingredients for the model-driven engineering of a prototype (RG3).

As was already indicated in the discussion chapter of [89], *"The whole process of generating and starting the web services, setting up the connection with Camunda, etc. requires several steps, but could ideally be done with less hassle. The utopian goal would be to achieve this through code generation as well, to allow for process validation through the integrated prototyping of a collection of processes and the supporting information system with just a few clicks."* Streamlining this process, by reducing the number of steps and by further integrating verification & validation, is a future goal, whereby we will also consider the consistency between the different layers of the Merode approach.

In order to evaluate the didactic contribution of a prototype like the example in this chapter, we plan to conduct an experiment with university students in the context of a course on Information Systems Modelling.

Chapter 5
Adapting the Information System Service Layer of Merode for code generation

5.1 Introduction

The meta-model for integrated domain and process modelling with Merode and BPMN presented in the previous chapter addresses the need for an abstract syntax and basic semantics for the integrated modelling of the enterprise layer and business process layer. In this chapter, we investigate the additional semantics required for the integration and develop a prototype modelling tool to demonstrate the feasibility of the proposed integration and its usability for code generation, as well as the missing concrete syntax (research objective 2 & 3). This will allow obtaining a view on the missing components and possible sources for filling the gaps. We will identify three gaps in the Merode architecture that need to be addressed to obtain a full integration for the semantics and concrete syntax. Each of these gaps is then addressed theoretically in Sections 5.3, 5.4 and 5.5 with a proof of concept. Section 5.6 presents the development of a prototype modeller.

Merode already benefits from a formal definition of the abstract syntax, concrete syntax and semantics for its enterprise layer, which includes data structures as well as data behaviour. The process layer of Merode allows the modeler to choose their own modelling language, and therefore 'borrows' the abstract syntax, concrete syntax and semantics from the chosen process modelling language. Therefore, the interaction between the enterprise layer and the process layer are defined informally, to allow for this flexibility. Formalizing the Information System Services Layer is only possible if the process modelling language is known. Therefore, this chapter will investigate the formalization of the semantics and concrete syntax for the ISSL of Merode under the assumption that BPMN is used for the BPL.

5.2 Identifying the gaps in the Merode approach for the integration with BPMN

As explained in Section 4.4.1, the ISSL of Merode consists of Input and Output services. The Output services are rather straightforward: they represent queries that can be run from a task in a business process to extract information from the database and present it to the user. Input services trigger one or more events. An Input service that triggers

© The Author(s), under exclusive license to Springer Nature Switzerland AG 2026
C. Verbruggen, *Advancing Multi-modelling in MDE for Integrated Domain
and Business Process Modelling*, Lecture Notes in Business Information Processing 576,
https://doi.org/10.1007/978-3-032-13876-7_5

multiple events at once is called a complex input service. The trigger of multiple events in one service can be necessary for user friendliness and/or consistency reasons. A complex input service for the sake of user friendliness simply groups business events that are often performed together to save the user some time. The need for complex input services for the sake of consistency is dictated by the EDG. If the EDG contains a mandatory dependency, objects of the master object type need to have at least one object of their dependent object type as soon as they are created. For example, in Figure 5.1 an instance of Order needs to be linked to an instance of OrderItem as soon as it is created. Creating a master object without creating a dependent object at the same time, is defined to be an inconsistent atomic event. To resolve the inconsistency, these objects need to be created at the same time, a functionality that is obtained by defining a consistent composed event that triggers both the creating event for the master object and the creating event for its required depending object. For example, the consistent composed event crNewOrder combines crOrder and crOrderItem. The consistent composed event is rolled back in case one of the atomic events it is made up of cannot be executed. Similarly, the master object needs to have at least one dependent object until the moment the master object is ended, and, due to referential integrity, a master object cannot be ended if it still has a living dependent. Therefore, the (last) dependent and the master object need to be ended simultaneously, thus also requiring the definition of a consistent composed event that combines the ending of the master object with the ending of the dependent object. For example, the composed event EVendOrderWithLastOrderItem triggers EVendOrderItem and EVendOrder. This composed event will end a single order item and the order it is part of. If this composed event is invoked for an order that has multiple order items, the atomic event EVendOrder will violate the referential integrity constraint, and the entire composed event is rolled back. For a mandatory many dependency, instances of the dependent object type can be created or ended with an atomic event as long as it is not the first or last dependent of a master object. For a mandatory one dependency, the master object always has at least one but never more than one dependent. Therefore, ending the dependent should always be done simultaneously with creating a new dependent for that master object (or ending the master object itself as described above).

Based on these considerations, the first gap is to develop guidelines for the construction of the required consistent composed events for Merode models that contain mandatory dependencies. These guidelines are explained in section 5.3. The second gap is the specification of parameter values when methods are tiggered on the instance level. Since methods are triggered via business events, which are triggered via input services, the consistency of parameter values accross the methods, business events and information services needs to be considered. This gap is addressed in section 5.4. The third gap is the executability from the perspective of the BPMN model. In section 5.5, we investigate the issues that need to be considered in this regard and how they can be addressed.

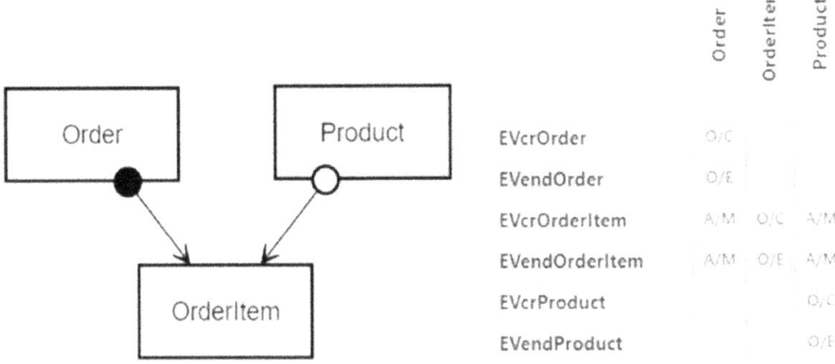

Figure 5.1 Example of an EDG for a web shop with a mandatory dependency between Order and OrderItem

5.3   Guidelines for defining Consistent Composed Events

Before defining input services for user friendliness, the modeler should always start by identifying the inconsistent atomic events, and defining consistent composed events to replace them.

Table 5.1 inconsistent atomic events that need to be replaces by consistent composed events for a single dependency

	Optional many	Optional one	Mandatory many	Mandatory one	
crM				crMwithFirstDependent	
endM				endMwithLastDependents	
crD				crMwithFirstDependent crNewD	OR
endD				endMwithLastDependent crNewD	OR

Table 5.1 describes the atomic events that are inconsistent for each of the four dependency types in Merode, and which consistent composed events should replace them. However, an EDG can have many different combinations of dependencies. If several mandatory dependencies are combined, defining consistent composed events becomes much more complex. For example, let's consider an EDG where a dependent object type has two master object types, and both dependencies are mandatory many (see Figure 5.2). To create an instance of the first master object type (m1 is an instance of M1), there needs to be an instance of the dependent object type (d is an instance of D). But for d to exist, there also needs to be an instance of the second master object type (m2 is an instance of M2). Therefore, to create m1, a composed consistent event is needed that creates m1, m2 and d simultaneously. Now we might want to create a second instantiation of M1 (m1') and D (d'), but use the existing object m2 as master of d'. In that case, we need

another consistent composed event to m1' and d' without creating a new instantiation of M2. With an infinite amount of potential combinations of dependencies, developing a single procedure to define all required consistent composed events for any given EDG is not possible. The modeler will have to define these themselves based on their EDG. However, we can provide some guidelines to simplify the task.

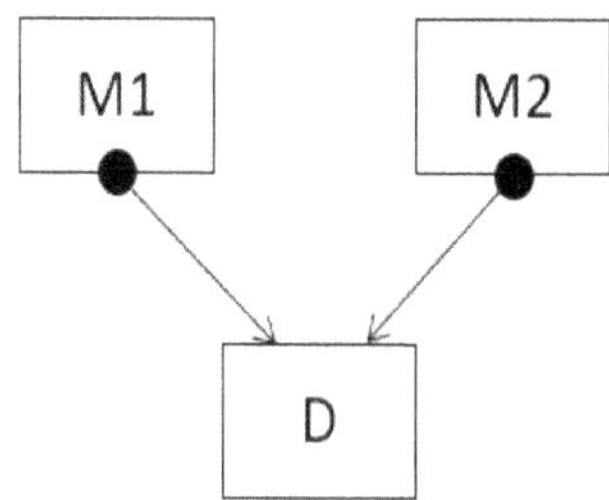

Figure 5.2 EDG with one dependent object type (D) and two master object types (M1 and M2) where both dependencies are mandatory many.

5.3.1   Guidelines for 1 master object type with one dependent object type

GUIDELINE 1: Reduce the EDG along the optional dependencies.

As shown in Table 5.1, the events in a single optional dependency are always consistent. When considering an EDG with more than one dependency, we reason that the required composed events never contain both a master object and a dependent object from the same optional dependency. For example, Figure 5.3 shows a random EDG with several mandatory dependencies. If we want to create an instance of object type A, instances of object types B and D are also required, but not of object type C. The instance of object type B also requires an instance of object type E, but not of object type F. Similarly, the created instance of object type D does not immediately require an instance of object type G. Therefore, the composed event only needs to consist of 'crA', 'crB', 'crD' and 'crE'. We can reduce the EDG along the optional dependencies by simply removing these dependencies from the diagram and only considering the remaining sub-graphs. The consistent composed events that result from these sub-graphs will be sufficient to ensure the consistent creation of instances for the original EDG.

When applying this to the example from Figure 5.1, only the object types Order and OrderItem remain, as shown in Figure 5.4.

GUIDELINE 2: Apply the consistent composed event patterns when possible

For a single mandatory dependency, the consistent composed events described in Table 5.1 are sufficient. These patterns are illustrated in Figure 5.5: a master object needs to be created simultaneously with its first dependent object, a master object needs to be ended simultaneously with its last dependent object, and for a mandatory one dependency, a new depedent object for an existing master object needs to be created at the same time as the ending of the previous dependent object for that master.

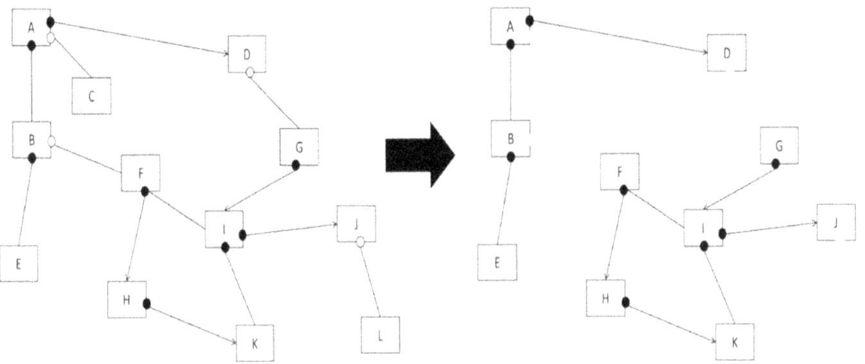

Figure 5.3 Random EDG with several mandatory dependencies before (left) and after (right) applying Guideline 1

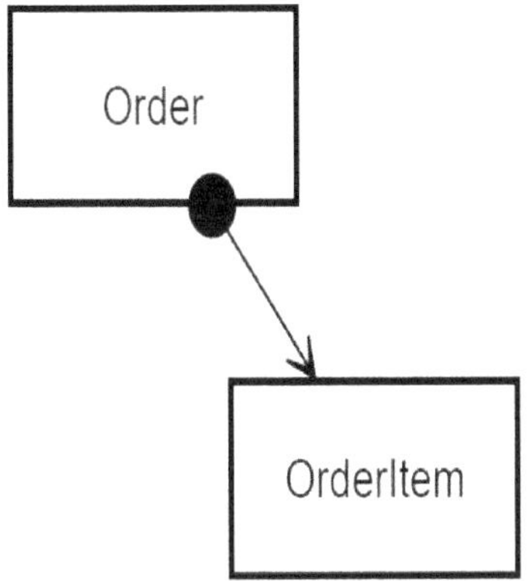

Figure 5.4 The web shop example of Figure 5.1 after applying Guideline 1

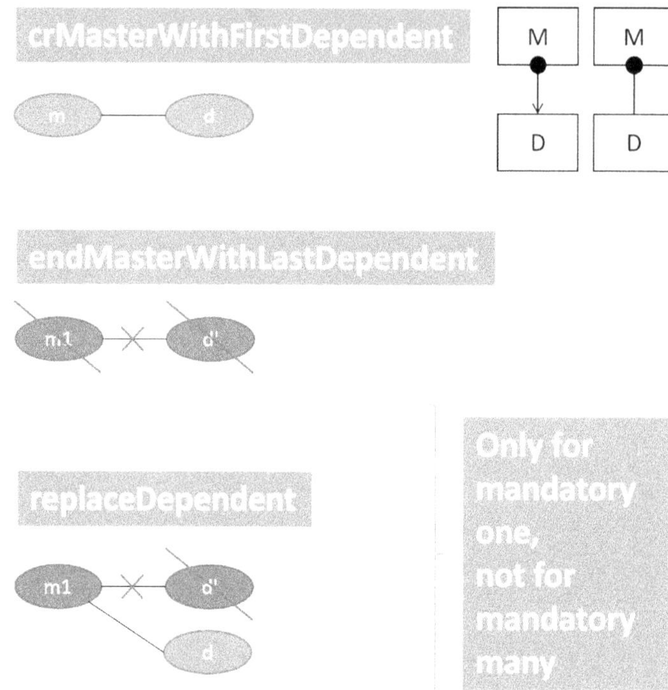

Figure 5.5 Patterns for a single mandatory dependency

When considering situations where a single master object type has several mandatory dependent object types, we can simply combine the patterns for each of the dependents and remove the duplicate atomic events for the creation of master objects, as described in Guideline 3 and illustrated in Figure 5.6.

When applying these patterns to the web shop example from Figure 5.4, we need to define the consistent composed events EVcrOrderWithFirstOrderItem (which triggers EVcrOrder and EVcrOrderItem) and EVendOrderWithLastOrderItem (which triggers EVendOrderItem and EVendOrder). The consistent composed event EVreplace-OrderItem is not required since an order can have multiple order items at the same time, which allows replacing an order item for a given order in two atomic steps without violating the referential integrity constraint.

GUIDELINE 3: Order the atomic events so that the composed event is made up of as follows: first all the ending events, ordered bottom to top, and then all the creating events, ordered top to bottom (endD > endM > crM > crD)

This guideline ensures the consistent composed events are presented in a clear way. It also ensures that referential integrity is respected during the execution of the composed event, which is important during code generation. This is also demonstrated in Figure 5.6.

When applying this to the web shop example, that means that the consistent composed events are defined as follows: EVcrOrderWithFirstOrderItem = EVcrOrder.EVcrOrderItem and EVendOrderWithLastOrderItem = EVendOrderItem.EVendOrder.

5.3.2   Guidelines for n master object types with one (shared) dependent object type

For and EDG where n object types have one shared dependent object type, the same guidelines apply as in section 5.3.1. However, the patterns for Guideline 2 need to be adapted to fit all different possible configurations of mandatory many and mandatory one dependencies in this type of EDG. This section describes the six required patterns. When these patterns are applied to a single mandatory dependency, the patterns in Figure 5.5 and Table 5.1 are obtained. To illustrate the patterns in this section, we will consider a web shop where both the Product and the Order have a mandatory many dependency with OrderLine, as illustrated in Figure 5.7.

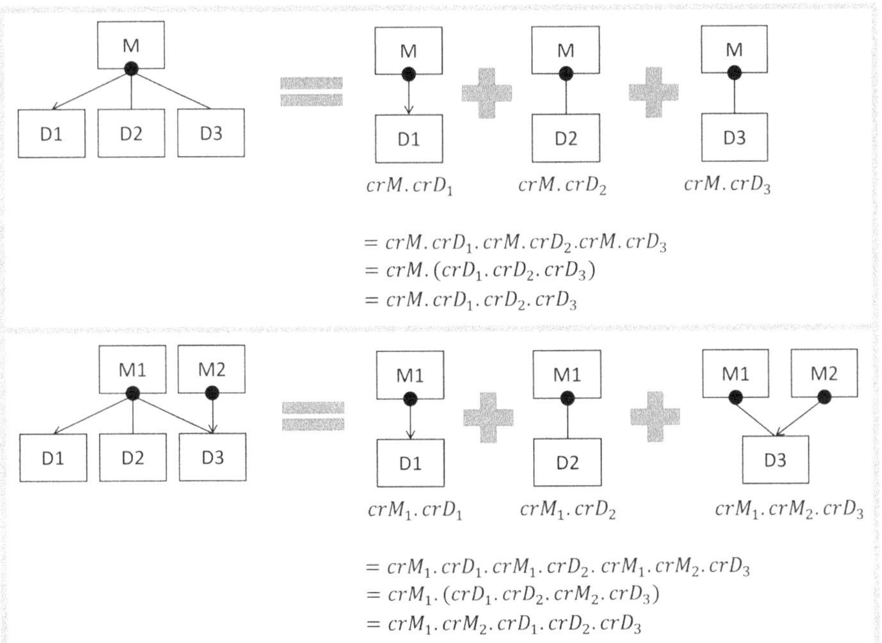

Figure 5.6 Examples of consistent composed events to create an object m for an EDG where object type M has n dependents D1, …, Dn

Figure 5.7 Web shop example with two mandatory many dependencies (left) and with a mandatory many dependency and a mandator one dependency (right).

The patterns were constructed by iterating over all possible scenarios for this type of EDG. Figure 5.8 summarizes the patterns and provides a visual representation. The patterns follow the following notation:

$\vec{M}$:set of all master object types

$\vec{m}$: set of instances, one of each master object type

$M_i \in \vec{M}$: master object type i

m_i: instance of M_i

D: the dependent object type

$D \leftarrow M_i$: the dependency between the master object type M_i and the dependent object type D

$D \leftarrow M_i = MAX *$: the dependency $D \leftarrow M_i$ has a maximum multiplicity of many

$D \leftarrow M_i = MAX 1$: the dependency $D \leftarrow M_i$ has a maximum multiplicity of one

Pattern 1: crAllMastersWithFirstDependent

The first pattern is simply creating instances of all master object types and of the dependent object type simultaneously. It is formally defined as:

$$crM_1.crM_2.(\dots).crM_n crD$$

In the web shop example in Figure 5.7, this will result in EVcrOrder.EVcrProduct.EVcrOrderItem.

Pattern 2: endMastersAndDependent

The second pattern mirrors the first pattern, as it ends a dependent object with all its master objects. It is formally defined as:

$$endD.endM_1.endM_2.(\dots).endM_n$$

In the web shop example in Figure 5.7, this will result in EVendOrderItem.EVendOrder.EVendProduct.

Pattern 3: crDependentAndOneMaster(M_i)

Pattern 3 is used in scenarios where we want to create a new instance of the dependent object type, with only a new instance of one master object type (M_i). For the creation of the dependent object type, one instance of each master object type is required. Therefore, we use existing instances of the master object types other than M_i. . (see Figure 5.8 for a visual representation).

In case all dependencies in the EDG are of the type mandatory many, Pattern 3 is simply $crM_i.crD$. However, if one or more dependencies in the EDG are of the type mandatory one, the pattern becomes more complex. To handle this complexity, we define two Boolean variables x and y. The variable x is 1 if the EDG contains only one master object type M_i (formally : $\vec{M} \setminus M_i = \varnothing$) or if all of the master object types other than M_i have mandatory many dependencies $\left(\forall M_j \in \vec{M} \setminus M_i : D \leftarrow M_j = MAX * \right)$. If this is the case, existing instances of the other master object types can be used for the creation of the dependent instance without issue, as they can have multiple dependent objects at once. However, if at least one of the other master object types have a mandatory one dependency (x=0), this means that all instances of that master object type have exactly one living dependent object already, and creating a second dependent object for such an instance would leave the database in an inconsistent state. In that case, the existing dependent object needs to be ended first. Pattern 3 then becomes $endD.crM_i.crD$. However, if the dependency between M_i and D is mandatory one, ending the existing dependent object will result in an instance of M_i without dependent objects, leaving the database in an inconsistent state. To resolve this, the instance of M_i also needs to be ended. In that case, the pattern becomes $endD.endM_i.crM_i.crD$. To combine these three cases into a single pattern the variable y is defined as a Boolean variable that equals 1 if the dependency between M_i and D is mandatory one ($D \leftarrow M_i = MAX\,1$). Therefore, Pattern 3 is formally defined as:

$$(1 - x)\left[endD.(y)endM_i \right].crM_i.crD$$

$$\text{With } x = 1 | (\vec{M} \setminus M_i = \varnothing) \vee \left(\forall M_j \in \vec{M} \setminus M_i : D \leftarrow M_j = MAX * \right)$$

$$y = 1 | D \leftarrow M_i = MAX\,1$$

Note that for an EDG with only one master object type, x automatically becomes 1, and Pattern 3 equals Pattern 1.

In the web shop example with two mandatory depedencies in Figure 5.7 (left), this will result in two consistent composed events: EVcrOrder.EVcrOrderItem and EVcrProduct.EVcrOrderItem.

If the EDG has a mandatory one dependency (Figure 5.7, right), the resulting consistent composed events are EVendOrderItem.EVcrOrder.EVcrOrderItem and EVcrProduct.EVcrOrderItem.

Pattern 4: endDependentAndOneMaster(M_i)

Pattern 4 mirrors Pattern 3, as it is used in scenarios where we want to end an existing instance of the dependent object types, as well as an instance of one master object type (M_i). The existing instances of the master object types other than M_i are not ended (see Figure 5.8 for a visual representation).

Similar to Pattern 3, we can distinguish three different cases, characterised by the multiplicities of the dependencies in the EDG. These cases are defined with the same two Boolean variables x and y as in Pattern 3. The first case occurs when all master object types other than M_i have mandatory many dependencies (x = 1). Then, Pattern 4 is defined as $endD.endM_i$. assuming all other master objects of the dependent object that is ended have more than one living dependent, this will leave the database in a consistent state. If this is not the case and at least one master object type other than M_i has a mandatory one dependency (x = 0), each instance of that master object type has exactly one dependent object, and ending this dependent object requires the creation of a new dependent object. To create this new dependent object, we need to consider the multiplicity of the dependency between M_i and D. If this dependency is mandatory many (y = 0), creating a new instance of D can be done without issue and the pattern becomes $endD.endM_i crD$. However, if the dependency is mandatory one (y = 1), creating a new instance of D also requires creating a new instance of M_i and the pattern becomes $endD.endM_i.crM_i.crD$. Using the variables x and y as defined in Pattern 3, all three scenario's can be combined and formally defined as:

$$endD.endM_i.(1 - x)\big[(y)(crM_i).crD\big]$$

Note that for an EDG with only one master object type, x automatically becomes 1, and Pattern 4 equals Pattern 2. Also, if x = 0 and y = 1, Pattern 3 and Pattern 4 are the same. This is also depicted in Figure 5.8.

In the web shop example with two mandatory depedencies in Figure 5.7 (left), this would result in two consistent composed events: EVendOrderItem.EVendOrder and EVendOrderItem.EVendProduct.

If the EDG has a mandatory one dependency (Figure 5.7, right), the resulting consistent composed events are EVendOrderItem.EVendOrder.EVcrOrderItem and EVendOrderItem.EVendProduct.

Pattern 5: assignNewDependentToAllMasters

Pattern 5 is used in scenarios where we have a set of master objects that share a dependent object, and for each of these master objects, we want to create a (separate) new dependent object (see Figure 5.8 for a visual representation). Again, the multiplicities of the dependencies play a major role in the definition of this pattern. If all dependencies are mandatory many, the atomic event crD is consistent (see Table 5.1) and is sufficient for this pattern. However, if at least one of the dependencies is mandatory one, there is at least one master object that already has a dependent object and that cannot have more than one dependent objects. Thus, the existing (shared) dependent object should be ended first. While this condition can be characterized with the already defined variables x and y, we define a new Boolean variable z to reduce the complexity of the formula. The variable z is defined as 1 if all dependencies are mandatory many.

After ending the dependent object, each master object should be considered separately. For example, when considering master object m_1 (instance of M_1), instances of the other object types $M_2 \ldots M_n$ are required for the creation of a new dependent object d_1 (instance of D). We can assume that for each of the object types $M_2 \ldots M_n$, we already have at least one instance (if not, we can apply Pattern 1 first). If all dependencies between $M_2 \ldots M_n$ and D are mandatory many dependencies, a new dependent object d_1 can be created immediately. If one of these dependencies $(D \leftarrow M_j)$ is a mandatory one dependency, a new instance of this master object type M_j needs to be created first. This logic is applied for all master objects of the initial (shared) dependent object. The complete pattern is formally defined as:

$$(1 - z)endD.[\forall M_i \in \overrightarrow{M} : \left[\forall M_j \in \overrightarrow{M} \setminus M_i : crM_j | D \leftarrow M_j = MAX\,1\right].crD]$$

with

$$z = 1 | \forall M_i \in \overrightarrow{M} : D \leftarrow M_i = MAX *$$

$$\text{or}: \ z = 1 | x = 1 \wedge y = 0$$

In the web shop example with two mandatory depedencies in Figure 5.7 (left), no new consistent composed events are required.

If the EDG has a mandatory one dependency (Figure 5.7, right), the resulting consistent composed events are EVendOrderItem.EVcrProduct.EVcrOrderItem and EVendOrderItem.EVcrOrderItem.

Pattern 6: connectExistingMasters($\overrightarrow{m}_1, \ldots, \overrightarrow{m}_i, \ldots, \overrightarrow{m}_n$)

Pattern 6 is used in scenarios where we have n separate instantiations of the EDG and for each instantiation, we select one master object in such a way that the final selection of master objects contains one instance of each master object type. Then we want to create a shared dependent object for this set of master objects, connecting the initially separated instantiations of the EDG. To further clarify, this pattern uses n separate instantiations of the EDG, each with their own set of master objects ($\overrightarrow{m}_1, \ldots, \overrightarrow{m}_i, \ldots, \overrightarrow{m}_n$) and their own dependent object ($d_1, \ldots, d_i, \ldots, d_n$). The pattern selects m_i from $\overrightarrow{m}_i$ for the creation of the new shared dependent object d (see Figure 5.8 for a visual representation).

The first step is to make m_i available for a new dependent in each set of master objects $\overrightarrow{m}_i$. If the dependency between M_i and D is mandatory many, m_i is already available for a new dependent. If the dependency between M_i and D is mandatory one ($y = 1$), the existing d_i needs to be ended first. In order to end d_i, we need to consider the multiplicities of the dependencies between the master object types other than M_i and D (applying similar logic as in Pattern 4). If one of the other object types (M_j) has a mandatory one dependency with D, we should first create a new instance of M_j.

Once all master objects in the selected set ($m_1 \in \overrightarrow{m_1},...,m_i \in \overrightarrow{m_i},...,m_n \in \overrightarrow{m_n}$) are available for a new dependent object, the pattern closes with the creation of this shared dependent object. The pattern is formally defined as:

$$\forall \overrightarrow{m}_i : (y)\left[endD(d_i).(\forall m_j \in \overrightarrow{m_i} \backslash m_i : endM_j|(D \leftarrow M_j = MAX\,1))\right].crD$$

In the web shop example with two mandatory depedencies in Figure 5.7 (left), no new consistent composed events are required.

If the EDG has a mandatory one dependency (Figure 5.7, right), no new consistent composed events are required for order, but the consistent composed event EVendOrderItem.EVcrOrderItem is required for Product.

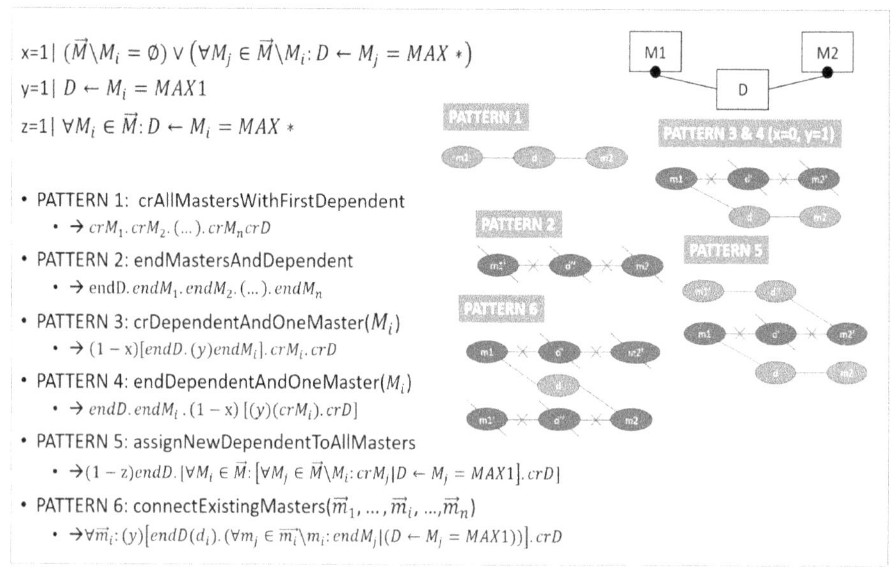

x=1| $(\overrightarrow{M} \backslash M_i = \emptyset) \vee (\forall M_j \in \overrightarrow{M} \backslash M_i : D \leftarrow M_j = MAX\,*)$

y=1| $D \leftarrow M_i = MAX1$

z=1| $\forall M_i \in \overrightarrow{M} : D \leftarrow M_i = MAX\,*$

- PATTERN 1: crAllMastersWithFirstDependent
  - → $crM_1.crM_2.(...).crM_ncrD$
- PATTERN 2: endMastersAndDependent
  - → $endD.endM_1.endM_2.(...).endM_n$
- PATTERN 3: crDependentAndOneMaster(M_i)
  - → $(1-x)[endD.(y)endM_i].crM_i.crD$
- PATTERN 4: endDependentAndOneMaster(M_i)
  - → $endD.endM_i.(1-x)[(y)(crM_i).crD]$
- PATTERN 5: assignNewDependentToAllMasters
  - → $(1-z)endD.[\forall M_i \in \overrightarrow{M} : [\forall M_j \in \overrightarrow{M} \backslash M_i : crM_j|D \leftarrow M_j = MAX1].crD]$
- PATTERN 6: connectExistingMasters($\overrightarrow{m}_1, ..., \overrightarrow{m}_i, ..., \overrightarrow{m}_n$)
  - → $\forall \overrightarrow{m}_i : (y)\left[endD(d_i).(\forall m_j \in \overrightarrow{m_i} \backslash m_i : endM_j|(D \leftarrow M_j = MAX1))\right].crD$

Figure 5.8 Patterns for n master object types that share one dependent object type where all dependencies are mandatory. The illustrations demonstrate the patterns for an EDG with two master object types where all dependencies are mandatory many dependencies.

The patterns and guidelines provided in this section only cover a subset of all potential EDGs. Further research is required to prove that all potential EDGs can be covered by composition of these patterns. However, EDGs that are part of well-designed Merode models tend to use mandatory dependencies sparingly, given that these types of dependencies have a significant impact on the flexibility of the resulting system. As a result, applying guideline 1 (reducing the EDG along the optional dependencies) will often result in very simple remaining sub-graphs that are already covered by the patterns in this section.

5.4 Adding attributes

To complete the definition of input and output services, it is essential to allow the modeler to specify which parameters the user can provide for an input service, and which queries they can execute with output services. Without this option, the only way to generate functional code is to use provide parameters for all attributes of all objects involved in the service, which has two major disadvantages. First, the user will have to manually enter all attribute values, even if some values don't change. This can lead to unnecessary repetitive work, reducing the user friendliness of the system. Second, this would introduce potential data quality challenges, as users can easily make mistakes and unintentionally change values. Finally, it also makes it impossible to implement different levels of authorization permissions: users would either have full read/write access on all attributes of an object type, or read-only access. In some situations, it can be necessary that certain users are allowed to change some attribute values, but not all (e.g., a student is allowed to change their contact details in the system of the university, but not their final grade).

Including parameters in the definition of input and output services is thus a crucial element for (useful) code generation. However, this is already done well in several object-oriented modelling approaches, so we can incorporate existing theories in Merode that have been thoroughly tested and evaluated. In this case, we choose to look at the OO-method developed by Pastor and Molina as it is similar to Merode in the sense that it follows an object-oriented approach where different models are used to address different perspectives. For both approaches, these perspectives include the data perspective, both from a static (data structure) and from a dynamic (data behaviour) viewpoint. The two main differences are that Merode only allows relationships between classes that express existence dependency and that the Merode approach is event-driven meaning that business events drive not only the execution of services but also the coordination between objects. This is a major benefit of Merode, as means the modeler does not need to specify object interactions in a seperate object interaction model, which is the case for the OO-method. Additionally, the OO-method includes a functional and presentation model, which is not part of the Merode approach. However, previous research has been done on the generation of user interfaces for software applications developed with Merode [107], [108].

5.4.1 Comparing the Merode approach with the OO-method

Before incorporating elements of the OO-method in the Merode approach, we provide an overview of the OO-method and how its concepts relate to the concepts of Merode. This is not a complete analysis, but an overview of the most relevant elements of both methods. To illustrate both methods, we use the Car Rental example that is used throughout the handbook describing the OO-method [109]. The Merode handbook uses a very similar example to illustrate input and output services [102], which we will adapt to match the example for the OO-method. The Car Rental example consists of company that rents out cars to its clients [109].

The OO-method consists of four models: the object model, the dynamic model, the function model and the presentation model.

The object model presented [110] in represents the static data model as a class diagram where each class has attributes and services, and several types of relationships between classes can occur. Figure 5.9 shows the object model for the Car rental example on the left, which consists of two classes "Vehicle" and "Client", each with attributes and services. The relationship between both classes is that of and Agent class (Client) and a server class (Vehicle), where the client can trigger services defined in the server class [110]. The right side of Figure 5.9 presents the same model in Merode notation, where a third class "Rental" is used to model the contract between the Client and the Vehicle. Renting and returning vehicles is captured with the creation and ending of Rental objects. The definition of attributes is not visually included in the EDG in Merode, but the modelling tool Merlin provides a dialog window where attributes can be defined. This is also shown in Figure 5.9. Defining events which are used in input and output services in the ISSL, is done in the OET (see Figure 5.10). For example, the event EVrent corresponds to an owned creating method for the object type Rental, and acquired modifying methods for Client and Vehicle (see section 4.4.1 for a more detailed explanation of acquired methods and event propagation). In the OO-method, attributes have a data type similar to Merode attributes, but also have additional properties ('type', 'identifier', 'size', 'default value', 'required on creation' and 'nulls allowed'). The services fulfil the same function as input services in Merode, but in the OO-method, they are always part of a class. Similar to the input services of Merode, a service in the OO-method can be atomic (comprising of a single event) or molecular (comprising of multiple events). An event in the OO-method can be a creation event, a destruction event, an own event or a shared event. The main difference with Merode is that in Merode, existence dependency and the propagation rule dictate which events are shared, and that creation and destruction events can also be shared events. In the OO-method, services consist of one or more arguments that correspond to the class(es) of the event(s) that are triggered by the service, each with at least the properties 'name', 'data type', 'size' and 'null values accepted'. In the OO-method, 'molecular' services are called transactions or operations. Transactions should always be executed either completely or not at all, meaning that if one of the events in the transaction throws an error, all previous events of that transaction should be rolled back. This is also the case for composed events and complex input services in Merode. Operations can be partially executed in case one of the events throws an error. In this case, the operation simply stops and the next events are not executed, but a roll-back is not required. Finally, the object model in the OO-method also contains static and/or dynamic integrity constraints, which correspond to invariants and pre-/postconditions in Merode.

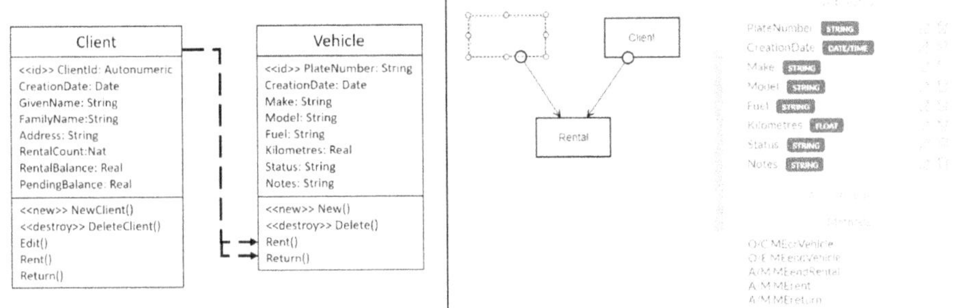

Figure 5.9 Left: The Car Rental example adapted from [110]. Right: The Car Rental example in the Merode approach. This figure shows the EDG and the attributes and methods of the object type Vehicle.

	Vehicle	Client	Rental
EVcrVehicle	O/C		
EVendVehicle	O/E		
EVcrClient		O/C	
EVendClient		O/E	
EVedit		O/M	
EVrent	A/M	A/M	O/C
EVreturn	A/M	A/M	O/M
EVendRental	A/M	A/M	O/E

Figure 5.10 The OET for the Car Rental Example in the Merode approach.

The dynamic model presented in [111] consists of state transition diagrams for each class in the object model and an object interaction diagram. State transition diagrams correspond to FSMs in Merode (Figure 5.11, right), with the added element that for each state transition, the agents that are allowed to trigger the state transition are defined. This is illustrated in Figure 5.11 on the left where creating new vehicles and deleting vehicles from the system can only be done by administrators, while registering the renting and returning of vehicles can be done by all agents (administrators and clients). The second component of the dynamic model in the OO-method consists of object interaction diagrams. An object interaction diagram defines triggers and global transactions and operations. A trigger defines an automatic execution of an event, transaction or operation when a certain condition becomes 'true'. This functionality is captured in the Business Process Layer in Merode. Global transactions and operations are transactions and operations that trigger events from several different classes, whereas transactions and operations that trigger only events from a single class are called local transactions and operations. In Merode, both local and global transactions correspond to complex input services, while local and global operations can be modelled in the BPL by having a single task trigger multiple input services.

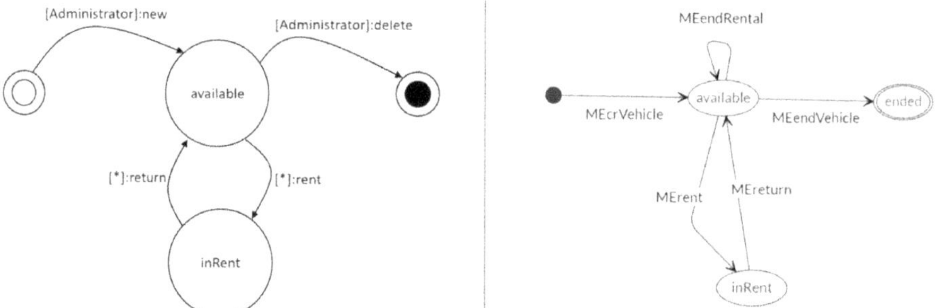

Figure 5.11 Left: A possible State Transition Diagram for the Vehicle class in the OO-Method. Right: The FSM for the Vehicle object type in the Merode notation

The functional model presented in [112] captures how event executions affect the attribute values of objects. This is not yet part of Merode, therefore, the developer needs to implement this manually in the body of the methods that are generated based on the OET. In the OO-method, these effects are called 'evaluations' and can be grouped in three categories: state evaluations (where the new attribute value is independent of the previous attribute value), cardinal evaluations (where the new attribute value is calculated by adding or subtracting a given number from the initial value), or situation evaluations (where the new attribute value is dependent on the previous attribute value). For each of these three groups, the evaluations can be captured in a table. The state evaluations table has columns 'event', 'attribute' and 'evaluation effect'. The cardinal evaluations table also includes the columns 'evaluation condition' and 'action' (adding or subtracting). Finally, the situation evaluations table has the columns 'event', 'attribute', 'previous value' and 'evaluation effect'. Defining the evaluations for each atomic event also defines how the execution of transactions and operation will affect the attribute values of objects, given that the transactions and operations are made up of atomic events. Several examples of evaluation tables can be found in [112]. Table 5.2 presents the example provided in [112] for situation evaluations where the level of vehicles is updated from entry-level ("E") to mid-level ("M"), from mid-level to top-level ("T") and from top-level back to entry-level.

Table 5.2 Situation evaluations for the event "UpdateLevel" of the Vehicle class, adapted from [112]

Event	Attribute	Previous value	Evaluation effect
UpdateLevel	Level	"E"	"M"
UpdateLevel	Level	"M"	"T"
UpdateLevel	Level	"T"	"E"

The fourth model of the OO-method is the presentation model described in [113]. This is a PIM detailing what the user interface should contain. The presentation model consists of three levels: a system access structure (level 1), interaction units (level 2) and basic elements (level 3). The first level captures the access rights of users to the system. The second level captures changes that a user can perform within the system by triggering services or manipulating (collections of) objects. The basic elements defined in level 3 are the building blocks of the interaction units, for example, data entry, filters and navigation. The Merode approach does not include these elements, although previous research has been done on the generation of user interfaces for software applications developed with Merode. Similar to the OO-method, this research starts from a PIM (the abstract user interface) which can be transformed to a PSM (the concrete user interface) [114].

5.4.2   Enhancing the Merode approach with elements from the OO-method

The comparison above demonstrated that the Merode approach mostly lacks the possibility to define events and non-default input and output services with their parameters, as well as the functionalities that are captured in the OO-method by its functional model.

In the OO-method, the arguments of an event are defined using a table with the columns 'name' (of the argument), 'data type', 'size' (for arguments of data type 'string'), 'default value', 'nulls allowed' where each row represents an argument that corresponds to an attribute of the class that is affected by the event. This table can be used as-is to define parameters of event types in Merode. Input services can now be defined similarly to transaction in the OO-method: The name of the input service followed by its parameters in brackets equals a sequence of atomic events where the parameter values of the atomic events correspond to the input service parameters, for example:

InputServiceName(IS_param1, IS_param2)

= EventName1(IS_param1).EventName2(IS_param2)

The functional model of the OO-method can easily be adapted to the Merode approach. The column 'event' can be replaced by 'method', as it are method and not business events that actually change objects in Merode. Alternatively, the column 'event (type)' can be kept if a column 'object type' is added. In that case, the method in question can be derived from the OET. The column 'Attribute' is kept, but since Merode does not enforce that attributes of different object types have unique names (e.g., both the object types Professor and Student can have an attribute 'name'), a column 'object type' is needed to uniquely identify the attribute. The other columns that can be part of a functional model in the OO-method are kept as-is ('evaluation effect', 'evaluation condition', 'action' and/or 'previous value'). This is demonstrated in Table 5.3.

Table 5.3 The situation evaluations table (Table 5.2) adapted for the definition of methods in the Merode approach

Event Type	Object Type	Attribute	Previous value	Evaluation effect
UpdateLevel	Vehicle	Level	"E"	"M"
UpdateLevel	Vehicle	Level	"M"	"T"
UpdateLevel	Vehicle	Level	"T"	"E"

5.5   Integration with BPMN process models

Modelling the coordination between data-models and process models is a complex task, as demonstrated in [115]. In order to generalize the modelling of this coordination, several concerns need to be taken into consideration.

First, it is not enough just to link a single task in a process model to a single object type in a data model. Generally speaking, a single task instance could affect multiple instances of the same object type (for example, the task "Cancel all Orders" will affect each instance of the object type "Order"), and a single instance of an object type could be affected by multiple instances of the same task (for example, if "Apple" is an instance of the object type "Product Type", every time a Customer orders a certain quantity of apples, the value of the attribute "Stock" of the object "Apples" will go down). However, in some cases the modeler should be able to limit the interaction between a task in a process model and an object type in a data model. For example, an instance of the task "Pay Order" should only affect one instance of the object type "Order", and an instance of the object type "Order" should only be affected by one (successful) instance of the task "Pay Order" and "cancelMyOrders" should only affect all orders of the customer invoking the action. A single task in a process could also affect instances of different object types. In that case, it should also be possible to identify these instances.

A second concern to be taken into account is that the mapping between object types in a data model and tasks in a process model should contain all the required information on how the instances of the task will affect the data objects. A task can affect instances of data objects by creating new instances, deleting instances, updating values of attributes or changing the state of the object in its lifecycle.

The third concern is that some process modelling languages already capture data as model constructs (for example, BPMN). However, these constructs are usually not related to each other, and only exists within the context of the process. This can have implications for redundancy and consistency in the overall system that is modelled. Even if the modelling tool uses a dictionary to capture data objects, the relationships between these objects are not defined by the modeler. Now that we link a process model to a data model, we should reconsider which data should be captured by the process model. For example, if a process model deals with the placement and handling of a single order, it makes sense to model the unique ID of the order that is handled as a data construct of the process. However, the information of the Customer that placed the order is not specific to the process instance and can be looked up in the database via the ID of the order. By not modelling the Customer as a separate data object, but retrieving the information from the database using the Order ID, we can make sure the information is consistent with the Customer database. We should consider what would be "good practice" when it comes to including data-constructs in process models when they are combined with data models.

A final concern to handle is that tasks are not atomic occurrences and that completing them usually takes several steps. Both in the BPMN and the CMMN specifications, this is captured by the fact that an activity (BPMN) or a task (CMMN) has a lifecycle [7], [116]. To further illustrate this concern, we will consider the BPMN specification. The lifecycle of an activity in BPMN is illustrated in Figure 5.12. According to the BPMN specification [7], input data is evaluated when the activity is in the state "ready". If all the required data is available, the activity will move to the sate "active". In this state, the activity is executed. If no errors occurred during the execution, the activity moves to the state "completing" where it waits for non-interrupting event handlers to finish. The activity will trigger "data output sets" when it is in the state "completed". However, this does not take into account the constraints that result from a data model, and once an activity is in the state "completed", the lifecycle of the tasks no longer allows error handling which might be required to deal with these constraints. For example, an activity can trigger an input service to create a new loan for a book in a library (where Book and Loan are object types, Loan is existence dependent on Book and a book can have at most one loan). If the book already has a loan, the triggered input service will throw an error stating that the business event crLoan was not executed. The business process should be able to handle this error. Therefore, we need to consider at which points in this lifecycle the actual changes to the data objects will occur. Additionally, it might not always be possible to automatically determine which object instance(s) should be affected when a task is executed, requiring manual user input. We should consider how this user input can be added to a process model with minimal changes to the model itself, while still respecting the lifecycles of activities.

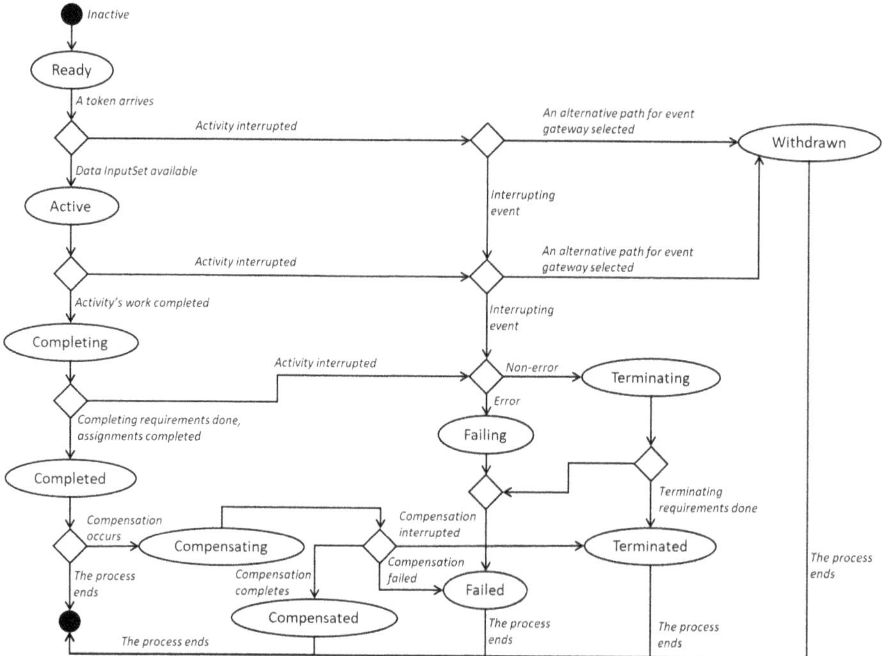

Figure 5.12 Lifecycle of an Activity according to the BPMN specification (section 13.3.2)

The first two concerns are addressed by the definition of input and output services in the ISSL of Merode, as described in section 4.4.1 and [117]. to address the third concern, we propose the following guideline on the choice between modelling a data element as a data construct in a business process model or as an object type in the domain model: a data element should only be modelled as a data construct in the process model if (1) it denotes the ID of the object that is being handled by an instantiation of the process, (2) it denotes information that is only relevant for an instantiation of the process, but should not be stored in a persistent manner in the system, or (3) it denotes temporary information that is already known and/or needed for the execution of a task, but will only be stored persistently at a later point in the process. An example of the third condition would be a simple web shop model where clients can place orders for products, but the order is only created after the customer has triggered the event 'order'. In that case, the products that are selected for the order can be stored as process variables until the order itself is created. To address the fourth and final concern, we propose that input and output services should be triggered in the "active" state of BPMN tasks, where errors that occur only because of the data perspective can be caught and can result in an interruption of the task. Now, tasks simply need to be linked to the input and output services they trigger, which can be done with a table.

In order to generate code for a complete Merode model that addresses all three layers, the elements in sections 5.3 (defining composed consistent events), 5.4 (defining parameters for events and defining complex input services) and 5.5 (defining which activities trigger which input and output services) can now be incorporated in the existing tools.

5.6   Development of a Prototype modeler

The goal of this section is to present the necessary extensions to the existing Merode tools in order to model the connections between the Merode model and the BPMN process model. The Merode tools do not yet allow the user to define complex input services. In this next section, we will explain how the tools were extended in order to support complex services triggering several business events or combining input and output services.

The Camunda tool suite is used for modelling and deploying processes, for the reasons explained in [1]: Camunda is open source and provides a modelling tool and a platform for the execution of the process model. The Camunda Modeler allows the model to be extended with implementations for the tasks. This makes it possible to invoke the input and output services. The Camunda BPM platform consists of three different viewpoints. The first viewpoint is the Camunda Tasklist which allows users to start a new process and to interact with the active tasks of a running process. The second viewpoint is the Camunda Cockpit, where the deployed processes can be managed. It also provides a view on the running instances of the process deployments. Finally, Camunda Admin provides a view on the users and their authorizations.

Merlin Extension

We developed a prototype of the Merlin extension as a separate modelling tool (see Figure 5.13). This tool allows the user to import an mxp file generated by Merlin, extend it with complex input services and link input services with a BPMN model. On the left side of the screen, the user can create input services and links to the BPMN model, while the right side of the screen provides an overview of the created input services and links. Once an mxp file has been uploaded, the user can start defining complex input services Just like a simple input service, a complex input service can only be triggered for an instance of the object type that owns it. Therefore, the user first has to decide which object type is the owner of this complex input service. Then, the user can select events owned by this object type or one of its (indirect) dependents to compile a complex input service. For each of the selected events, it is possible to add a filter that will be applied to the instances of the relevant object type. For example, when one candidate has been hired for a job, you might want to end all other applications that are still in the state "eligible". In that case, you can filter the instances of the Application object type by their state. In fact, this filter defines an output service. This filter already offers a lot of functionality that will suffice in most cases. However, in a future iteration of the tool, it would be possible to allow the user to define an output service as an SQL query as well. Once the user has selected the required events for the complex input service, they can save the input service and continue to add new complex input services.

The tool also allows the user to define the link between the tasks in their BPMN model and the Merode model by means of the input and output services (see Figure 5.14). First, the user can upload a .bpmn file. For example, a BPMN model that has been created in the Camunda Modeler tool. Then the user will see a table on the right side of the screen, with one row per task from the BPMN model. For each task, the user can then select which input service (simple or complex) they want to link to this task. Finally, the tool provides a button "Download models" that allows the user to generate the three model files that are needed for code generation in a zipped folder. The three files are the original mxp file, a new mxp file with the defined complex input services and the BPMN file that has been extended with the input services that are called by the tasks.

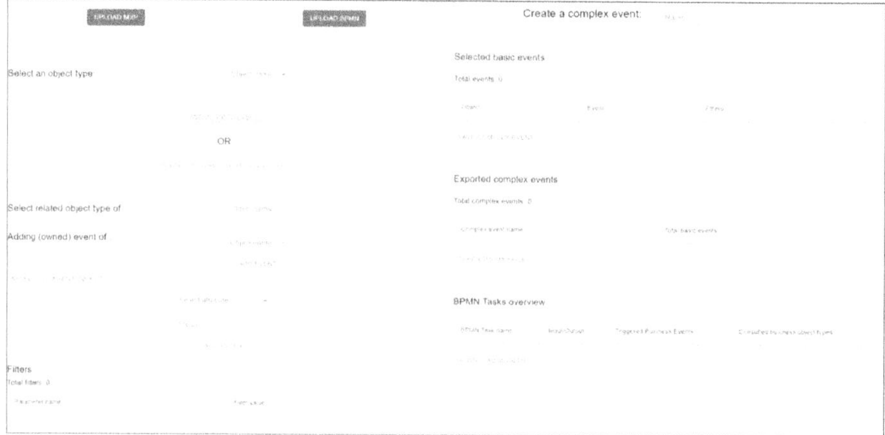

Figure 5.13 Prototype of the Merlin extension

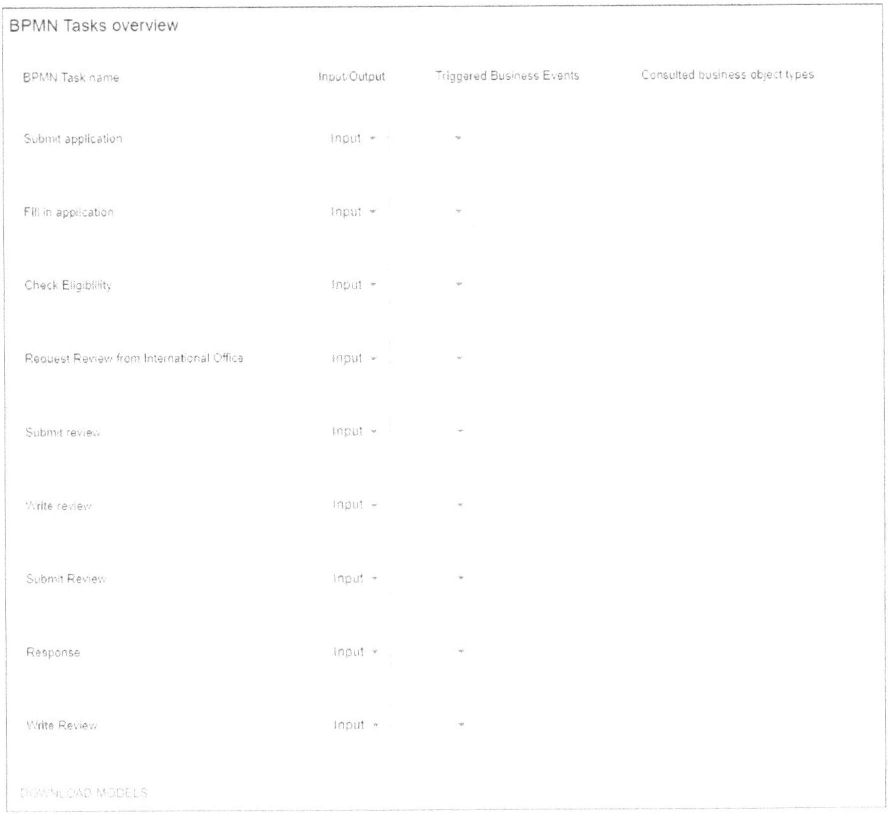

BPMN Tasks overview

BPMN Task name	Input/Output	Triggered Business Events	Consulted business object types
Submit application	Input		
Fill in application	Input		
Check Eligiblility	Input		
Request Review from International Office	Input		
Submit review	Input		
Write review	Input		
Submit Review	Input		
Response	Input		
Write Review	Input		

DOWNLOAD MODELS

Figure 5.14 Prototype of the Merlin extension - closeup of the BPMN component

Code Generator

In order to create a working prototype of the database that can be used in combination with a process engine like Camunda, the Merode Code generator also needed to be extended with more detailed output services, complex input services and links between the Merode model and the BPMN model. The output services were already partially implemented in the Code generator, namely to select an instance based on its id or to select all instances of a given object type. However, this needed to be extended to allow the user to filter the instances based on attributes or their state. In order to implement the complex input services, a new event handler was created called the "MerodeComplexEventHandler". This event handler will transform the complex input services as defined in their mxp file into code that will check whether the sequence of events is executable according to the model, and if so, will execute the events in the correct sequence. Finally, the Code generator will create a default Eclipse project that contains the needed components in order to run the BPMN process with the Camunda Process engine. The generated Eclipse project invokes the input services as REST web-services, which trigger changes in the Merode database application which is run separately. As this is a default project, the user can still enrich their bpmn model by manually adding implementation supported by Camunda. For example, to edit the user interface that actors in the process will encounter when performing their tasks.

5.7 Conclusion

This chapter presents the extensions required to complete the integration between Merode and BPMN. The gaps in the layered architecture of Merode were identified and a proof of concept for their solutions was proposed. Our implementation shows that it is possible to combine the Merode tools with a BPMN modelling tool and process engine like Camunda by means of an event-driven approach. In this chapter we presented the core aspects that are needed to achieve this integration. Both the modelling tool Merlin and the code generation tool have been extended with the capacity to model and generate code for complex input services and output services. Additionally, Merlin was extended in order to define the links between BPMN tasks and the IS Services. Finally, the Code generator creates a default project that can be used to run the process in the Camunda Process Engine.

Chapter 6
iDOCEM - Defining a Common Terminology for Object-Centric Event Logging and Data-Centric Process Modelling

This chapter was previously published in [118] and [119] and demonstrates the use of the MERODExBPMN integration by using the meta-model as a basis for defining a common terminology for object-centric event logging and data-centric process modelling.

6.1 Introduction

In the business process lifecycle, models can be approached from two perspectives: on the one hand models are used to create systems (possibly after analysis and redesign), and on the other hand, systems in use produce (event) logs that are used to discover the models representing the structure of the systems through the use of algorithms based on data [120]. These discovered models can be the starting point of a new cycle of analysis, redesign, implementation, etc. Especially when the log is extracted from a black box system, only the data in the log is available to reconstruct the process models. Therefore, proper logging of implemented processes in line with system design is a critical element for process discovery. Recently, the consideration of the integration of data and process aspects has seen a surge in interest, both from a model-for-design as from an automatic model discovery perspective. In particular, recent process mining efforts have revised the task of extracting an event log from the analysed information system from a single to a multi-object perspective [121]. To serve this purpose, various new efforts have proposed new solutions for analysing and modelling object-centric processes including object-centric visualization tools [122], log sampling and filtering techniques [123], and object-centric Petri nets [124]. To enable these analyses and modelling efforts, various object-centric logging formats have been proposed, such as eXtensible Object-Centric (XOC) [125], the Object-Centric Behavioural Constraint (OCBC) model [126], Object-Centric Event Logs (OCEL) [121], and more recently Data-aware Object-Centric Event Logs (DOCEL) [127]. These logging formats are discussed in more detail in Section 6.2.3. Likewise, data-aware process modelling has seen a surge in interest as well. Steinau at al. [93] performed an in-depth analysis of no less than 17 different data-aware process management approaches and captured this in the DALEC framework (Data-centric Approach Lightweight Evaluation and Comparison framework). However, it seems that the model-for-design research domain and the automatic model discovery research domain use different conceptualisations of data/object-aware systems. Especially the concept of an event needs to be aligned, as this is the main concept that the domains have in common.

In an ideal situation, when (designed) models are implemented, the resulting information systems are equipped with logging functionalities that allow the rediscovery of the models based on which the information systems were implemented. This is represented in Figure 6.1. However, one of the conclusions of Steinau at al. [93] is that while many data-centric process modelling approaches cover the *design phase* of the business process lifecycle, there remain substantial gaps for the support of next phases of the lifecycle of a business process i.e. *implementation and execution* and *diagnosis and optimization*. To support each phase and the transition from one phase to the next, additional research is needed to define and develop good support for process monitoring, diagnosis discovery and optimization through proper logging built into the information systems at implementation time. Therefore, it is important that the concepts of the model-for-design research domain and the automatic model discovery research domain are aligned. The mismatch between these domains is illustrated in more detail in Section 6.4.3 and can be summarized with the following five misalignment issues:

1. Logging functionalities of systems in use do not necessarily comply with a process log format such as XES, OCEL or DOCEL.
2. Logging formats lack clarity on which granularity level they use to record events.
3. Attributes might be considered static according to the logging format, while they are considered dynamic according to the modelling approach.
4. Lifecycles of objects are not included in the object-centric logging formats.
5. Logging formats lack a clear logging policy that describes which information should be captured in order to discover object relationships.

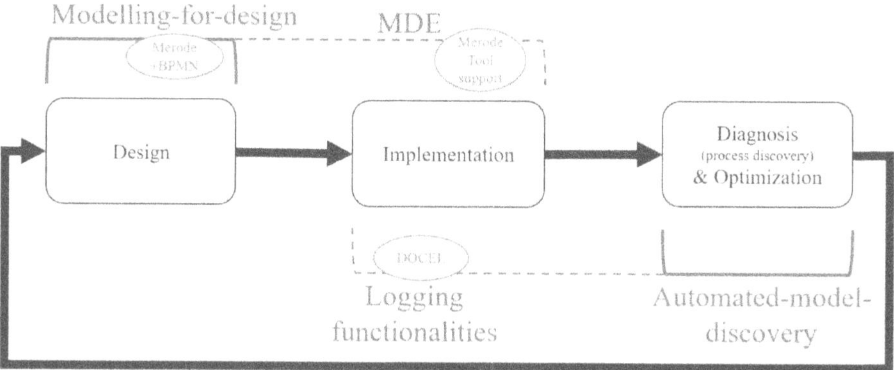

Figure 6.1 The three phases of the BPM lifecycle and how the other key concepts of this chapter are related to these phases

The goal of this chapter is to investigate the concepts and terminology used in the different phases of the business process lifecycle: the design phase, the implementation phase (including the implementation of logging) and the discovery phase, and to align the terminology across all these phases. Figure 6.1 illustrates how the domains of modelling-for-design and automated-model-discovery cover the three phases of the BPM lifecycle. The domain of modelling-for-design covers mostly the design phase, but has implications for the implementation of the system, especially in projects that use model-driven engineering approaches. On the other hand, the automated-model-discovery domain covers mostly the Diagnosis & Optimization phase, but is greatly affected by the logging functionalities that are implemented in the system. Achieving terminology alignment across phases and domains will enable researchers to incorporate knowledge of other phases of the lifecycle into novel research projects. For example, researchers focusing on the design phase could formulate modelling guidelines that lead to efficient logging in the implementation phase. On the other hand, researchers focussing on the implementation phase could analyse data and software quality as a function of design choices. Furthermore, Steinau et al. [93] conclude that while there are many tools available to support the design phase, there is a lack of tool support for the monitoring the execution of processes and for diagnosing and optimising processes. Alignment between modelling (in the design phase) and logging (in the implementation phase) facilitates better integrated tool support across the different phases, which in turn could greatly reduce the costs (monetary, time and effort) required for companies to implement state-of-the- art model-driven engineering and process/decision mining techniques developed by academia. iDOCEM is a first step towards improving tool support for monitoring, diagnosing, and optimising processes, as is discussed in more detail in Section 6.8.3.

The alignment of terminology is achieved by proposing a meta-model that aligns the DOCEL and the Merode meta-model with a unified terminology. This is then illustrated with a running example. This chapter presents an extension of the alignment that was presented at BPMDS 2023 [118]. In particular, this extends the original iDOCEM meta-model by adding eight meta-classes, ensuring complete alignment with the Merode meta-model. In addition, this chapter provides a detailed grounding in the Merode approach with an extensive running example. Furthermore, new logging formats have been added to the comparison: OCEL 2.0, event knowledge graphs, and OCED. To validate iDOCEM, the original paper is extended with a thorough test of the proposed meta-model through the IKAE case. For this purpose, a prototype application is generated using the Merode prototyper and is then adapted in order to generate a DOCEL-compliant event log. These actions mimic the manual execution of the defined business processes. The case study thus allows to establish the feasibility of generating a proper DOCEL log, and to identify the remaining challenges. This is further discussed in section 6.7.

The rest of this chapter is structured as follows: Section 6.2 covers related work and is followed by Section 6.4 that provides the details of a running example, including concrete examples of the misalignment issues listed above. Subsequently, Section 6.5 presents the meta-model iDOCEM that aligns the terminology in different phases of the cycle, and next, Section 6.6 shows how iDOCEM captures all concepts from the Merode approach and DOCEL, and how these concepts are related to other logging formats.

Section 6.7 discusses the implementation of event logging in a Merode application. Finally, Section 6.8 provides a discussion of iDOCEM by comparing it to related work, Section 6.9 discusses the limitations and future work and Section 6.10 concludes the chapter.

6.2 Related Work

This section first discusses research on artefact-centric process modelling (Section 6.2.1), followed by research on aligning data and process modelling (Section 6.2.2), object-centric logging formats (Section 6.2.3) and the discovery of artefact- centric processes (Section 6.2.4). The Section concludes with an identification of the research gap (Section 6.2.5).

Note that the literature sometimes uses the terms "artefact" and "object" interchangeably. Steinau et al. [93] provide an extensive discussion of different process modelling approaches, illustrating how these terms relate to each other. In short, from a modelling perspective, both artefacts and objects are general data representation constructs, where an artefact has a wider meaning as it includes a lifecycle model [93]. Thus, the term "artefact" subsumes the term "object" conceptually. However, in the domain of process mining, the term "object" seems to be used more often. In this section, we will use the terms "artefact" and "object" as they are used by the publications we discuss. As of Section 6.4, we will use the term "artefact" as defined here, and the term "object" as defined by the Merode approach (i.e. an instance of a class in a data model, see Section 6.5, Table 6.1).

6.2.1 Artefact-centric Process Modelling

The idea that a business process (model) can use and affect multiple objects or can be defined by means of a set of connected subprocesses, each related to an object or artefact, is not new. For example, Proclets have already been proposed back in 2001, whereby a business process consists of multiple proclets with each proclet being the subprocess of a certain artefact [128]. Since then various object-centric representation formats have been proposed such as Colored Petri nets (CPN) [129] where each colour represents a different object in object-centric Petri nets [124]. An extension on object-centric Petri nets was proposed in [130] with Catalogue and Object-aware Nets (COA) where transitions can have guards and data can be directly extracted from databases. Another proposal is Guard-Stage-Milestone (GSM) where the interaction between artefact instances is graphically visualized in a declarative manner [131] and a BPMN extension with the possibility to model data objects to have complex data dependencies was also proposed [132]. More complete overviews can be found in [93] and [133]. Finally, [134] proposes a modelling approach for business processes with a many-to-many interaction. The proposal defines a core concept called unbounded dynamic synchronization of transitions allowing to synchronize multiple business processes.

6.2.2 Aligning Data and Process Modelling

In the field of data-aware process modelling, several frameworks have been proposed to align data modelling and process modelling. The BALSA framework [135] introduces four dimensions in order to structure artefact-centric process modelling approaches: business artefacts, macro lifecycles, services and associations. Data modelling is addressed through business artefacts and macro lifecycles, and process modelling is addressed through defining services and as- sociations. The services are in essence tasks and associations are links between the services, and between services and macro lifecycles. The paper also lists a number of challenges identified by practitioners at IBM. Interestingly, they already suggest applying process mining techniques in artefact-centric settings. In [136], the authors propose to link UML and BPMN models with the use of the Object-Constraint Language (OCL) allowing to execute these models with for example SQL-based relational databases. In the PHILharmonicFlows framework [133], a set of requirements for the support of data-aware process modelling is presented, followed by a framework detailing the characteristics of data-aware processes. In [93], existing data-aware process modelling approaches are first compared to each other and classified by means of a systematic literature review. The detailed comparison throughout all phases of the business process lifecycle results in a comprehensive set of criteria for full support of data-aware processes. One of the findings of this paper is that tool support mainly focuses on the design phase, but is lacking for the implementation and execution phase, and especially for the diagnosis and optimization phase. Recently, in [115] the gap between the *Design and implementation and execution* phase was addressed by developing a formal link between business process modelling and domain modelling and demonstrating how data-aware processes can be co-designed and deployed in combination with a full-fledged domain model and ensuing set of applications services. This resulted in Merode being a well-developed data-aware process modelling approach that satisfies the large majority of the criteria put forward in [133]. As stated in [137], proposals for new data-aware process modelling notations often lack in usability, especially regarding the integration of data and processes. The Merode approach mitigates this issue as it is based on the popular modelling standards of UML for class diagrams and state charts, allows for the use of BPMN for process modelling and provides support in many forms. Additionally, Merode has a layered, event-driven architecture (see Section 6.4.1), the main benefit of it being that events are used to coordinate behaviour at different granularity levels, meaning that events and their relation to object types are well defined. Since events play a central role, the Merode approach is also well suited to support the creation of event logs. Finally, Merode provides automatic code generation for a prototype application. This will facilitate further experimentation and the implementation of a DOCEL log for a generated Merode prototype application. The main concepts of Merode are recapitulated in Section 6.4 by means of a running example.

6.2.3 Object-centric Logging Formats

To store object-centric process data, various logging formats have been proposed with the first proposals being the eXtensible Object-Centric (XOC) [125] logs and the Object-Centric Behavioral Constraint (OCBC) model [126]. They suffer, however, from scalability issues related to the storage of attributes and object-object relations with each event. To address this issue, the more scalable OCEL (1.0) [121] has been proposed. Certain problems remain with the proposal of OCEL, mainly related to attribute storage. In the case an attribute is updated, according to OCEL, this has to be stored together with the events. This entails however that whenever more than one object participates in an event, this attribute cannot be correctly allocated nor to the correct object type nor to the correct individual object. As a result, crucial information related to the business process and the data objects is lost. The importance of attributes is acknowledged with the proposal of DOCEL [127] which allows to unambiguously link each updated attribute value to the specific event that updated it and to the object the attribute belongs to. Recently, OCEL 2.0 [138] was proposed. The main improvement on OCEL 1.0 is that dynamic attributes are incorporated in the logging format (similar to DOCEL), as well as object relations. However, while the dynamic attributes are now linked to a timestamp, it is not yet possible to always uniquely identify which event triggered the creation, update or deletion of a dynamic attribute value [139]. Finally, OCED[1] is a meta-model that served as a starting point for OCEL 2.0 as well as for event knowledge graphs (EKGs). We choose DOCEL as the best of breed object-centric logging format to base our alignment effort on, because it supports both unambiguous object-attribute allocation, as well as attribute-event allocation.

6.2.4 Discovery of Artefact-centric processes

Besides works that study how to represent artefact centric processes or investigate logging formats, various studies investigated the extraction of artefact-centric knowledge within a process context. For example, how to support many-to-many relations between artefacts in state-based artefact lifecycle models was investigated in [140]. In [141] an algorithm is proposed to automatically discover the object-lifecycle of each data object involved in a business process. In [142] an algorithm is developed for the transformation of XES logs to OCEL logs. This algorithm is dependent on the correct discovery of artefact-event associations and object-attribute associations whilst the transformation of OCEL to DOCEL logs proposed in [143] depends on the correct discovery of dynamic attributes and their object-attribute associations. The semi-automatic discovery of data models from event logs has been investigated in [144]. The study in [124] investigated how object-centric Petri nets can be extracted from an object-centric event log and also illustrates how a process can be viewed from different viewpoints. In [145], the authors propose a method to simulate an object-centric process based on an object-centric log. Their approach is not based on mainstream modelling languages such as UML or BPMN. The previous works focused more on discovering artefact centric models but disregarding the interactions artefacts can have between one another. The study in [146] investigates an end-to-end approach to discover an artefact-centric process model containing the business objects, lifecycles and their interactions from an ERP system database containing unusual executions. In [147] an approach to discover interacting state machines from all involved artefacts in the process is proposed. The approach was implemented as a ProM plug-in taking as input an XES event log. The modelling approach proposed by Fahland [134] was extended and evaluated using both synthetic and real life event

---

[1] https://www.tf-pm.org/resources/oced-standard

logs [148]. The authors of [149] propose a novel data storage format in which event data is stored in labelled knowledge graphs. Subsequently, the authors of [150] investigate how process mining can be performed on such event knowledge graphs. Finally, [106] proposes an approach for conformance checking on artefact-centric process models. The artefact-centric process models are expressed in the BAUML framework, which consists of UML class diagrams, UML state machine diagrams, UML activity diagrams and OCL operation contracts. In this approach, the BAUML model is transformed into a Petri net that reflects the sequence constraints of the UML activity diagram. Additionally, the cardinality constraints of the UML class diagram and the guard conditions of the UML state machine diagrams are incorporated. This Petri net can then be used for formal verification and conformance checking. These publications, even though not exhaustive, show the interest in artefact-centric knowledge extraction from a process context. However, none of them provide a clear conceptual alignment between the design, logging and monitoring phases of the BPM cycle.

6.2.5   Research Gap

The above overview of the related work suggests that the focus lies either on the creation and analysis of the logs, whereby the data modelling formalisms used in the system design are not taken into account, or, that the focus lies on the formalism used to design and implement a system, but that the logging, and subsequent monitoring, analysis and diagnosis is underdeveloped (cfr. The conclusion of Steinau at al. [93]). To the best of the authors' knowledge, Gonzales et al. [151] is the only related work that focuses on the alignment problem. They aim to connect the data and process perspective, in order to support process mining in a data-aware setting. They provide a meta-model connecting both perspectives and a detailed description of the developed tool support applied in several real-world settings. However, the approach is based on the XES specification, and hence the event logs do not link events to objects in an unambiguous manner, and there is no support for object-centric logs nor for an artefact-centric perspective on the global system. Furthermore, they do not provide support for modelling.

6.3   Methodology

Integrating two meta-models is a very challenging task. Osman et al. [152] provide an overview of the three steps that are required for holistic ontology integration: matching, merging/aligning and repairing. These steps were followed for the construction of iDO-CEM. First, the corresponding elements in both meta-models were identified (matching). In this step, we analysed the abstract syntax and semantics of both models and identified the elements that represent the same concepts, as well as several elements that seem aligned but represent different semantics. This step was done in an iterative approach over several meetings with the authors of the Merode and DOCEL meta-models. The final result of the matching is incorporated in Table 6.2. The misalignment issues are described in section 6.4.3. In the second step (alignment), only the elements from both meta-models that fully overlap in their semantic meaning are merged, while other elements with similar but not the same semantics are connected (e.g. Event in DOCEL and BusinessEvent in Merode). These connections resulted in several new elements that bridge concepts from both meta-models. Finally, the resulting meta-model was critically evaluated by the authors of both the Merode and the DOCEL meta-model, addressing the repairing phase of ontology integration according to Osman et al. [152]. We iterated over these three steps until all authors were satisfied with the result.

6.4 Background and Running Example

To ease the further explanation of concepts we make use of a running example that describes the buying of goods at the (fictitious) IKAE shop, whereby the scope is restricted to the goods available at the self-service department.

Description *At IKAE, goods are stored in an alley at a certain place. The place has up to five shelves. Only shelf zero is reachable by the customers. When the stock level at shelf zero drops below a certain threshold (e.g. five pieces), a stock movement is automatically requested. At periodical intervals, the requested stock movements are collected and assigned to a forklift driver. The forklift driver will execute the requested stock movements by moving a pallet of goods from an upper shelf to the reachable shelf zero. When a customer arrives at the cashier (or self-checkout), a new receipt is started. The customer card is scanned first to identify the customer. If the customer has no card, the receipt is made for an "anonymous" customer. Then each product is scanned. If the barcode cannot be scanned, the cashier can enter the product number manually. If needed, a quantity can be added. Otherwise, the default quantity is always 1. Each scanned product adds a line to the receipt. Simultaneously, the quantity in stock at shelf zero is decreased with the corresponding quantity on the receipt line. The checkout process ends with the customer paying the receipt. The buying of a product can always be cancelled. In rare situations (e.g. the customer cannot pay), an entire receipt can be cancelled as well.*

6.4.1 Merode Model

The main benefit of Merode in the context of this chapter is that it allows a systematic allocation of events to participating object types, which will be explained later in this section. In future work, the rules of existence dependency can be leveraged to rediscover the EDG from a limited amount of information, thereby addressing the scalability issue of object-centric event logs.

In the EDG for the case in this chapter (Figure 6.2), the object type RECEIPT is ED on the object type CUSTOMER, because the *customer* that a *receipt* belongs to cannot change after the *receipt* has been created. Since a receipt can contain several *products*, and *products* can be listed on several *receipts*, there is no ED relationship between the object types RECEIPT and PRODUCT. The many-to-many relationship between RECEIPT and PRODUCT needs to be further specified with a new object type RECEIPTLINE to represent the appearance of a *product* on a *receipt*. Each *product* has several *stock locations*. When a *product* is moved from one *stock location* to another, this is registered as a

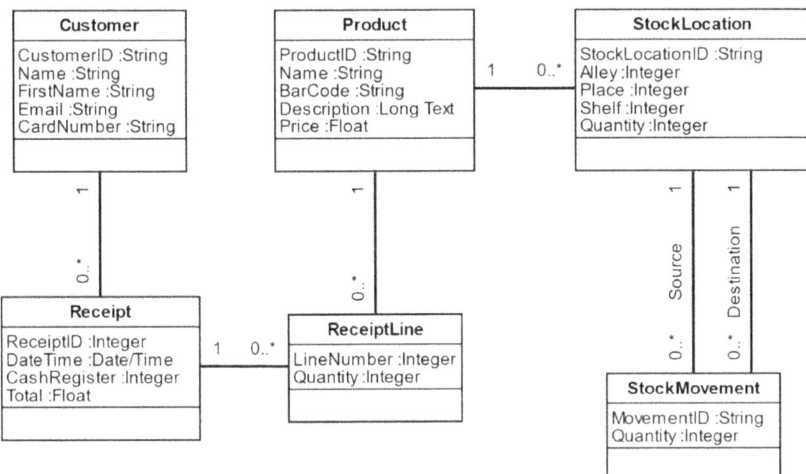

Figure 6.2 The EDG

StockMovement that is ED on two stock locations: the *source stock location* and the *destination stock location*.

The **Object Event Table (OET)** shown in Figure 6.3 maps the event types (rows) to the object types (columns) that participate in the event type. An event type can create, modify or end instances of a given object type, which is represented with "*/C", "*/M" and "*/E", respectively. If an event type is owned by an object type, this is indicated with "O/*". The owner of an event type corresponds in most cases to the natural "home" of that type of events, e.g. RECEIPT is the owner of the EVPAY event type. As each dependent object always has a reference to its master objects, master objects can "see" and therefore implicitly participate in all the events that affect their dependents. Therefore, master object types "acquire" the event types that are "owned" or acquired by their dependent object types. This is indicated with "A/*". For example, the event type EVCRRECEIPTLINE is a creating event type that is "owned" by RECEIPTLINE (O/C). The master object types of RECEIPTLINE (RECEIPT and PRODUCT) acquire the event type EVCRRECEIPTLINE as a modifying event type. PRODUCT has no master itself, but RECEIPT has the master CUSTOMER. Therefore, CUSTOMER also acquires EVCRRECEIPTLINE as a modifying event type.

When an object type participates in an event type (i.e., the cell for that row and column contains "O/C", "O/M", "O/E" or "A/M"), the effect of an occurrence of the event type on an instance of the object type is specified in a corresponding method. At the very least, a method will trigger a transition in the FSM of the object type, but an additional implementation can be added to a method. For example, for RECEIPTLINE, the method MECRRECEIPTLINE will create a new instance of RECEIPTLINE, while for RECEIPT, the method MECRRECEIPTLINE will adjust the value of the attribute TOTAL of RECEIPT.

In Merode, each object type has exactly one **Finite State Machine (FSM)**. At the moment of deployment, exactly one FSM should be implemented. FSMs impose sequence constraints on the methods of a given object type, and thus on the event types. In the IKAE case, CUSTOMER, PRODUCT and STOCKLOCATION have a default FSM. Thus, no sequence constraints are imposed for these object types, except that their instances should be created with an "*/C"-method and ended with an "*/E"-method. RECEIPT, RECEIPT-LINE and STOCKMOVEMENT have non-default FSMs that specify additional sequence constraints (Figure 6.4).

	Customer	Receipt	ReceiptLine	Product	StockLocation	StockMovement
EVcrCustomer	O/C					
EVendCustomer	O/E					
EVcrReceipt	A/M	O/C				
EVendReceipt	A/M	O/E				
EVcrReceiptLine	A/M	A/M	O/C	A/M		
EVendReceiptLine	A/M	A/M	O/E	A/M		
EVcrProduct				O/C		
EVendProduct				O/E		
EVcrStockLocation				A/M	O/C	
EVendStockLocation				A/M	O/E	
EVcrStockMovement				A/M A/M	A/M A/M	O/C
EVendStockMovement				A/M A/M	A/M A/M	O/E
EVPay	A/M	O/M				
EVCancelReceipt	A/M	O/E				
EVCancelAcquisition	A/M	A/M	O/E	A/M		
EVmoveGoods				A/M A/M	A/M A/M	O/M
EVCancelStockMovement				A/M A/M	A/M A/M	O/E
EVadjustStockLevel				A/M	O/M	
EVmodCustomer	O/M					
EVmodProduct				O/M		
EVmodStockLocation				A/M	O/M	

Figure 6.3 The OET

The **Information System Service layer** contains transactions (called input services) that trigger one or more business events and SQL queries that retrieve data from the Enterprise Layer (called output services). For example, when a *customer* buys a certain *product*, two business events need to be triggered: the product and the quantity that the customer is buying need to be added to the customer's receipt (*EVcrReceipt-Line*), and the stock level of the product in the system needs to be reduced by the same quantity (*EVadjustStockLevel*). Both event types can be grouped in an input service ISregisterProductOnReceipt.

The **Business Process layer** defines the business processes. Merode does not impose a specific business process modelling language, but suggests the use of BPMN given its status as de facto standard for this task. Figure 6.5a illustrates the process of a cashier serving a customer. Figure 6.5b shows the sub-process for scanning a single product for that customer. Figure 6.5c shows the process of the store manager who has to plan the stock movements that need to be executed, and Figure 6.5d shows the process of a forklift driver when they are assigned a new stock movement.

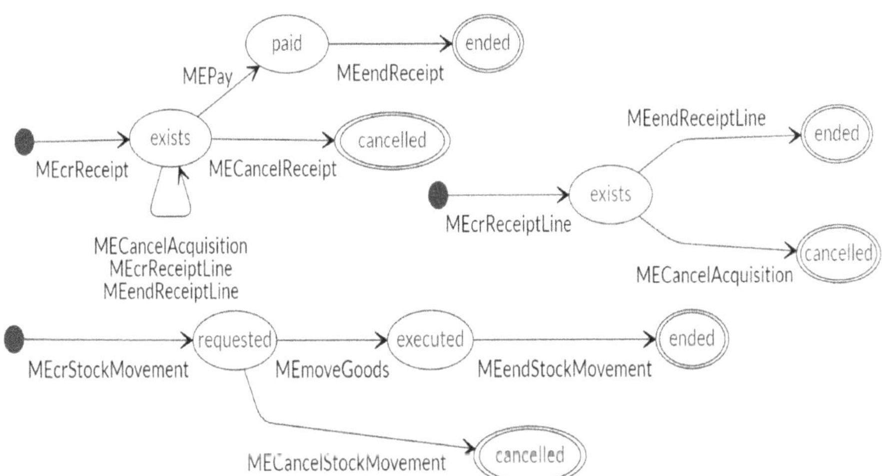

Figure 6.4. The non-default FSMs of the IKAE case

The automated service task REGISTER PRODUCT ON RECEIPT in the process of scanning a given product for a given receipt (Figure 6.5b) illustrates the different granularity levels of processing in data-aware process modelling. In this example an instance of the activity *Register Product on Receipt* can invoke an input service (*ISinvocationRegisterProductOnReceipt*) that will in turn trigger two business events: *EVcrReceiptLine* (for the specific *product* and *receipt*, with the correct *quantity* of items bought by the *customer*) and *EVadjustStockLevel* (for the same *quantity* to reflect the change in the stock levels). In turn, and as can be seen from the OET, the business event *EVcrReceiptLine* will trigger four method executions (*MEcrReceiptLine* for the creation of the new *receipt line* object, *MEcrReceiptLine* for the involved *product*, *MEcrReceiptLine* for the involved *Receipt* which will adjust the value of the attribute "Total" of the *receipt* and *MEcrReceiptLine* for the *customer* that the involved *receipt* belongs to). Similarly, the business event *EVadjustStockLevel* will trigger two method executions (*MEadjustStockLevel* for the "shelf zero" *stock location* of the involved *product* and *MEadjustStockLevel* for the involved *product* itself). A benefit of the different granularity levels during the design phase is that modellers can reuse IS services and/or event types. For example, the event type EVADJUSTSTOCKLEVEL is also triggered when the stock levels of the products are replenished.

6.4.2 DOCEL format

DOCEL (Data-aware Object-Centric Event Logs) is an event log format that builds on the OCEL (1.0) standard [127]. The DOCEL meta-model refines the concept of an attribute into the classes "Static Event Attribute", "Static Object Attribute" and "Dynamic Attribute". A DOCEL log consists of a table for the events (with columns for the linked objects and the static event attributes), a table for each object type (with columns for the static object attributes) and a table for each dynamic attribute (with a column for the value and for the linked event and object).

From the perspective of Merode, all attributes except for object identifiers are considered dynamic attributes (see issue 3 below). However, to obtain a DOCEL log, attributes that are not changed within the time frame of the logging should be considered static. For the running example, creating a new customer and their first receipt would be logged in the DOCEL event log as shown in Figure 6.6 (top). The static attributes of the customer (Customerid and Cardnumber) would be logged in the DOCEL Customer log as shown in Figure 6.6 (bottom left) and the dynamic attributes of the customer would be logged in the DOCEL dynamic attribute logs as shown in Figure 6.6 (bottom right).

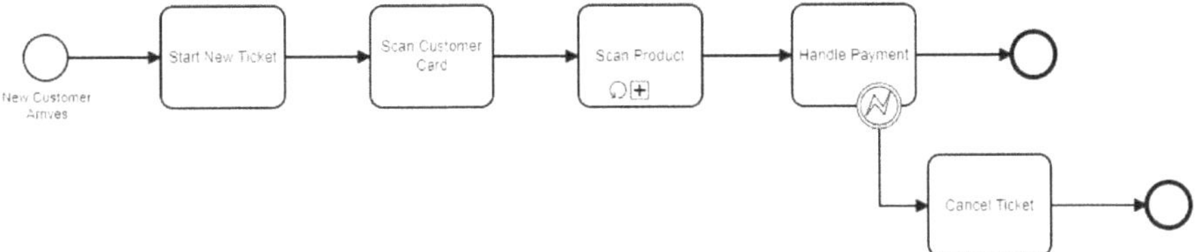

(a) The process of a Cashier serving a customer

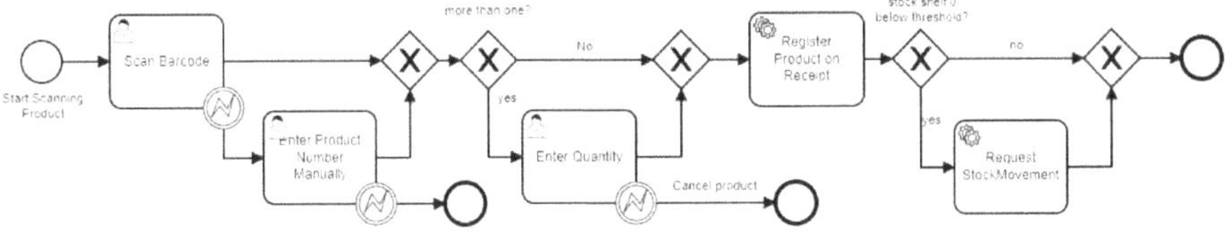

(b) The process of scanning a product

(c) The process of planning the stock movements

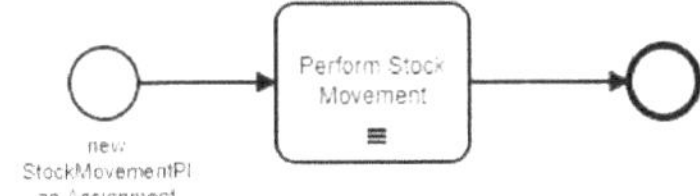

(d) The process of a Fork Lift Driver executing stock movements

Figure 6.5 The different processes of the IKAE case

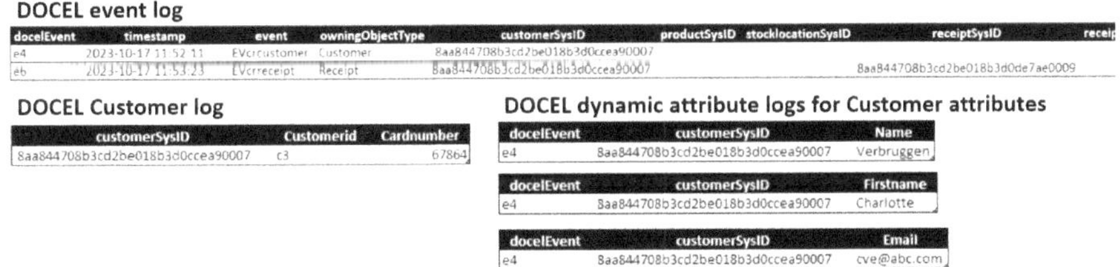

DOCEL event log

docelEvent	timestamp	event	owningObjectType	customerSysID	productSysID	stocklocationSysID	receiptSysID	receip
e4	2023-10-17 11:52:11	EVcrcustomer	Customer	8aa844708b3cd2be018b3d0ccea90007				
e6	2023-10-17 11:53:23	EVcrreceipt	Receipt	8aa844708b3cd2be018b3d0ccea90007			8aa844708b3cd2be018b3d0de7ae0009	

DOCEL Customer log

customerSysID	Customerid	Cardnumber
8aa844708b3cd2be018b3d0ccea90007	c3	67864

DOCEL dynamic attribute logs for Customer attributes

docelEvent	customerSysID	Name
e4	8aa844708b3cd2be018b3d0ccea90007	Verbruggen

docelEvent	customerSysID	Firstname
e4	8aa844708b3cd2be018b3d0ccea90007	Charlotte

docelEvent	customerSysID	Email
e4	8aa844708b3cd2be018b3d0ccea90007	cve@abc.com

Figure 6.6 Example of a DOCEL log

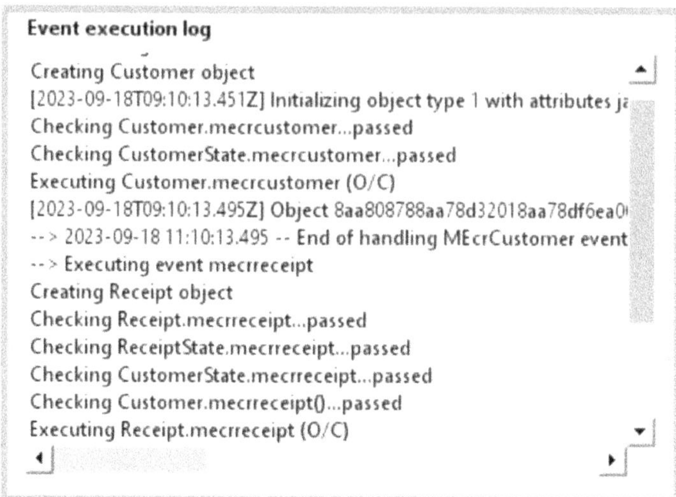

Figure 6.7 The log generated by the Merode prototyper

6.4.3 Misalignment Issues

Issue 1: Compliance with Process Log Formats. From the perspective of Merode, the domain model can be automatically transformed into a working prototype application that includes logging of events. The way logging is conceived in this prototype has nevertheless a number of shortcomings from a process mining perspective. The logging functionality tracks each attempted triggering of business events, including the failed attempts that result from violating some constraint defined in the models. Figure 6.7 shows an example of the log of the creation of a customer and their first receipt. Even though the log contains information about an action's start, execution, cancellation or completion, the current logging was developed with the aim of providing model-understanding support for modellers, and does not follow any process log format such as XES, OCEL or DOCEL. The Merode log shown in Figure 6.7 is therefore incomplete and not suited for process mining. Reverting to another artefact-centric modelling approach will not solve the issue: in [93], criterion D14 "Support for monitoring" is unsupported by all considered modelling approaches.

Issue 2: Recording Granularity of Events. When considering the issue from a process mining perspective, the main problem is the lack of clarity about which granularity level of events is logged and has to be logged according to the selected logging format. As DOCEL (and other event log formats) only contains the notion of "event", such logging does not allow distinguishing whether a logged "event" refers to a business process task or a more fine-granular invocation of individual operations on an object. For example, as described above, the service task "Register Product on Receipt" invokes an "EVcrReceiptLine" business event that affects the state of the receipt of the customer, the receipt, and the product and creates a receipt line object. For the product that is added to the receipt, the task will also update the stock location that is accessible to customers (shelf zero) by adjusting the value of the attribute "Quantity". Depending on how the logging is set up, the logging may be done at the level of the entire task or at the level of the operations on individual objects, or a single log may even contain a mix of events at different granularity levels. The lack of clarity in this matter complicates the correct interpretation of log information.

Issue 3: Static vs Dynamic attributes. Additionally, both domains consider different timeframes resulting in a different perspective on static and dynamic attributes. The modelling domain considers objects from their creation until their end-of-life. Thus, if an attribute of a class is static, its value needs to be set at the moment of the creation of each object (instance of that class), and this value can never change. Therefore, attributes are rarely static from the modelling perspective, except for object identifiers. On the other hand, event logs take a snapshot of the system for a given period. If the value of an attribute of an object does not change within this period, it is considered static. The domain of single object event logging usually makes a distinction between (static) trace attributes (where a trace relates to a single object) and (dynamic) event attributes. Therefore, DOCEL also makes the distinction between static and dynamic attributes. For example, if we consider a log containing data from a time period where the prices of the products are not adjusted, the attribute Price will be considered static from an object-centric event logging perspective. However, from a system design perspective, it makes more sense to make this a dynamic attribute, allowing the price of a product to change over time.

Issue 4: Logging Lifecycles. Even though all the object-centric process logging proposals are aimed at storing object-centric processes, none of them include the notion of object lifecycles or states as separate meta-objects within their meta-model. This is mainly due to the fact that data is considered from a pure database perspective, rather than from a domain modelling perspective. As the execution of an event may cause transitions from one state to the next (e.g., the event "EVPay" will put the receipt in the state "paid") , having information about the states before and after the event execution allows distinguishing between positive and negative events: logging the event "EVPay" in itself does not provide information about the success or failure of the payment, unless the resulting state is logged as well. The logging standards do not ensure this information to be logged. For example, XOC starts from the redo logs of databases rather than considering the application logic issuing the database manipulation statements. A domain model may typically contain additional business logic besides the pure data aspects, and logging needs to capture this information properly.

Issue 5: Lack of Logging Policy. Finally, the lack of a policy on what data to log may mean that not all object relationships are discoverable with the DOCEL log, as the choice of what to log is up to the system developer, who might not be aware of all the implications of their choice for system discovery afterwards. For example, when paying a receipt, the developer might choose to log only the data of the affected receipt object, but not of the related customer. This makes that the complete object model behind a process model might not be completely discoverable with the produced log.

6.5 iDOCEM - Integrated Data- & Object-Centric Event Meta-model

The first challenge in aligning object-centric event logs with data-centric conceptual models is matching the terminology used by both domains. Then, the Merode meta-model and the DOCEL meta-model [127] can be integrated by creating a new meta-model (iDOCEM).

The full Merode meta-model with a description can be found on the Merode website[2]. The DOCEL meta-model is presented in [127]. The Integrated Data- & Object-Centric Event Meta-model (iDOCEM) is represented in Figure 6.8 and can be consulted online[3] in more detail. To document the origin of each element in iDOCEM, we applied colour highlighting as suggested by Djurica et al. [153]: elements that originate only from Merode are highlighted in blue, elements that originate only from DOCEL are highlighted in green, elements that originate both from Merode and DOCEL are highlighted in orange, and new elements are highlighted in red. In order to maintain the readability of the model, several simplifications were performed:

- Not all attributes are represented. Attributes that were taken from the DOCEL meta-model are mentioned explicitly, but besides that, each class may contain more attributes, such as identifiers.
- The Class 'Data Type' is not included to minimize the number of crossing associations. In the full model, the 'Data Type' class is connected to the 'ISS Parameter', 'Static Event Attribute', 'Event Parameter', 'Method Parameter' and the 'Object Attribute' class. Data Types represent both basic types such as integer, boolean, float, character, etc. as well as complex types such as string, date, lists. Object Type is a subtype of Data Type as implementing associations results in attributes having the object type as data type.
- The meta-model contains only the elements from the Merode meta-model that are relevant for this problem. For example, the parts related to Inheritance of object types have not been included.

---

[2] https://merode.econ.kuleuven.be/merodemeta-model.html
[3] https://merode.econ.kuleuven.be/iDOCEM_SoSyM.html

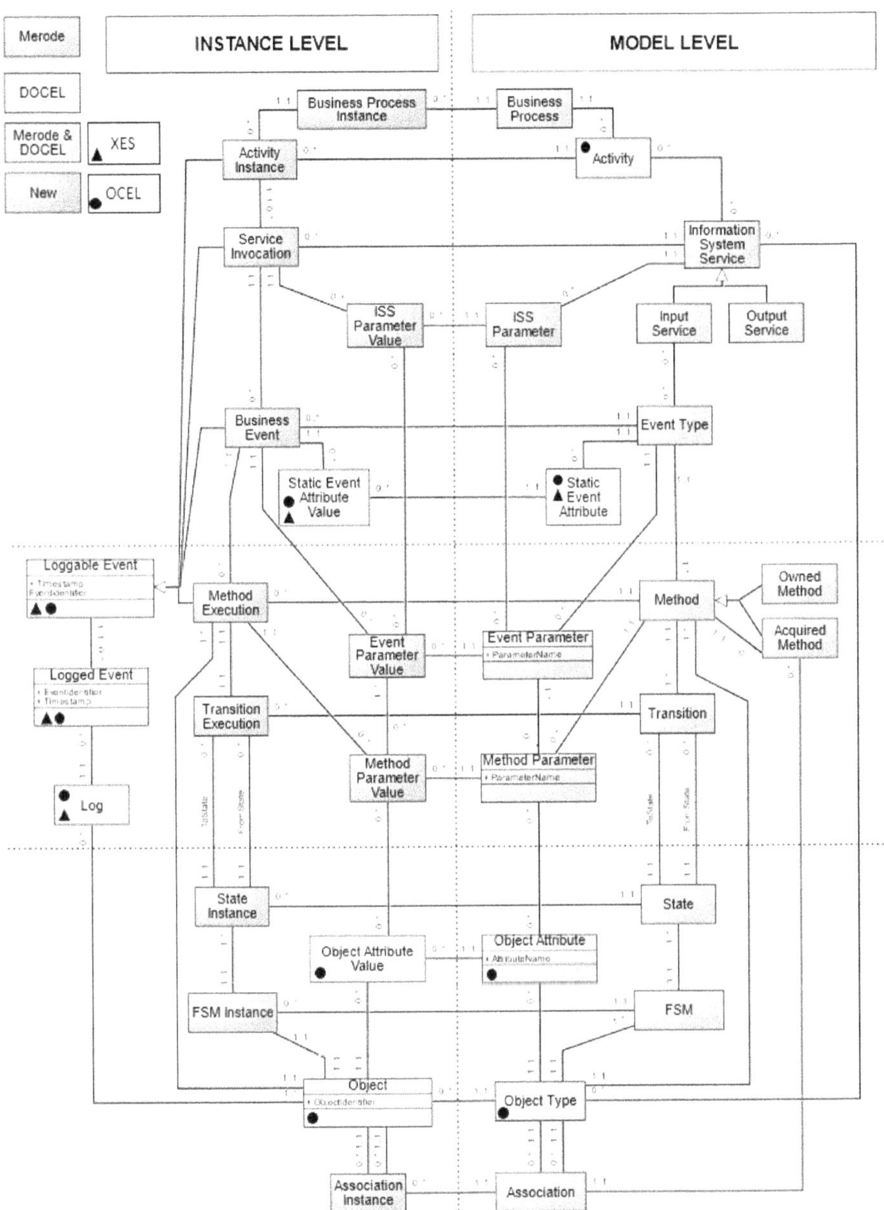

Figure 6.8 The iDOCEM meta-model

iDOCEM has six zones (shown in Figure 6.8). On the one hand, the meta-model is split into an instance level (left) and a model level (right). On the other hand, the meta-model is divided in three areas that deal with data objects, their attributes and their associations (bottom), activities and events (top), and the methods and parameters that connect events to objects (middle). The definitions of the entities used in iDOCEM are provided in Table 6.1, where the third column provides an illustrative example from the IKAE case. The cardinalities at the instance level (on the left) mostly mirror the cardinalities at the model level (on the right). An exception is the association between BUSINESS EVENT and ACTIVITY INSTANCE: while an EVENT TYPE can be triggered in multiple ACTIVITIES (e.g., EVADJUSTSTOCKLEVEL is triggered both when a customer buys a product, and when the stock is replenished), a BUSINESS EVENT is always triggered by exactly one ACTIVITY INSTANCE (when Monique buys an office table, the stock level of shelf zero of the office tables is adjusted). The elements that come from the Merode meta-model and the DOCEL meta-model are coloured in blue and green, respectively. Elements that appear in both meta-models are coloured in orange and new elements are coloured in red. Next, elements that appear in XES or in OCEL are indicated with a triangle and circle respectively. This is further discussed in Section 6.6.

The most challenging aspect of combining the meta-models is defining the correspondence between events and activities, as their definitions in the Merode approach (and artefact-centric process modelling in general) differ slightly from the definitions used in process log meta-models. In the Merode approach, an ACTIVITY INSTANCE (e.g., registering the office table that Monique is buying on her receipt) in a BUSINESS PROCESS INSTANCE (scanning products for Monique's receipt) can trigger zero, one, or multiple BUSINESS EVENTS via a SERVICE INVOCATION (e.g., the service invocation *ISinvocationRegisterProductOnReceipt* triggers *EVcrReceiptLine* for *Monique's receipt* and the product *office table*, and *EVadjustStockLevel* for the 'shelf zero' stock location of the product *office table*). The business events in turn trigger method executions, affecting the objects (*MEcrReceiptLine* in object *Monique + MEcrReceiptLine* in object *Monique's receipt + MEcrReceiptLine* in object *office table + MEadjustStockLevel* in object *stocklocation shelf zero of office table + MEadjustStockLevel* in object *office table*).

On the other hand, an event in an event log either represents the execution of an activity instance, a service invocation, a business event, or even a method execution, depending on the granularity level of logging. In iDOCEM, we man- age this disparity by creating LOGGABLE EVENT as an abstract superclass of Activity INSTANCE, SERVICE INVOCATION, BUSINESS EVENT and METHOD EXECUTION. The class LOGGED EVENT captures when a LOGGABLE EVENT is included in a LOG. A LOGGABLE EVENT can occur several times as a LOGGED EVENT in different LOGS.

Both in DOCEL and in Merode, object types (e.g. Customer, Receipt, Product) and event types are related in a many-to-many way. In the Merode meta-model, this many-to-many association is further specified into the meta-object METHOD. In the Merode approach, an EVENT TYPE (e.g., EVCRRECEIPTLINE) is related to one or multiple METHODS, one for each OBJECT TYPE that is defined to be affected by the EVENT TYPE (e.g., EVCRRECEIPTLINE affects CUSTOMER, RECEIPT and PRODUCT). The METHOD captures how an EVENT TYPE affects an OBJECT TYPE, i.e. the METHOD may create an instance of the OBJECT TYPE (an OBJECT), change the value of an attribute of the involved OBJECT and/or perform a transition in the object's lifecycle (e.g., in RECEIPT, MECRRECEIPTLINE updates the value of the attribute TOTAL with price of the product(s) added to the receipt). Each OBJECT TYPE is always involved in at least two EVENT TYPES (one for the creation of object instances, and one for ending the life of those instances), while each EVENT TYPE should always affect at least one OBJECT TYPE to be considered in scope of a domain model. DOCEL, however, does not have such a clearly defined policy regarding object-event relations. Instead the only requirement it has is that it assumes that each LOGGABLE EVENT directly interacts with the relevant OBJECTS involved in that LOGGABLE EVENT. Just like event types in Merode, each LOGGABLE EVENT should at least be dealing with one OBJECT and each OBJECT should at least be involved in one LOGGABLE EVENT to be considered in scope of the object-centric process. However, from a process perspective, there are no requirements regarding the presence of LOGGABLE EVENTS that create and delete OBJECTS since a business process can be a snapshot and thus certain OBJECTS may already have been created before or maybe deleted after the business process snapshot.

The Merode meta-model allows INFORMATION SYSTEM SERVICES, EVENT TYPES and METHODS to have attributes (called ISS PARAMETER, EVENT PARAMETER and METHOD PARAMETER), but does not define a relationship between the attributes of an OBJECT TYPE and an INFORMATION SYSTEM SERVICE, EVENT TYPE or METHOD: it is assumed that this relationship is set in the programming code that defines a METHOD's implementation. For example, QUANTITY may be a parameter of the EVCRRECEIPTLINE event type, and the code inside the methods MECRRECEIPTLINE will ensure to write this data in the correct place. In DOCEL on the other hand, DYNAMIC ATTRIBUTES of OBJECTS are also linked to the LOGGABLE EVENT that changes the value of the attribute. To incorporate this into iDOCEM, EVENT PARAMETER and METHOD PARAMETER are linked, and the latter is linked to the OBJECT ATTRIBUTE class.

Table 6.1 Terminology used in iDOCEM

Entity	Definition	Example
Business Process	Model of a business process.	BPMN diagram for the Cashier process
Business Process Instance	Occurrence of a *business process*.	Serving a single customer according to the Cashier process
Activity	The concept of a task in a business process.	Scan Customer Card
Activity Instance	Occurrence of an *activity*.	Scan Monique's Customer Card
Information System Service	The abstract superclass of Input Service and Output Service. Information system services are services rendered by the information system to support the execution of activities.	*Abstract classes do not have instances*
Input Service	An input service can query the objects in the database and trigger business events.	The input service *ISregisterProductOnReceipt* triggers the business events *EVcrReceiptLine* and *EVadjustStockLevel*

(*continued*)

Table 6.1 (*continued*)

Entity	Definition	Example
Output Service	An output service can query the objects in the database.	The output service *OSinspectStock* presents the quantity available at each *stocklocation* of a given *product*
Service Invocation	The invocation of an information system service by an activity instance triggering one or more business events	The activity instance where Monique's purchase of office tables is registered on her receipt will trigger a service invocation for the information system service *ISregisterProductOnReceipt*
ISS Parameter	An information system service has an ISS Parameter for each event parameter required to trigger the event types and/or for each object attribute required to query the database objects.	The ISS *ISregisterProductOnReceipt* has the ISS Parameters ReceiptID, ProductID and LineNumber for the EVcrReceiptLine event type, the ISS Parameters StockLocationID, Alley, Place and Shelf for the EVadjustStockLevel event type, and the ISS Parameter Quantity for both event types.
ISS Parameter Value	Value of an *ISS Parameter*.	When Monique buys five office tables, the ISS Parameter Value for Quantity is five.
Event Type	Type of real-world event that is relevant for the system and may trigger state changes in objects.	EVcrReceipt
Business Event	Occurrence of an *event type*.	The cashier creates a new receipt for Monique
Static Event Attribute	Attribute that is inherently linked to an *event type* and cannot be changed, such as the event identifier or timestamp.	Time of creation of a receipt
Static Event Attribute Value	Value of a *static event attribute*.	The time at which Monique's new receipt was created
Method	Procedure according to which the instance of the given *object type* is created, modified or ended as a result of the occurrence of the given *event type*.	Implemented procedure for creating a receipt

(*continued*)

Table 6.1 (*continued*)

Entity	Definition	Example
Owned Method	Method for event type of which the object type is an owner, i.e. is the most dependent object type of all participants to the event type.	Procedure MEcrReceiptLine in the class ReceiptLine
Acquired Method	Method for an event type for which the participation is due to the object type being a master of some other object type participating in the event type.	Procedure MEcrReceiptLine in the class Receipt
Method Execution	Occurrence of either an *Owned Method* or an *Acquired Method*.	Execution of the code when Monique's new receipt is created
Loggable Event	The abstract superclass of Activity Instance, Business Event and Method Execution that groups elements that can be logged in an event log.	*Abstract classes do not have instances*
Logged Event	*loggable event* that is included in a *log*.	Logging of the creation of Monique's new receipt
Log	Stored collection of *loggable events*.	Log of the Cashier process
Event Parameter	Parameters related to an *event type*, i.e. placeholder for a value that should be supplied when triggering a *business event* and its *methods*, resulting in a change in the *objects*.	Parameter "CashRegister" for the EVcrReceipt event type
Event Parameter Value	The value(s) given with each *event parameter*.	"5" as value of the CashRegister where Monique is being served
Method Parameter	Placeholder for a value that should be supplied when invoking the *method*.	Parameter "CashRegister" for the MEcrReceiptLine method in the object type Receipt
Method Parameter Value	The value(s) given with each *method parameter*.	Recording "5" as the value of the CashRegister when Monique's receipt is created
Object Attribute	Attribute of an *object type* that can be changed throughout the lifecycle of that *object type*.	Attribute "CashRegister" in object type Receipt
Object Attribute Value	Value(s) given to an *object attribute* by means of a *method execution*.	The value of the attribute CashRegister for Monique's new receipt is "5"

(continued)

Table 6.1 (continued)

Entity	Definition	Example
Object Type	Entity/Class in a data model.	Customer, Receipt, ...
Object	Instance of an *object type*.	Monique, Monique's new receipt, ...
Association	Relationship between two *object types*.	Customer has 0..* Receipts
Association Instance	Link between two *object instances*.	Receipt 12345 is linked to Monique
FSM	An *object type* has exactly one FSM in a system, defining the sequences constraints imposed on the event types by the object type.	FSM of Receipt
FSM Instance	Statechart Machine that manages the state of a given *object*.	FSM for Monique's new receipt
State	A *state* exists within the context of an *FSM* and represents a stage in the lifecycle of an *object type*.	State "paid" in the FSM of Receipt
State Instance	Actual value of a *state* for a given *object* (object being in this state or not).	Value of state "paid" for Monique's new receipt is "false"
Transition	A *transition* specifies how a *method* causes an *object type* to transition from one *state* to another *state*.	Transition from exists to paid in the FSM of Receipt
Transition Execution	Occurrence of a *Transition* where a *method execution* causes an *object* to transition from one *state instance* to another.	The execution of the method MEpay on Monique's receipt causes it to transit from the state "exists" to the state "submitted"

6.6 Aligning the Terminology of Existing Logging Formats

This section aligns iDOCEM's terminology with XES, OCEL, DOCEL, and Merode, and explains the differences and equivalences between logging formats and Merode.

XES [154] is a commonly-used business process logging format that logs a process from the perspective of a single object type. Each process execution instance is called a trace, which is the execution of a specific case which may coincide with (a part of) a lifecycle of an object in a process. OCEL [121] is an object-centric event log format allowing to store the logs of object-centric processes and currently the most widely used log format for object-centric processes. Before OCEL, OCBC models [126] were introduced together with the XOC logging format [125] to respectively represent and store object-centric process logs. Both suffer from scalability issues related to the storage of a relevant data model and all its attributes with each event [121]. Due to this and the absence of a meta-model in their proposal, OCBC and XOC are not included in the terminology alignment.

The alignment of terminologies between iDOCEM, XES, OCEL, DOCEL and Merode can be found in Table 6.2. EKGs are not included in this table, since they follow the OCED meta-model. In this table, a cell contains '/' when the meta-model does not contain a class equivalent to the corresponding class in the iDOCEM meta-model. If the meta-model contains a class that has similar but not exactly the same functionality to the corresponding class in iDOCEM, the name of the class is marked with a '*'. If the meta-model contains exactly the same class as the iDOCEM meta-model, the cell is marked with a '='.

Table 6.2 Terminology Alignment between iDOCEM, XES, OCEL 1.0, OCEL 2.0, DOCEL and Merode

iDOCEM	XES	OCEL 1.0	OCEL 2.0	DOCEL	Merode	OCED
BUSINESS PROCESS	/	/	/	/	=	/
BUSINESS PROCESS INSTANCE	Trace*	/	/	/	/	/
ACTIVITY	/	=	=	=	IS Supported Task	=
ACTIVITY INSTANCE	Event*	Event*	Event*	Event*	/	Event*
INFORMATION SYSTEM SERVICE	/	/	/	/	=	/
INPUT SERVICE	/	/	/	/	=	/
OUTPUT SERVICE	/	/	/	/	=	/
SERVICE INVOCATION	/	/	/	/	=	/
ISS PARAMETER	/	/	/	/	=	/
ISS PARAMETER VALUE	/	/	/	/	=	/
EVENT TYPE	/	/	/	/	=	/
BUSINESS EVENT	Event*	Event*	Event*	Event*	/	Event*
STATIC EVENT ATTRIBUTE	Attribute*	Attribute*	Event Attribute	=	/	Event Attribute Name
STATIC EVENT ATTRIBUTE VALUE	Value*	Attribute Value*	Event Attribute Value	Attribute Value*	/	Event Attribute Value
METHOD	/	/	/	/	=	/
OWNED METHOD	/	/	/	/	=	/
ACQUIRED METHOD	/	/	/	/	=	/
METHOD EXECUTION	Event*	Event*	Event*	Event*	/	Event*
LOGGABLE EVENT	Event*	Event*	Event*	Event*	/	Event*
LOGGED EVENT	Event	Event	Event	Event	/	Event
LOG	=	=	=	/	/	=
EVENT PARAMETER	Attribute*	Attribute*	Object Attribute*	Dynamic Object Attribute*	Event Parameter	Object Attribute Name*
EVENT PARAMETER VALUE	Value*	Attribute Value*	Object Attribute Value*	Attribute Value*	/	Object Attribute Value*
METHOD PARAMETER	Attribute*	Attribute*	Object Attribute*	Dynamic Attribute*	Method Attribute	Object Attribute Name*
METHOD PARAMETER VALUE	Value*	Attribute Value*	Object Attribute Value*	Attribute Value*	/	Object Attribute Value*
OBJECT ATTRIBUTE	Attribute*	Attribute*	Object Attribute	Dynamic/Static Attribute*	Attribute*	Object Attribute Name
OBJECT ATTRIBUTE VALUE	Value*	Attribute Value*	Object Attribute Value	Attribute Value*	/	Object Attribute Value
OBJECT TYPE	/	=	=	=	=	=
OBJECT	/	=	=	=	/	=
ASSOCIATION	/	/	qualifier*	/	=	Object Relation
FSM	/	/	/	/	=	/
FSM INSTANCE	/	/	/	/	=	/
STATE	/	/	/	/	=	/
STATE INSTANCE	/	/	/	/	=	/
TRANSITION	/	/	/	/	=	/
TRANSITION EXECUTION	/	/	/	/	=	/

Table 6.2 shows that compared to XES and OCEL, iDOCEM distinguishes more between different kinds of attributes depending on whether they belong to OBJECTS or BUSINESS EVENTS. XES only contains the meta-object ATTRIBUTE and ATTRIBUTE TYPE but these can only be linked to either an EVENT or a TRACE which is not always equivalent

to an OBJECT. OCEL distinguishes between object and event attributes with the distinction that object attributes cannot be changed over time and that event attributes cannot be unambiguously linked to an object. DOCEL solves this by having both DYNAMIC ATTRIBUTES and STATIC ATTRIBUTES that belong to an OBJECT and/or EVENT. In domain modelling, all object attributes are dynamic, since the value of an attribute must be set at least once in the life cycle of its object. Hence, iDOCEM does not distinguish between static and dynamic object attributes.

Because iDOCEM links METHOD EXECUTIONS to BUSINESS EVENTS, which are considered individually or as a group via a SERVICE INVOCATION of an ACTIVITY INSTANCE, it provides a finer logging granularity that is missing in XES, OCEL or DOCEL, where the results of methods are only represented in EVENTS and are not linked to specific ACTIVITIES. For example, if a product is registered on the receipt of a customer (activity instance that triggers the business event *EVcrReceiptLine*), a *ReceiptLine* is created and the total amount of the *receipt* is updated (2 method executions, see Section 6.4.1). If only the business event *EVcrReceiptLine* is logged with the corresponding event parameter values for the event parameters LINENUMBER and QUANTITY, there is no record of the fact that the method MECRRECEIPTLINE is executed for the *receipt*, and thus that the object attribute value *Total* of the *receipt* is changed. In iDOCEM, the link between METHOD EXECUTIONS and BUSINESS EVENTS is made explicit. Finally, iDOCEM stands apart from XES, OCEL, and DOCEL in its explicit inclusion of multiple object lifecycle meta-objects such as FSM, FSM INSTANCE, STATE, STATE INSTANCE, TRANSITION, TRANSITION EXECUTION, in the meta-model. This makes that iDOCEM is more artefact-centric compared to XES, OCEL, and DOCEL as the inclusion of these object lifecycles is more explicit.

6.7 Extracting a DOCEL Log from a Merode Application

To validate the proposed iDOCEM meta-model and the feasibility of generating DOCEL-compliant logs from an application, we implement a log generator for the running case. This amounts to performing a descriptive, scenario-based evaluation as well as a functional test according to Hevner [10]. Figure 6.9 shows the pipeline from Merode-model to event log. First a Merode model (EDG, OET and FSMs) is created in the Merlin modelling tool. From this model, the Merode prototyper can automatically generate a prototype of a desktop application. This application contains a changelog of the database in SQL format, as well as the original (incomplete) Merode log (see Figure 6.7). The Merode log tracks updates at a fine-granular level as not only the invocation of an event is logged, but also the invocation of the underlying operations on the individual objects. Nevertheless, attribute values are not logged. These are present in the SQL changelog, but not linked to eventIDs. At this point the system developer can manually adjust the generated code to add logging functionalities to the prototype application. Now, this prototype can be used to manually simulate workflows, and all performed action will be recorded in full detail (including attribute values) in an adjusted event log[4].

---

[4] A more detailed explanation of this pipeline, including the required input file and the obtained output files, can be found at https://merode.econ.kuleuven.be/iDOCEM_SoSyM.html

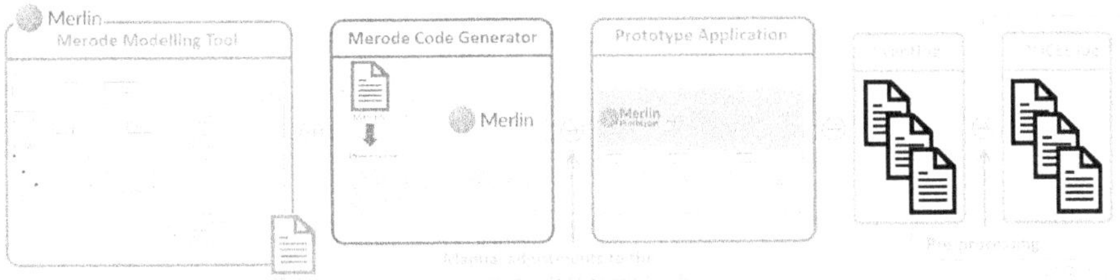

Figure 6.9 The pipeline from a Merode model to an event log

6.7.1   Extracted DOCEL Log for Business Events

Extracting the exact DOCEL format directly from an existing system is not feasible. In particular, from a (long running) information system's perspective, it is not possible to differentiate between static and dynamic attributes at runtime: over time, all attributes are considered to be dynamic. Therefore, we create a DOCEL log in two steps. First, we generate a raw log where all attributes are incorporated in the object type tables (Figure 6.10a). In a following pre-processing step, the tables for the dynamic attributes can be extracted from the generated raw log, resulting in a log that fully complies with the DOCEL standard (Figure 6.10b). In this pre-processing step, we need to determine which attributes are static and which attributes are dynamic within the time window covered by the log. For the running example, we will consider an attribute as a dynamic attribute if there is at least one object for which the value of this attribute changes in the context of the extracted log.

6.7.2   Logging at Different Granularity Levels

The example in Section 6.7.1 shows how the BUSINESS EVENTS of a Merode application can be logged. The iDOCEM meta-model (Figure 6.8) also contains the classes METHOD EXECUTION, SERVICE INVOCATION and ACTIVITY INSTANCE as subclasses of LOGGABLE EVENT. In this Section, we will discuss the logging of instances of these subclasses.

METHOD EXECUTIONS are already logged by the generated prototype application, as shown in Figure 6.7. However, this logging does not follow a formal logging standard. Following the implementation of the logging of business events in the DOCEL format, implementing the logging of method executions in the DOCEL format is now fairly straightforward. Figure 6.10c presents an example of a DOCEL log that includes method executions.

DOCEL event log

docelEvent	timestamp	event	owningOT	customerSysID	productSysID	receiptSysID	sto
e0	17/10/2023 11:42	EVcrproduct	Product		8aa844708b3cd2be018b3d0442130001		
e1	17/10/2023 11:49	EVcrcustomer	Customer	8aa844708b3cd2be018b3d0a5ce50004			
e2	17/10/2023 11:50	EVcrcustomer	Customer	8aa844708b3cd2be018b3d0bb1bb0006			
e3	17/10/2023 11:51	EVmodcustomer	Customer	8aa844708b3cd2be018b3d0bb1bb0006			
e4	17/10/2023 11:52	EVcrcustomer	Customer	8aa844708b3cd2be018b3d0ccea90007			
e5	17/10/2023 11:52	EVmodcustomer	Customer	8aa844708b3cd2be018b3d0ccea90007			
e6	17/10/2023 11:53	EVcrreceipt	Receipt	8aa844708b3cd2be018b3d0ccea90007		8aa844708b3cd2be018b3d0de7ae0009	

DOCEL Customer log

docelEvent	timestamp	event	customerSysID	Customerid	Name	Firstname	Email	Cardnumber
e1	17/10/2023 11:49	EVcrcustomer	8aa844708b3cd2be018b3d0a5ce50004	c1	Snoeck	Monique	abc@abc.com	15348
e2	17/10/2023 11:50	EVcrcustomer	8aa844708b3cd2be018b3d0bb1bb0006	c2	Vanthienen	Jan	abc@xyz.com	57316
e3	17/10/2023 11:51	EVmodcustomer	8aa844708b3cd2be018b3d0bb1bb0006	c2	Vanthienen	Jan	xyz@xyz.com	57316
e4	17/10/2023 11:52	EVcrcustomer	8aa844708b3cd2be018b3d0ccea90007	c3	Verbrugen	Charlot	cve@abc.com	67864
e5	17/10/2023 11:52	EVmodcustomer	8aa844708b3cd2be018b3d0ccea90007	c3	Verbruggen	Charlotte	cve@abc.com	67864

(a) The raw event log and Customer log produced by the prototype application

DOCEL event log

docelEvent	timestamp	event	owningOT	customerSysID	productSysID	receiptSysID	st
e0	17/10/2023 11:42	EVcrproduct	Product		8aa844708b3cd2be018b3d0442130001		
e1	17/10/2023 11:49	EVcrcustomer	Customer	8aa844708b3cd2be018b3d0a5ce50004			
e2	17/10/2023 11:50	EVcrcustomer	Customer	8aa844708b3cd2be018b3d0bb1bb0006			
e3	17/10/2023 11:51	EVmodcustomer	Customer	8aa844708b3cd2be018b3d0bb1bb0006			
e4	17/10/2023 11:52	EVcrcustomer	Customer	8aa844708b3cd2be018b3d0ccea90007			
e5	17/10/2023 11:52	EVmodcustomer	Customer	8aa844708b3cd2be018b3d0ccea90007			
e6	17/10/2023 11:53	EVcrreceipt	Receipt	8aa844708b3cd2be018b3d0ccea90007		8aa844708b3cd2be018b3d0de7ae0009	

DOCEL Customer log

customerSysID	Customerid	Cardnumber
8aa844708b3cd2be018b3d0a5ce50004	c1	15348
8aa844708b3cd2be018b3d0bb1bb0006	c2	57316
8aa844708b3cd2be018b3d0ccea90007	c3	67864

DOCEL dynamic attribute logs for Customer attributes

docelEvent	customerSysID	Name
e1	8aa844708b3cd2be018b3d0a5ce50004	Snoeck
e2	8aa844708b3cd2be018b3d0bb1bb0006	Vanthienen
e4	8aa844708b3cd2be018b3d0ccea90007	Verbrugen
e5	8aa844708b3cd2be018b3d0ccea90007	Verbruggen

docelEvent	customerSysID	Firstname
e1	8aa844708b3cd2be018b3d0a5ce50004	Monique
e2	8aa844708b3cd2be018b3d0bb1bb0006	Jan
e4	8aa844708b3cd2be018b3d0ccea90007	Charlot
e5	8aa844708b3cd2be018b3d0ccea90007	Charlotte

docelEvent	customerSysID	Email
e1	8aa844708b3cd2be018b3d0a5ce50004	abc@abc.com
e2	8aa844708b3cd2be018b3d0bb1bb0006	abc@xyz.com
e3	8aa844708b3cd2be018b3d0bb1bb0006	xyz@xyz.com
e4	8aa844708b3cd2be018b3d0ccea90007	cve@abc.com

(b) The DOCEL event log, Customer log, and dynamic attribute logs for the Customer attributes after preprocessing

DOCEL event log

EventID	timestamp	EventName	owningObjectType	invokedBy	customerSysID	productSysID	receiptSysID	receiptlineSysID	sto
e0	17/10/2023 15:07	EVcrcustomer	Customer		8aa844708b3dbead018b3dbfc77b0001				
e1	17/10/2023 15:08	EVcrproduct	Product			8aa844708b3dbead018b3dc0dc6f0004			
e2	17/10/2023 15:09	EVcrreceipt	Receipt		8aa844708b3dbead018b3dbfc77b0001		8aa844708b3dbead018b3dc151be0007		
e4	17/10/2023 15:09	receipt.MEcrreceiptline		e3			8aa844708b3dbead018b3dc151be0007		
e5	17/10/2023 15:09	product.MEcrreceiptline		e3		8aa844708b3dbead018b3dc0dc6f0004			
e6	17/10/2023 15:09	customer.MEcrreceiptline		e3	8aa844708b3dbead018b3dbfc77b0001				
e3	17/10/2023 15:09	EVcrreceiptline	ReceiptLine			8aa844708b3dbead018b3dc0dc6f0004	8aa844708b3dbead018b3dc151be0007	8aa844708b3dbead018b3dc18327000a	

DOCEL Receipt log

docelEvent	timestamp	event	receiptSysID	ReceiptId	DateTime	CashRegister
e2	17/10/2023 15:09	EVcrreceipt	8aa844708b3dbead018b3dc151be0007	1	17/10/2023	4
e4	17/10/2023 15:09	receipt.MEcrreceiptline	8aa844708b3dbead018b3dc151be0007	1	17/10/2023	4

(c) Logging method executions of the business event EVcrreceiptline

Figure 6.10 Logging at different granularity levels for the IKAE case

The Merode prototyper does not yet support the automatic code generation for the Information System Services Layer and the Business Process Layer. However, the generated prototype application can be extended with information system services and integrated with a process engine like Camunda, as discussed in [115]. In order for a task in a business process to affect the data objects, the task should invoke a business event via an input service [88]. The interaction between tasks and data objects is therefore covered by the logging of business events and method executions. The logging of the service invocations and activity instances can therefore be done in the DOCEL event log table, independently of the object tables. The main implementation challenge is synchronizing the logging done by the BPM engine and the logging done by the prototype application.

A prime advantage of iDOCEM is that it contains a participation policy between objects and (loggable) events participation policy due to the concepts of the Merode approach. A consistent participation policy is important because relations between OBJECT TYPES need to be kept stable across the execution of a business process. If this participation policy is not consistent or correct, it might not be possible to discover the complete object-centric process since not all objects are linked correctly to the right event, hence missing certain aspects of the process, e.g., with a business event *EVcrStockMovement* both the *sourceLocation* and the *destinationLocation* need to be provided. However, if no *sourceLocation* is linked to that event then the forklift driver cannot know from which stock location they should move the products for that *EVcrStockMovement* business event. iDOCEM already contains a relationship between OBJECT, METHOD EXECUTION, BUSINESS EVENT, SERVICE INVOCATION and ACTIVITY INSTANCE, defining the participation of LOGGABLE EVENTS to OBJECTS. The Merode meta-model[5] specifies this relationship even further given that each association must express existence dependency, and object types can acquire methods from their dependents [88]. As such an unambiguous and consistent object-event participation policy is defined.

6.8 Discussion

In this section, we will address the five issues that were raised in the Problem Illustration. The rest of this section will discuss how iDOCEM compares to related work, and its added value from the data-aware process modelling perspective.

6.8.1 Addressing the Five Issues

Section 6.4.3 highlighted five issues that might occur due to misalignment between the data-aware process modelling and the object-centric event logging domains. In section 6.7.1 we demonstrated how the Merode tools can be used to address the first issue, making sure that logging functionalities follow a process log format. The second issue (the lack of granularity in how logging formats record events) was addressed in section 6.7.2. The third issue (static versus dynamic attributes) was addressed in the iDOCEM meta-model (Section 6.5) by using several different attribute/parameter meta-classes. Additionally, Section 6.7.1 demonstrates how this issue can be handled when extracting DOCEL logs from Merode applications. The fourth issue concerns the fact that logging formats do not include lifecycles of objects in their meta-models. This issue was addressed by directly linking the transitions in a lifecycle to method executions in the iDOCEM meta-model (Section 6.5), which are loggable events. Finally, while the concept of the EDG in Merode provides an interesting starting point for developing a logging policy that describes which information should be captured in order to discover object relationships this was not yet addressed in detail in this chapter, as it would require additional analysis and testing. This is considered future work.

---

[5] https://merode.econ.kuleuven.be/merodemeta-model.html

6.8.2 Comparison to Related Work

Section 6.2.5 introduces the only other publication ([151]) proposing a meta-model for the same problem. The main differences between both meta-models are listed here.

- While iDOCEM uses two meta-levels (the model level and the instance level), G. López de Murillas et al. use three meta-levels by adding the notion of *object versions*. iDOCEM does not contain an OBJECT VERSION class, this is instead captured by an OBJECT which can have several OBJECT ATTRIBUTE VALUES for the same OBJECT ATTRIBUTE. The same applies for EVENT PARAMETERS, METHOD PARAMETERS and STATIC EVENT ATTRIBUTES. iDOCEM assumes that the data model is kept stable during a process execution leaving database structure evolution out of scope at this point.
- According to [151], the process and data sides of the meta-model are only connected to each other at the most granular level. In iDOCEM, the connections between the OBJECT TYPES, ATTRIBUTES/PARAMETERS, EVENT TYPES and ACTIVITIES are explicitly modelled at the model level as well, while this is missing in [151].
- In [151] EVENTS (and ACTIVITY INSTANCES) are grouped into CASES, which are then grouped into LOGS. iDOCEM directly groups LOGGABLE EVENTS into LOGS as the cases can be retrieved using filtering operations on the log.
- Both [151] and iDOCEM include a class (LOGGABLE) EVENT. However, the former defines an event on a more coarse level than the latter. In their meta-model, an ACTIVITY INSTANCE can be related to several EVENTS that define the type of operation (read, write, delete, ...) and/or the lifecycle value of the ACTIVITY INSTANCE (start, complete, ...). In iDOCEM, LOGGABLE EVENTS can also represent the trigger of SERVICE INVOCATIONS or individual METHOD EXECUTIONS. More specifically, a LOGGABLE EVENT is further specialized via inheritance in four granularity levels. The relationship between the loggable events at the different granularity levels are specified in the meta-model by means of the 1-to-many associations between the four subclasses.
- In [151] only the relationship between ATTRIBUTE and CLASS is modelled, while iDOCEM makes a distinction between different types of attributes (STATIC EVENT ATTRIBUTE, OBJECT ATTRIBUTE, EVENT PARAMETER and METHOD PARAMETER) and how they relate to the other classes.

It is important to mention that some modelling languages have been developed specifically for the purpose of capturing the information extracted by means of process mining. These modelling languages do align well with the respective event data models on which they were designed, i.e., Petri nets [155] and XES [154], or OCPN [124] and OCEL [121]. However, every proposal has been designed with certain assumptions in mind. This chapter argues that for certain issues the current proposals do not sufficiently satisfy all the needs that processes might have, such as multiple granular logging facilities and a clear mapping between the different granularities. Secondly, these modelling languages do not sufficiently take into account the artefact-centric dimensions such as life-cycles, changing attribute values or even object relations.

When comparing iDOCEM to mainstream process formalisations in the area of business process management, one can note three main differences. First, most process algebras assume that all behavioural aspects of a system are captured by the same algebra, i.e. that the algebra is "encompassing" in its capability of describing system behaviour, whereas iDOCEM combines two different algebras to capture behaviour. This is significantly different from algebras such as Proclets, object-centric Petri nets and other Petri net variants. And while [156] also combines imperative and declarative modelling, the combination results in a unified algebra for processes. For the business process layer, iDOCEM assumes the use of a process modelling language, as well as a formalisation by means of Petri nets [105]. The process layer does not include data aspects itself, but invokes services to create, modify, end or retrieve data from the object types in the domain layer. This interaction with the domain layer relies on message sending, in particular, by invoking input and output information services. Second, the behavioural aspects captured in the domain layer are formalised by means of state charts and, while rooted in the object-oriented paradigm, the objects do not communicate by means of message passing. Rather, the notion of joint synchronisation on business events is used, the formalisation of which is rooted in the process algebra CSP [28] and its operators for parallel composition (‖), unbounded interleaving ($\sim$) and iteration (*) (see [99], [100] for details). This synchronous participation to common business events bears some similarity with object-centric Petri nets [124]. Third, in the domain layer, relations between objects are not maintained as part of the processes themselves. The relations between objects are kept as part of the data model (and implemented e.g. via foreign keys). Objects thus "know" what their related objects are, and depending on the cardinality of associations, the lifecycle of a master object type will run in parallel with the unbounded interleaving composition of the processes of its dependents (max. cardinality of many) or the iteration of a process of its dependents (max. cardinality of one). This has been described in detail in [99], [100]. The implementation of the ‖, $\sim$ and * operators is realised by means of an intermediate event-handling layer, responsible for broadcasting the event to all participating objects and coordinating their answer: either all participants accept to execute the corresponding action successfully or the event is refused and all (if any) performed actions associated to the event are rolled back. The participating objects themselves will verify the observation of maximum cardinality and referential integrity constraints using the information contained in the data model (concepts of "Object Type" and "Association" in iDOCEM). The implementation of the event handling mechanism is based on event-based architectures, as described in [99]. Because of the event handling mechanism, all communication between Business Processes and Objects is channelled via the event handler. The input services can furthermore trigger several events in sequence, thus allowing for implementing cascading effects, such as a cascading delete, as multi-event transactions (see chapter 9 of [88]). The interested reader is referred to [88], [99], [100], [157] for more details.

6.8.3   Contribution of iDOCEM for Data-Aware Process Modelling with Merode

Several sets of evaluation criteria can be considered to identify the added value of iDO-CEM for data-aware process modelling. The set proposed in the PHILharmonicFlows framework [133] focuses mostly on the design phase of the business process lifecycle, while the set of criteria proposed in the DALEC framework [93] covers all phases of the business process lifecycle at the expense of a smaller set of criteria for the design phase.

Since the focus of this chapter concerns the other phases of the business process lifecycle, the DALEC framework is more suitable to evaluate the added value of iDOCEM. The DALEC framework also provides a detailed description of each criterion, and when it can be considered partially or fully supported. Merode already provides partial or full support for almost all criteria of the PHILharmonicFlows framework [133], and hence also largely meets criteria D01-D12 proposed by the DALEC framework.

The integration of Merode with DOCEL into iDOCEM yields improved support for two additional criteria. In view of the conclusion of Steinau at al. [93] that there remain substantial gaps for the support of last phases of the lifecycle of a business process i.e. *implementation and execution* and *diagnosis and optimization*, we review to what extent iDOCEM opens an avenue for better support of these phases.

D14 - Support for Monitoring As discussed in Section 6.4.3, the Merode prototyper supports the generation of event logs. However, the log is incomplete and not suited for process mining. In order to provide full support for this criterion, monitoring should be possible for "all aspects" of the object types, FSMs and processes in real time and at run time [93], including complete event logs. iDOCEM supports setting up better logging by making the connection between ACTIVITY INSTANCES, SERVICE INVOCATIONS, BUSINESS EVENTS, METHOD EXECUTIONS and LOGS explicit. Thereto, the current logging facilities in the Merode-generated applications should be adjusted to include more detailed and formalized logging. Section 6.7 demonstrated the feasibility through manual adjustment of the code. Given that the to be added code is identical for all events (up to the elements' names), we expect that this can be built into code generator without too many problems. In the future, this will allow us to capitalize on the opportunity to include process mining in order to gain more insight in user behaviour.

D23 - Tool support for Diagnosis and Optimization The systematic literature review reported in [93] did not find a single approach that provides support for diagnosis and optimization. In the diagnosis and optimization phase, "event logs are evaluated based on Business Activity Monitoring (BAM) and process mining techniques" [93]. While the Merode approach was not included in this literature review, it also lacks tool support in this area. iDOCEM provides a first step towards performing process mining on the execution of the modelled process, by aligning the concepts of data-aware process modelling approaches and object-centric event logs, and demonstrating the implementation of a running example. iDOCEM in combination with the Merode-tool opens up opportunities for generating artificial DOCEL event logs for which the ground truth is available. Such DOCEL event logs with companion ground truth model would offer interesting benchmarks for the validation of object-centric conformance checking and object-centric process discovery.

6.9 Limitations and Future Work

A first limitation if the work presented in this chapter is that the alignment of concepts in iDOCEM is based on the concept definitions used in a specific artefact-centric modelling approach, and a specific object-centric logging standard (Merode and DOCEL respectively). The results of this chapter are therefore specific to Merode and DOCEL. However, aligning both research domains in general would have been a much more complex task, given that definitions within a domain can vary across approaches. For example, the concept of an object lifecycle is defined differently in Merode and in the PHILharmonicFlows approach. By aligning the concepts of specific approaches, we provide an example for the alignment of other approaches. For example, the alignment of the PHILharmonicFlows approach and the DOCEL logging format can now be achieved by mapping PHILharmonicFlows on the Merode concepts.

A second limitation is that the current log format of the applications generated by the Merode prototyper do not yet follow any log storage standard. In order to extract a log in the DOCEL standard, the generated code needs to be manually adapted as explained in Section 6.7. Furthermore, as the logging by the prototype application only pertains to the application component, tasks in the business process that are executed without support of the application, and tasks that only consult information but do not trigger events, are not logged yet. This corresponds to logging in information systems that do not make use of process engines. As such, in its present form, the current log format provides only a partial view of the executed processes. Section 6.7 nevertheless demonstrates the feasibility of extracting a DOCEL log from an artefact-centric application generated from a Merode model. Since we demonstrated how to implement this in a generated Merode application, it is now possible to incorporate it in the Merode prototyper in the future, eliminating the task of manually programming the logging functions. By the fact that iDOCEM includes the meta-objects needed to capture the process elements, the format is also capable of describing the logs of a process-aware information system. The implementation of logging at the business process level is also briefly discussed in Section 6.7.2.

Finally, after implementing the required logging functions for a DOCEL log, the events need to be manually executed or simulated in the Merode prototype to populate the event log. In the future, we are planning to extend the Merode modelling tool to include the Information System Service layer, completing the integration of the domain model and the business process model. This will also facilitate the development of an event log generator that provides a more complete log by also including the logging of output service invocations and that allows for the automatic simulation of an artificial event log based on input from the user. However, as is explained in more detail in [158], capturing all the different objects, their lifecycles, interactions while respecting the process itself make this problem difficult to implement and to scale efficiently. Moreover, the study conducted in [159] provides an overview of the available single-point of view simulation models as well as an overview of different possible simulation parameters such models can contain. It does not, however, consider the artefact dimension but rather mainly focuses on the control-flow dimension of process simulation. This model can be used in the future to develop and compare the planned object-centric process log simulation tool. Another interesting research direction is whether event knowledge graphs [149] can also be extracted from a Merode prototyper as knowledge graphs also have their own advantages regarding query execution and storage optimisation.

6.9.1 Conclusion

This chapter identifies a misalignment between the model-for-design research domain and the automatic model discovery research domain in the context of data/object-aware processes. This misalignment is illustrated with a running example. The main contribution of this chapter is the Integrated Data- & Object-Centric Event Meta-model (iDOCEM) which aligns the concepts of the Data-aware Object-Centric Event Log (DOCEL) and an artefact-centric modelling approach (Merode). The terminology used in iDOCEM is also aligned with the terminologies of XES, OCEL and DOCEL. The chapter also discusses how the Merode architecture and tools can be leveraged for the implementation of a DOCEL log, and demonstrates this with the running example. This demonstration illustrates the feasibility of generating code for object-centric logging, and eventually developing an object-centric event log generator.

Part IV
Evaluation

Chapter 7
TEC-MAP: a taxonomy of evaluation criteria and its application to the multi-modelling of data and processes

This chapter was previously published in [160] and [161].

7.1 Introduction

The domain of Enterprise Information Systems Engineering uses many different conceptual modelling languages and methods to specify the requirements of a system under development. The resulting models can add value in several ways – the models can simply be used as documentation of the specifications, the models can be used to facilitate communication between developers and other stakeholders, or the models can be used for automatic code generation. The complexity of the systems under development may require addressing multiple perspectives with different models. Amongst the perspectives to be addressed we find data, processes, user interfaces, security, privacy, goals, etc. The modeller will thus have to choose the appropriate (set of) modelling languages according to their specific modelling goal. For example, the database of a system can be modelled with a UML Class Diagram or an ER model while the work processes it needs to support can be modelled with BPMN process models, EPCs or coloured Petri nets. Given that the different aspects relate to a single system, ideally, the models that capture the different perspectives should be aligned and consistent to ensure their integration. Multi-modelling approaches combine several conceptual modelling languages to provide integrated support to address different perspectives of a system under development. For example, combining different UML diagram types can be considered a multi-modelling approach, as well as using enterprise modelling frameworks such as ARIS [162] and 4EM [163]. Each candidate (set of) modelling language(s) comes with advantages and disadvantages. Combining BPMN with (E)ER diagrams to address process and data modelling will require coming up with one's own alignment and consistency rules as these languages were defined independently from each other. But also multi-modelling languages come with their limitations: UML does not provide precise rules on the combined use of diagram types, activity diagrams come with a more limited set of modelling constructs compared to BPMN, and, in contrast to e.g. 4EM, UML does not address goal modelling. To make an informed choice in this matter, the modeller should select a number of criteria relevant to their problem domain and compare candidate (multi-) modelling languages based on these criteria. This task is complicated in two respects: the number of perspectives to model and the resulting set of candidate modelling languages is quite large and existing sets of evaluation criteria cover only part of the aspects of the

© The Author(s), under exclusive license to Springer Nature Switzerland AG 2026
C. Verbruggen, *Advancing Multi-modelling in MDE for Integrated Domain and Business Process Modelling*, Lecture Notes in Business Information Processing 576,
https://doi.org/10.1007/978-3-032-13876-7_7

multi-modelling task, e.g. by not addressing the aspects related to the integration of multiple modelling languages. The overall goal of the research presented in this chapter is to provide support for the assessment of a chosen set of independent (multi-)modelling languages in a multi-modelling context. The contribution of this chapter is two-fold: on a theoretical level, the chapter provides an overview of existing evaluation frameworks in the literature, builds a more complete set of evaluation criteria and proposes a unified taxonomy for the classification of these evaluation criteria; on a practical level, the chapter provides guidance and support to the modeller for selecting the appropriate evaluation criteria for their problem domain.

The evaluation of multi-modelling approaches needs to consider the individual perspectives, and how integration is ensured. Many possible perspectives and combinations can be considered. In recent years several combinations have been investigated: goal modelling and process modelling (e.g. [164]), decision modelling and process modelling (e.g. [165]), data modelling and process modelling (e.g. [115]). Amongst these combinations, data + process modelling has attracted a lot of interest [93], and, interestingly, evaluation frameworks for this combination have been proposed as well (e.g. [93], [133]). This provides an interesting starting point for the research. Therefore, this chapter will primarily focus on the integrated multi-modelling of data and processes, including the process-related viewpoints of users and authorisations. The main reason for this choice is the relatively large number of proposals on data-aware process modelling, and the existence of evaluation frameworks in this domain.

The assessment of a data-aware process approach may be done from multiple perspectives: the adequacy of the modelling language used for each aspect e.g. in terms of their expressive power, the level of integration across different aspects, the ease of use of the method, tool support, etc. Various evaluation frameworks have been proposed to demonstrate the value of proposals for data-aware process modelling approaches. They differ in a similar way in their use of terminology and definitions, but also in their focus, the level of detail used to describe their criteria and how these criteria should be evaluated. Next to these specific evaluation frameworks, there are also well-established evaluation frameworks of a more general nature (e.g. Moody's Method Evaluation Model [92] and Krogstie's SEQUAL framework [166]). While these frameworks are not suitable for evaluating specific aspects related to combining data and process modelling (or any other modelling viewpoint), they do address other important aspects, such as utility, ease of use, model quality, etc. Such frameworks can also be applied to data-aware process modelling as well, and this would make it possible to address open problems in the field of data-aware process modelling [137]. Therefore, to contribute to the field, we not only pool and align existing frameworks in a meta-framework, but also expand the scope by considering frameworks that address general aspects such as understandability, ease of use, model quality, etc.

We address the lack of a comprehensive evaluation framework by making use of existing evaluation frameworks, as this offers the advantage of starting from proven and robust sets of criteria, while avoiding a bias towards specific solutions. At the same time, the diversity of frameworks allows for a good degree of comprehensiveness, while requiring the creation of a taxonomy to identify identical, similar or subsuming criteria. More concretely, we investigate the following research questions:

RQ1: what are the relevant evaluation frameworks for data-aware process modelling approaches, including general frameworks that can be applied to these approaches?

RQ2: what is the minimal set of dimensions and characteristics required to classify and summarize the evaluation criteria from the different evaluation frameworks identified in RQ1?

RQ1 will result in an overview of existing evaluation frameworks. RQ2 will result in a taxonomy for the classification of evaluation criteria. As a by-product of creating the taxonomy, all criteria will be classified since this is a requirement for finalising the taxonomy development. When referring to the taxonomy and all the classified criteria, we will use the term "populated taxonomy". The resulting comprehensive populated taxonomy is useful for comparing existing approaches, identifying aspects of existing approaches that are underdeveloped, or validating the proposal of a new approach. In a previous cycle of this research [160], we developed a **T**axonomy of **E**valuation **C**riteria for a **M**ulti-modelling **Ap**proach (TEC-MAP) based on nine well-known frameworks (five general frameworks, and four frameworks focusing on multi-modelling of (at least) data and processes). The different perspectives mentioned in this introduction cover one dimension of TEC-MAP. Additionally, we identified two other dimensions which we called the Pillar dimension (covering syntax, semantics, tool support and modelling guidelines) and the Phase dimension (covering the phases of the business process cycle). In this chapter we present the results of the second cycle of research that expands the previous work with a systematic search for more evaluation frameworks, and re-evaluates the proposed TEC-MAP by classifying the additional criteria found through the literature review which allows assessing its suitability and completeness. In addition, possible uses of TEC-MAP are explained by elaborating a set of guidelines for its application and presenting an example of an evaluation of several modelling approaches with TEC-MAP. While TEC-MAP is mostly intended to evaluate data-aware process modelling approaches, the inclusion of these two dimensions and the more general evaluation framework make it useful outside this context as well.

In the remainder of this chapter, section 7.2 first presents the systematic literature review and the overview of the different prominent evaluation frameworks that resulted from this search process. In section 7.3, we present the methodology used to construct the (meta-)taxonomy and classify the criteria. In section 7.4, we present the resulting (meta-)taxonomy TEC-MAP that can be used to categorize all criteria from the frameworks discussed in section 7.2 and the criteria are classified in TEC-MAP. Section 7.5 presents possible uses of the framework and related guidelines, and demonstrates the use through a practical application for the evaluation of the Merode modelling method, as well as a comparison between Merode, BAUML and 4EM based on the TEC-MAP framework. Finally, section 7.6 discusses the populated TEC-MAP and relates the summarized evaluation criteria to challenges and concerns identified by practitioners.

7.2 Inventory of Evaluation Frameworks

To address RQ1, we compiled an inventory of evaluation frameworks in two cycles. The first cycle was published in [160]. The second cycle was added for this paper.

7.2.1 Systematic Literature Review

The compilation of a set of frameworks was conducted in two cycles [8]. In the first cycle, we selected eight evaluation frameworks that are considered either seminal frameworks from the domain of conceptual modelling and information systems engineering (TAM [167], MEM [92], SEQUAL [166] and CMQF [168]), or prominent frameworks that are well-known in the data-aware process modelling community (BALSA [135], PHILharmonicFlows [133], MMQEF [169] and DALEC [93]).

For the second cycle we performed a systematic literature review according to Kitchenham's guidelines [32] aiming to find the most important and relevant evaluations frameworks for multi-modelling approaches, using two queries in Scopus and Web of Science. The first query is intended to find papers on evaluation frameworks for (conceptual) modelling approaches in general. This results in a set of papers from a wide variety of source publications, including conferences and journals from other, less relevant domains. After reviewing the titles of the source publications, the query is refined to sources that have the words 'system' or 'software' in their title. Both Scopus and Web of Science automatically perform lemmatization and search for spelling variations. This query still results in over 6000 publications, many of which focus on the evaluation of models, and not of the modelling language. Therefore, we added the term "framework" to the query. While the meaning of this term is slightly ambiguous, it is frequently used in literature on method evaluation and filters out many of the papers that focus on evaluating models instead of modelling languages. The full query used on Scopus is shown below (the same query is adapted for Web of Science).

QUERY 1

(TITLE-ABS-KEY("modeling language") OR TITLE-ABS-KEY("modeling method") OR TITLE-ABS-KEY("modeling approach") OR TITLE-ABS-KEY("conceptual modeling"))

AND (TITLE-ABS-KEY(evaluat*) OR TITLE-ABS-KEY(quality) OR TITLE-ABS-KEY(comparison))

AND TITLE-ABS-KEY(framework)

AND (SRCTITLE(system) OR SRCTITLE(software))

The second query is intended to find papers on frameworks for data-aware process modelling approaches, specifically. Again, the query is run both in Scopus and on Web of Science. We used the main four evaluation frameworks for data-aware process modelling (BALSA [135], PHILharmonicFlows [133], MMQEF [169] and DALEC [93]) as a golden standard for query 2, meaning that the results of the queries should include these publications to be considered a good selection. In this query, the term ("evaluat*", "quality" or "comparison") was dropped because it resulted in the exclusion of the BALSA framework. Again, we added the term "framework" to the query to filter out many of the papers that focus on evaluating models instead of modelling languages. The query as used in Scopus is shown below.

QUERY 2

(TITLE-ABS-KEY("data-aware process") OR TITLE-ABS-KEY("data-aware business process") OR TITLE-ABS-KEY("data-centric process") OR TITLE-ABS-KEY("data-centric business process") OR TITLE-ABS-KEY("art?fact-centric process") OR TITLE-ABS-KEY("art?fact-centric business process") OR TITLE-ABS-KEY("object-centric process") OR TITLE-ABS-KEY("object-centric business process") OR TITLE-ABS-KEY("object-aware process") OR TITLE-ABS-KEY("object-aware business process"))

AND TITLE-ABS-KEY(framework)

The first query results in 976 papers from Scopus and 303 papers from Web of Science. Since this query is used to find frameworks of a more general nature, the results are further refined by only selecting papers with more than 50 citations in order to focus on the most important frameworks. After removing duplicates, this results in 98 papers (84 papers on Scopus and 37 papers on Web of Science, with 23 duplicates). In order to be included in our selection of frameworks, the papers should either provide a concrete set of criteria, or they should present a framework structure that can be used to categorize criteria. Based on these inclusion criteria, a first screening on the title and abstract of the papers reduces the set to a total of 26 papers. If there is doubt about whether a paper complies with the inclusion criteria, the paper is also included. Finally, the content of the 26 remaining papers is screened on the same inclusion criteria, resulting in a final set of 9 papers.

The second query results in a set of 120 unique papers (114 papers in Scopus and 48 papers in Web of Science, with 42 duplicates). The same inclusion criteria are applied. The first screening on title and abstract reduces the set to a total of 68 papers. The second screening on the content of the papers further reduces the set to a total of 13 papers.

The final set that results from combining both queries thus counts 22 papers ([6], [91], [93], [133], [135], [137], [166], [168], [170], [171], [172], [173], [174], [175], [176], [177], [178], [179], [180], [181], [182], [183]). This set includes five of the eight papers selected in the first cycle ([93], [133], [135], [166], [168]), and many of the remaining 18 papers apply or are based on the eight frameworks from the first cycle. The next sections provide short descriptions of the final set of evaluation frameworks. The set of general evaluation frameworks was expanded with the one of Bork and Fill [6]. The literature review on data-aware process modelling yielded additional papers for the known frameworks that either illustrate (BALSA) or expand (PHILharmonicFlows) these frameworks, and a set of papers proposing own set of criteria to evaluate approaches (section 7.2.4). The evaluation frameworks differ in their scope, the level of detail they provide and their grouping of criteria. Some frameworks focus on user experience, while others focus on theoretical aspects. The frameworks with a more narrow scope also provide more detailed descriptions of their criteria and guidelines on how to measure the quality of an approach. Finally, each framework provides a different structure for grouping the criteria. All 9 frameworks were included in the creation of TEC-MAP in some capacity: DALEC [93], PHILharmonicFlows [133], BALSA [135], MMQEF [169], CMQF [168] and the Comparison Framework for Formal Aspects of Enterprise

Modelling Methods [6] were considered as input for the definition of dimensions and their characteristics, the MEM [92], CMQF [168], PHILharmonicFlows [133], [172], [173], [174], [175], [180] and Dalec [93] frameworks were used as sources for evaluation criteria to classify in the taxonomy. Indirectly, also the criteria from TAM [167], [184] and SEQUAL [166] were included, as their criteria are included in MEM and CMQF respectively. Below we briefly describe main characteristics of these frameworks: the origin, their popularity, their main focus, whether or not the framework provides measurements or specific quality criteria for the quality dimensions they address, and related papers (if any). We group the frameworks according to their being general frameworks for modelling in general, frameworks that are specific for data-aware process modelling and other related frameworks.

7.2.2 General Evaluation Frameworks

The Technology Acceptance Model (TAM). In 1985, Davis developed the Technology Acceptance Framework to evaluate the adoption of new technologies in the field of computer science [167]. This framework is very well adopted by the academic community, as the dissertation has over 10.000 Google Scholar citations. Davis developed two scales (each consisting of six Likert-scale questions) to measure the perceived usefulness and perceived ease of use [184]. This paper has received over 70.000 Google Scholar citations. For both papers, the number of citations still increases every year, proving that the computer science community considers this to be an important evaluation framework. A major benefit of the model is that it can be applied to a wide variety of new technologies.

The Method Evaluation Model (MEM). As TAM can be applied to a wide variety of technologies, many derivatives have been developed [185]. In 2003, Moody developed the Method Evaluation Model specifically for the evaluation of IS design methods [92]. This publication has over 300 Google Scholar citations. Moody states that the success of a method consists of two dimensions: actual efficacy and adoption in practice. In order to measure both dimensions, Moody combined the TAM with Methodological Pragmatism. According to Methodological Pragmatism, the validity of a method is not based on its correctness, but on its pragmatic success. Moody defines pragmatic success as "the efficiency and effectiveness with which a method achieves its objectives". An efficiency improvement is defined as "reducing effort required to complete the task" and an effectiveness improvement is defined as "improving the quality of the result". Moody does not provide measures for actual efficiency and actual effectiveness, stating that these measures depend on the (class of) method(s) that is (are) being evaluated. As a general guideline, he suggests that efficiency should be measured in time, cost and cognitive effort and that effectiveness should be measured in the quantity and quality of the results of the methods. The other two factors (perceived ease of use and perceived usefulness) should be measured as described by Davis in [184].

SEQUAL. The SEQUAL framework is an extension of on the work of Lindland et al. (the LSS framework) [91], which was published in 1994. The LSS framework focusses on the assessment of the semiotic quality of models. The SEQUAL framework was then further developed in several different publications from 1996 until 2006 [166], [186], [187]. The last iteration ([166]) has over 400 citations. The SEQUAL framework considers a conceptual model as statements, and groups these statements into sets related to the modelling domain, the modeler's knowledge, the external model, etc. [166]. The quality levels describe the coordination between sets [166]. Apart from suggesting set algebra definitions for the quality levels related to syntactic quality, the framework does not provide any metrics to measure the quality levels, as "the problem domain and the minds of the stakeholders are unavailable for formal inspection" [166]. One of the publications found in the expanded literature review is a book chapter on the SEQUAL framework [177].

The Conceptual Modelling Quality Framework (CMQF). The CMQF (2012) was developed based on the SEQUAL framework and the Bunge-Wand-Weber representation model (BWW) [168] which is an ontological theory published in 1990 that focusses on the modelling process [188]. CMQF has over 180 citations. It is a two-dimensional framework that integrates the SEQUAL framework and the BWW model into eight cornerstones. These cornerstones are divided vertically over the physical reality and the social reality and horizontally over the domain, the reference framework, the modelling language and the conceptual representation [168]. The framework then defines four layers of quality – the physical layer, the knowledge layer, the learning layer and the development layer – each with a number of quality types. The framework does not provide a way to objectively measure the quality types.

A Comparison Framework for Formal Aspects of Enterprise Modelling Methods. In 2014, Bork and Fill [6] developed a comparison framework for formal aspects of enterprise modelling methods. This framework has over 110 citations. The framework is based on the components of modelling methods as described by Karagiannis and Kühn [189]. According to the comparison framework of Bork and Fill [6], a modelling method consists of three main components: a modelling language, a modelling procedure and mechanisms and algorithms. The modelling language component in turn consists of syntax, semantics and notation. Finally, the semantics component consists of structural semantics (further split into type semantics and inherent semantics) and behavioural semantics, while the notation component consists of static notation and dynamic notation. The framework also describes when the specification of a component as a whole in a given modelling language can be considered formal, semi-formal or informal, however, it does not include any quality criteria.

7.2.3 Frameworks for data-aware process modelling approaches

Over the past fifteen years, several prominent frameworks have been developed specifically for integrating data and process modelling, including the BALSA framework [135], the PHILharmonicFlows framework [133], and the DALEC framework [93]. All these frameworks focus on combining the data and process perspective, and some also consider additional process-related perspectives such as users and authorisations. However, all approaches include at least the data perspective and the process perspective. While these frameworks address the same perspectives of an enterprise information system (data and processes), each uses slightly different terminology and definitions. The DALEC framework is based on a systematic literature review, comparing several approaches, including BALSA and PHILharmonicFlows. DALEC uses the overarching term "*data*-centric" process modelling, while BALSA is a framework for *artefact*-centric business processes, and defines a business artefact as corresponding to "key business-relevant objects, their lifecycles, and how/when services (a.k.a. tasks) are invoked on them" [135]. PHILharmonicFlows is a framework for *object-aware* process management. According to the authors of the framework, process support must consider "object behaviour as well as object interactions" [133], and provide "data-driven process execution and integrated access to processes and data" [133], in order to be object-aware. While one might be tempted to consider the terms "data", "artefact" and "object" as synonyms, the definitions given by the authors make clear that each framework has its own particular perspective on data. A similar analysis can be made for the behavioural aspects: each framework has its own perspective on how behaviour is addressed.

BALSA. The BALSA framework (2008) specifies four dimensions of artefact-centric business process modelling – Business Artefacts, Macro Lifecycles, Services and Associations [135]. The authors describe Business Artefacts as business object, their data and their relationships to other artefacts. Macro Lifecycles are described as the lifecycle of a Business Artefact, and can be represented as a finite state machine. A Service is described as "a unit of work meaningful to the whole business process" [135]. Associations are defined as a family of constraints on the changes that services make to artefacts. The BALSA framework can be used to construct an artefact-centric approach by selecting a set of model types that fit the four dimensions. However, the framework does not provide a set of criteria to evaluate the resulting approach.

Three other papers found in the second phase of the literature review use the BALSA framework: [179], [181], [183]. These three papers were written by the same team of researchers and build on each other. The papers demonstrate how different diagram types of UML can be used to cover the four dimensions of the BALSA framework.

PHILharmonicFlows. PHILharmonicFlows (2011) is a framework that specifies a set of requirements for the modelling and execution of object-aware process management systems [133]. It has over 290 citations. The authors state that support for object-aware processes requires considering the integration of the different building blocks of such a process (Data, Processes, Functions and Users). The list of requirements in the PHILharmonicFlows framework was composed based on a set of case studies [190]. The requirements are grouped by the building block they correspond to, and can be fully supported, partially supported or not supported.

Five other papers found in the second phase of the literature review use the PHILharmonicFlows framework and specify additional criteria: [172], [173], [174], [175], [180]. In [172], Chiao et al. demonstrate the development of a tool supporting the PHILharmonicFlows framework. On top of the criteria from the PHILharmonicFlows framework, they specify five additional requirements for this tool: use of visual models, enabling correctness-by-construction, persistent model storage, automated generation of user interface components and correct process enactment. Andrews et al. [174] leverage the PHILharmonicFlows framework to specify six requirements for fine-grained access control in object-aware process management systems: dynamic authorization of permissions and roles, role authorization depending on data, role authorization depending on relations, permission authorization depending on object state, permission authorization depending on data and scalable real-time permission and role authorization. In [173], Andrews et al. extend the PHILharmonicFlows framework to support process variants and versions with 5 requirements. Ciao et al. [175] propose a set of nine requirements for the Case Handling Paradigm to support object-aware processes. They demonstrate that the PHILharmonicFlows framework covers the requirements that are not yet covered by the Case Handling Paradigm. Finally, Chiao et al. [180] present an extension of the PHILharmonicFlows framework to support schema evolution. They add eleven requirements in total for structural changes at the static level, for changing active instances at the dynamic level and for the user.

MMQEF. The Multiple Modelling language Quality Evaluation Framework (2018) provides a reference taxonomy of IS concepts, and a methodology to "evaluate the quality of a set of modelling languages used in combination within an MDE context" [169], The method does however not include a set of explicit evaluation criteria. The reference taxonomy is based on the Zachman framework and consist of a Viewpoint dimension (Data, Function, Network, People, Time and Motivation) and an Abstractions dimension based on the Model-Driven Architecture (Computation-Independent Model, Platform-Independent Model, Platform-Specific Model, Physical Implementations)

DALEC. In 2019, Steinau et al. published a framework for the evaluation and comparison of data-centric process management approaches [93]. It has over 50 citations. First, they conducted a systematic literature review resulting in an in-dept comparison of 17 process modelling approaches described in 38 publications, including the PHILharmonicFlows framework. Based on this SLR, they defined a set of 24 criteria grouped along the phases of the business process lifecycle. Similar to the PHILharmonicFlows framework, the criteria can be fully supported, partially supported or not supported, however, the DALEC framework also defines for each criterion the required conditions for the criterion to be considered partially or fully supported.

7.2.4 Other related work

Besides the papers that explicitly refer to one of the afore-mentioned frameworks, several authors investigated some aspects of data-aware process modelling and develop their own set of criteria to evaluate approaches. Reijers et al. [137] argue that modelling method developers need to focus more on the human modeler when designing their methods. Therefore, they evaluate a set of data-centric process modelling approaches from the perspective of the user. They organized workshops with 29 practitioners to evaluate the quality statements made by the approaches regarding functionality, usability, efficiency, maintainability and portability. Among other techniques, they used the questionnaire developed by Moody for the Method Evaluation Model [92]. Fettke and Loos [178] proposed a procedure for the ontological evaluation of models that is based on the BWW model. Bendraou et al. [170] compared six UML-based languages on criteria developed for process modelling approaches. Luo and Tung [171] present a process modelling method as a set of perspectives (object, activity and role) and characteristics (formality, scalability, enactability, ease of use). The user should identify their modelling objectives and which perspectives and characteristics are required to select a business process modelling method. The authors provide an example comparison for two methods (data flow diagrams and role activity diagrams). Bernus et al. [182] present a framework for a "generic enterprise reference architecture and methodology" (GERAM) that covers the entire enterprise, including for example enterprise integration and products. Soffer et al.

[176] present a generic ERP modelling process, and criteria for modelling languages that should be satisfied specifically for ERP development.

7.3   Methodology

In order to summarize the criteria from all the evaluation frameworks, we need to create a taxonomy. We follow the iterative method for taxonomy development (see Figure 7.1) that was proposed by Nickerson et al. [191]. Section 7.3 describes the methodology for the construction of the taxonomy and the classification of the criteria, while the resulting dimensions, characteristics and argumentation for their design are detailed in Section 7.4.

7.3.1   Construction of the taxonomy

Nickerson et al. [191] define a taxonomy as *"a set of dimensions each consisting of a set of characteristics that sufficiently describes the objects in a specific domain of interest"* [191]. Below, we describe each step and Table 7.1 presents a summary of the process and the results. Detailed arguments and results are presented in section 7.4.

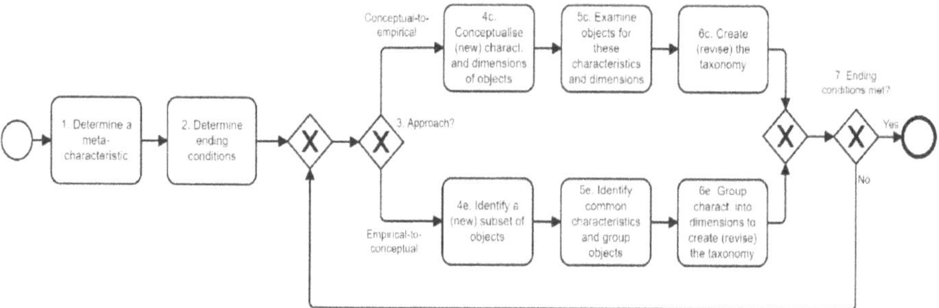

Figure 7.1 The method for taxonomy development, adapted from Nickerson et al. [191]

Preliminary steps. The **first step** of the method is to determine the meta-characteristic. Nickerson et al. describe the meta-characteristic as "the most comprehensive characteristic that will serve as the basis for the choice of characteristics in the taxonomy. Each characteristic should be a logical consequence of the meta-characteristic" [191]. Given that the purpose of our taxonomy is to provide an overview of evaluation criteria for data-aware process modelling approaches, we define the meta-characteristic as the characterization of evaluation criteria in the domain of multi-modelling.

The **second step** is to determine the ending conditions. Nickerson et al. define a minimal set of one objective and five subjective ending conditions: the taxonomy satisfies the definition of a taxonomy (objective), and the taxonomy is concise, robust, comprehensive, extendible and explanatory (subjective). We do not add any ending conditions to this set.

First iteration. The **third step** is to decide whether we follow the empirical-to-conceptual approach or the conceptual-to-empirical approach for the first iteration. The

Table 7.1 A Summary of the First Cycle of the Taxonomy Development (it. 1 and 2)

Step 1	Meta-characteristic	the positioning of evaluation criteria in the domain of data-aware process modelling			
Step 2	Ending conditions	the taxonomy satisfies the definition of a taxonomy the taxonomy is concise the taxonomy is robust the taxonomy is comprehensive the taxonomy is extendible the taxonomy is explanatory			
	Iteration 1		**Iteration 2**		
Step 3	Chosen approach	Empirical-to-conceptual	Step 3	Chosen approach	Conceptual-to-empirical
Step 4e	Objects	All 72 criteria of MEM, CMQF, PHILharmonic-Flows and Dalec	Step 4c	Char. Added	Abstract syntax, Concrete syntax, Modelling guidelines, Tool support
				Dim.	Pillar dimension
Step 5e	Char.	Design phase Implementation phase Model Evolution phase Data Objects viewpoint Lifecycles viewpoint Microservices viewpoint Process viewpoint Users viewpoint 8 coord. viewpoints	Step 5c	Classification	
Step 6e	Dim.	Viewpoint dimension, Phase dimension	Step 6c	Full taxonomy	See Figure 7-5
Step 7	Cond. met?	definition ✓ concise ✓ robust ✗ comprehensive ✓ extendible ✓ explanatory ✓	Step 7	Cond. met?	definition ✓ concise ✓ robust ✓ comprehensive ✓ extendible ✓ explanatory ✓

empirical-to-conceptual approach starts from available objects that need to be classified in the taxonomy, whereas the conceptual-to-empirical approach starts from the researcher's knowledge and understanding of the domain. In the first iteration, we use the empirical-to-conceptual approach based on the evaluation frameworks discussed in section 7.2.

In the empirical-to-conceptual approach, the **fourth step** is to identify a subset of objects. In this case, the subset of objects are the 72 evaluation criteria defined by the MEM, CMQF, PHILharmonicFlows and DALEC frameworks. Given that the criteria of TAM and the quality levels of SEQUAL are completely encompassed by the criteria of MEM and CMQF respectively, they were not included separately. When needed, criteria are split into sub-criteria so as to achieve similar granularity levels across the frameworks.

The **fifth step** is to identify the common characteristics and group the objects according to these characteristics and **the sixth step** is to group the characteristics into dimensions. In these steps, we add the Phase dimension and the Viewpoint dimension, as shown in Table 7.1. The dimensions, their characteristics and justification are described in Section 7.4.

At the end of each iteration, the **seventh step** is to evaluate the ending conditions. Given that the initial taxonomy satisfies the definition of a taxonomy by Nickerson et al., the objective ending condition is met. To evaluate the subjective ending conditions, Nickerson et al. [191] propose a guiding question for each condition, which we list in Table 7.2, however, the interpretation of these questions is still very open. Following these guiding questions, we consider the initial taxonomy to be concise as the number of dimensions (2) allows the taxonomy to be meaningful, without being unwieldy or overwhelming. We consider it comprehensive given that all objects from the sample can be classified. We consider it extendible given that more dimensions and characteristics can be added (see also the following iterations of the methodology), resulting in dynamic taxonomy that remains useful when new types of objects appear. For example, if we were to include evaluation frameworks for strategic modelling languages, the Viewpoint dimension could simply be extended with the required viewpoint(s). We consider the taxonomy explanatory given that the current dimensions clearly explain the nature of the objects without describing every single detail of a criteria. However, the initial taxonomy is not yet robust since there are some groups of criteria (where criteria share the same characteristics for each dimension) that need further differentiation. Since not all ending conditions are met, a second iteration is required.

Table 7.2 Guiding questions for the evaluation of subjective ending conditions, adapted from [191].

Subjective ending conditions	Guiding questions
Concise	Does the number of dimensions allow the taxonomy to be meaningful without being unwieldy or overwhelming?
Robust	Do the dimensions and characteristics provide for differentiation among objects (here: evaluation criteria) sufficient to be of interest?
Comprehensive	Can all objects or a (random) sample of objects within the domain of interest be classified? Are all dimensions of the objects of interest identified?
Extendible	Can a new dimension or a new characteristic of an existing dimension be easily added?
Explanatory	What do the dimensions and characteristics explain about an object?

Second iteration. In the second iteration, step 3 – 7 are repeated. In **step three**, we now decide to follow the conceptual-to-empirical approach so as to complement the insights obtained from studying the existing frameworks with insights from domain knowledge.

In the conceptual-to-empirical approach, **step four** is to develop characteristics and dimensions without considering actual objects, but by relying on the researcher's own knowledge and understanding of the domain. We decided to add the Pillar dimension as shown in Table 7.1.

In the conceptual-to-empirical approach, **step five** is to classify the existing objects according to the new dimensions and characteristics and **step six** is to add the new dimensions to the taxonomy. For example, we classify criterion D02 of the Dalec framework (specification of data representation constructs) under the Design phase characteristic in the Phase dimension, the Data Objects viewpoint characteristic in the Viewpoint dimension and the Abstract Syntax characteristic in the Pillar dimension. See section 7.4.4 for the complete results.

In **step seven** the ending conditions are re-evaluated. Given that the taxonomy satisfies the definition of a taxonomy by Nickerson et al., the objective ending condition is met. The taxonomy is still concise as the number of dimensions (3) are limited. Similar to step seven in the first iteration, it is comprehensive given that all objects from the sample can be classified. It is extendible and explanatory, given that more dimensions can be added and that the current dimensions explain the nature of the objects. Finally, the taxonomy is now also robust since all criteria are well-grouped and do not require further differentiation. Since all ending conditions are met, the taxonomy is finished.

Third iteration. The first and second iterations are performed as part of the first cycle of the framework. We perform a second cycle involving a third iteration to check whether the taxonomy resulting from the first two iterations reaches saturation, and to validate the Pillar dimension developed in the second iteration. By saturation, we mean that no new dimensions are added to the taxonomy. Therefore, we add 2 ending conditions (saturation of dimensions, and validation of the Pillar dimension). In **step 3** of this iteration, we follow the empirical-to-conceptual cycle with the aim to discover new frameworks and criteria in the second iteration of the literature review (see Section 7.2). In **step 4** of this iteration, we identify a new set of criteria extending the PHILharmonicFlows framework through the second iteration of the systematic literature review. In **step 5 and 6**, we review the dimensions and characteristics of the taxonomy based on the second iteration of the systematic literature review and re-classify the criteria where needed. This ultimately leads to the decision to include one more characteristic in the Pillar dimension, but saturation is reached. Thus, in **step 7**, we determine that the two new ending conditions are met.

7.3.2 Analysis of the criteria

Once the taxonomy has been constructed, we consider each group of criteria, meaning each set of criteria that falls under the same characteristics of each dimension. For each group, we determine which criteria are identical, subsuming or complementing each other. These criteria are accordingly adapted, resulting in the final populated taxonomy. It is important to note that criteria with sub-criteria should still be evaluated as well. There is no guarantee the evaluation of the sub-criteria alone is sufficient for a complete evaluation of the super-criterion.

7.4 Results

This section presents the final taxonomy: we first present the main reasoning behind each of the dimensions, and then proceed to the overall presentation of TEC-MAP.

7.4.1 The Phase Dimension

DALEC [93] uses the phases of the process management lifecycle to group their criteria. We adopted and slightly modified the phases as defined in [93] to accommodate for different views. The resulting lifecycle consists of the Design phase, the Implementation & Execution phase and the Diagnosis & Optimization phase [93]. MMQEF uses the MDA abstraction levels [169] where the Computation-Independent Model and the Platform-Independent Model cover the Design phase, and the Platform-Specific Model and the Physical Implementation cover the Implementation & Execution phase. Given that the criteria for different models in the design phase are the same, we align the taxonomy to the phases of DALEC.

7.4.2 The Viewpoint Dimension

PHILharmonicFlows categorizes their requirements according to the building blocks of an object-aware process (Data, Processes, Functions, Users) [133]. Similarly, BALSA defines 4 dimensions (Business Artefacts, Macro lifecycles, Services and Associations) [135]. Within the design phase, DALEC addresses data representation constructs (DRCs), object behaviour and object interaction [93]. Inspired by the ISO Architecture Description Standard [192], where each viewpoint is addressed by a different model kind, we define a set of 'viewpoints' based on these three frameworks – the Users viewpoint, the Data Objects viewpoint and three Behaviour viewpoints: the Lifecycles, Microservices and Process viewpoints. These dimensions also appear in MMQEF [169], albeit that MMQEF has just one behavioural viewpoint where all behavioural aspects are lumped together. Given that the Time and Network viewpoints of MMQEF are much less used in practice [193], and that Motivation is rather related to strategy, and that MMQEF does not provide any evaluation criteria, we leave these out.

The User Viewpoint covers the criteria related to information about the users of the to-be-developed system. The Data Object viewpoint deals with criteria related to the data objects, their attributes and associations. Steinau et al. [93] provide an overview of different data-aware process modelling approaches and how they define their "Data Representation Constructs" (DRCs). While many approaches define lifecycles as part of their DRCs, we define lifecycles as defining the states an object can be in and that constrain the operations that can be performed on an object. Therefore, we consider this as a separate viewpoint related to behaviour. The Process Viewpoint covers criteria related to overall processes (either declarative or procedural processes) and the Microservices Viewpoint deals with criteria related to 'tasks' in the processes.

Given that the authors of both the PHILharmonicFlows framework and the BALSA framework emphasize the importance of considering the coordination between the building blocks and dimensions respectively [133], [135], we will add 'coordination viewpoints' to categorize requirements that deal with this coordination. In what follows, each of the coordination viewpoints will be defined, whereby a coordination viewpoint takes care of defining correspondences between two viewpoints [192]. Figure 7.2 presents the viewpoints and the coordination viewpoints. In some cases, the coordination between viewpoints is trivial and does not require an explicit evaluation (cfr. Green dashed arrows). For these coordination viewpoints, we do not expect to find many evaluation criteria.

- **Lifecycles – Microservices (1).** Coordination between the lifecycles and the Microservices is not trivial: the data-aware process modelling approach needs to define how lifecycles and microservices are related. For instance, if an exam is in the state *running*, the professor should not be able to grade the exam. Once the exam is *submitted*, the professor can execute the microservice *grade the exam*. This will trigger the transition from *submitted* to *graded* for the exam.
- **Microservices – Process (2).** Processes enforce sequence constraints on Microservices. The coordination is an inherent part of the definitions of the processes and is therefore trivial.
- **Lifecycles – Process (3).** The sequence constraints imposed by the lifecycles should be compatible with those imposed by the processes. For example, if a process requires *shipping* before *invoicing an order*, the lifecycle of the order object should allow shipping in the *unpaid* state.
- **Data objects – Lifecycles (4).** Each data object has at least a default lifecycle. Given that a lifecycle always belongs to one data object, coordination (i.e. correspondence between data and lifecycles) follows from the definitions of the lifecycles. Nevertheless, consistency checking is needed at the semantic level to ensure consistency with the implicit default lifecycles and the behaviour implicitly defined through association and cardinalities in the data model. For example, if a customer can be associated to many invoices, the lifecycle of the customer should allow for the creation of many invoices.
- **Data objects – Microservices (5).** This viewpoint deals with the direct coordination between Microservices and data objects. Microservices should be able to create, modify and/or end data objects.
- **Data objects – Process (6).** Data object instances can be created, modified or ended during a process through the invocation of microservices. This viewpoint is therefore trivial as it results from the combination of (2) and (5).
- **Data objects – Users (7).** This viewpoint considers how Read and/or Write permissions for (attributes of) instances of data objects are granted to users. For example, professors can only view and manipulate the grades for the courses they teach.
- **Microservices – Users (8).** This viewpoint considers how permissions for the execution of microservices are granted to users. For example, students can view but not update their grades.
- **Lifecycle – Users.** Coordination between Lifecycles and Users is not required, given that users don't interact directly with lifecycles but only via Microservices. This coordination thus results from combining (8) and (1).
- **Process – Users.** Coordination between Process and Users results from combining (8) and (2). Users don't interact directly with the process as a whole: they interact with the individual microservices and their work is coordinated by means of control sequences, messages and data exchange. A user interacts with the entire process if they interact with all microservices of the process.

Figure 7.3 details how the TEC-MAP viewpoints cover the BALSA dimensions. For three of the four BALSA dimensions, the mapping to the TEC-MAP viewpoints is straightforward: the mapping of the BALSA Business Artefacts to the TEC-MAP Data Objects viewpoint, the mapping of the BALSA Macro Lifecycles to the TEC-MAP Lifecycles viewpoint, and the mapping of the BALSA Services to the TEC-MAP

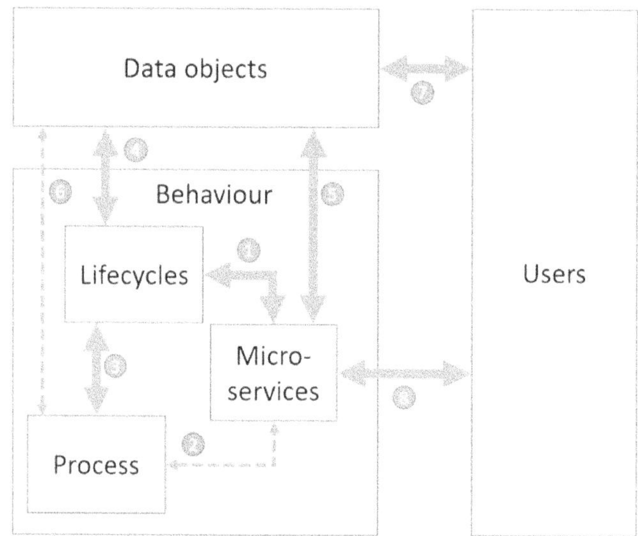

Figure 7.2 The Viewpoints and Coordination Viewpoints (arrows). The trivial coordination viewpoints are depicted as green dashed arrows

Microservices viewpoint. As stated in Section 7.2.2, the BALSA Associations can represent both associations between BALSA Services, and association between a BALSA Service and a transition in a BALSA Lifecycle. Therefore, the BALSA Associations dimension is mapped to the two corresponding coordination viewpoints in TEC-MAP: the Lifecycles – Microservices coordination viewpoint and the Microservices – Process coordination viewpoint.

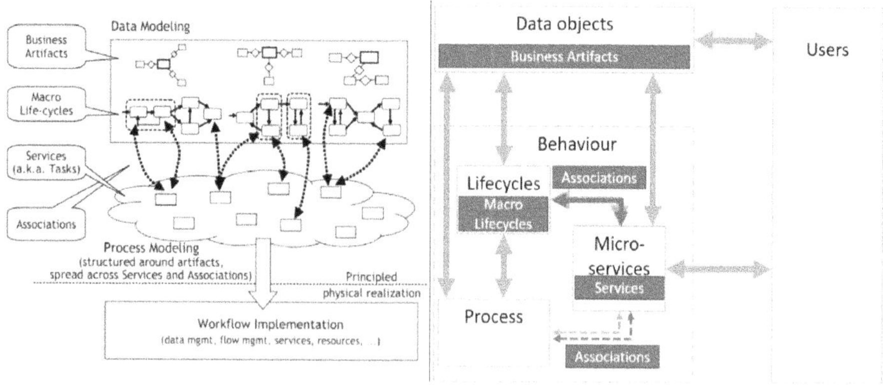

Figure 7.3 The BALSA framework [135] (left) and the BALSA framework mapped onto the viewpoints of TEC-MAP (right)

Figure 7.4 details how the TEC-MAP viewpoints cover the PHILharmonicFlows building blocks. For three of the four PHILharmonicFlows Data building blocks, the mapping to the TEC-MAP viewpoints is straightforward: the mapping of the PHILhar-monicFlows Data building block to the TEC-MAP Data Objects viewpoint, the mapping of the PHILharmonicFlows Users building block to the TEC-MAP Users viewpoint and the mapping of the PHILharmonicFlows Processes building block to the TEC-MAP Process viewpoint. As Künzle et al. state that the purpose of the PHILharmonicFlows Functions is separating the data logic and the process logic from the function logic by providing "for automatically creating end-user components, such as worklists, form-based activities, and overview tables containing relevant object instances" [133]. Therefore, the PHILharmonicFlows Functions building block cannot be mapped on a TEC-MAP viewpoint. Mapping it on the TEC-MAP Implementation phase is a better fit.

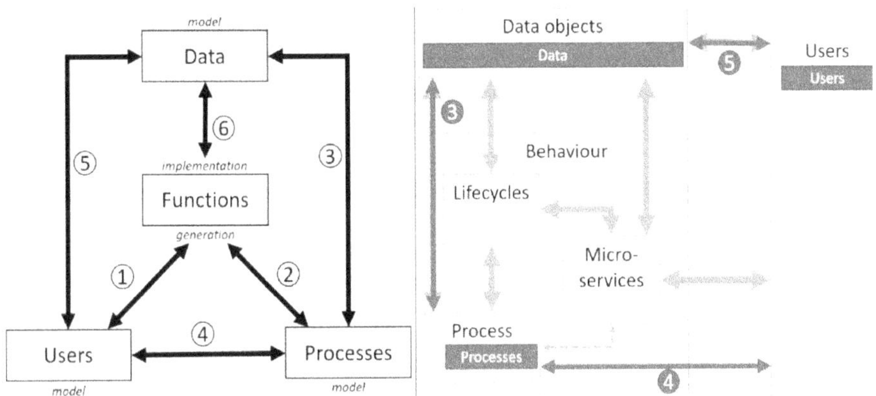

Figure 7.4. PHILharmonicFlows building blocks, adapted from [133] (left) and the PHILhar-monicFlows building blocks mapped onto the viewpoints of TEC-MAP (right)

Mapping DALEC onto the TEC-MAP viewpoints is straightforward – the DRCs are mapped onto the Data Objects viewpoint, object behaviour is mapped onto the three behaviour viewpoints and object interaction is mapped onto the coordination viewpoints related to the Data Objects viewpoint.

7.4.3 The Pillar Dimension

Criteria within the same criteria groups can still vary in what aspect they address. Some criteria deal with formal quality, others with tool support, etc. Therefore, we define the third dimension as the pillar dimension. The five pillars of a modelling approach are the abstract syntax, the concrete syntax and the semantics that make up the modelling language, the modelling guidelines that contain modelling rules and best practices, and tool support for all phases and viewpoints.

These pillars are supported by the literature [194], [195]. When considering modelling languages, the physical layer of CMQF distinguishes between the ontological constructs of a modelling language and its vocabulary and grammar [168]. This corresponds to Kleppe's advice of complementing the abstract syntax of a modelling language (or its meta-model) with a concrete syntax and semantics [196]. Additionally, the comparison framework by Bork and Fill describes five main components of a modelling method as syntax, semantics, notation, modelling procedure and mechanisms and algorithms [6]. The syntax, semantics and notation make up the modelling language.

The definitions of each pillar used in this taxonomy are based on [4], [5], [6], [196], [197]. Abstract syntax expresses the model elements and their relationships via a meta-model. Concrete syntax specifies the representation of the abstract syntax, meaning the notation. This distinction between abstract and concrete syntax is supported by the work of Erwig [4]. He also provides an alternative to the use of meta-models for the visual representation of the abstract syntax that is founded in mathematics. An abstract syntax often has multiple concrete syntaxes, for example a visual notation and an XML notation. The work of Fondement and Baar [5] supports the definitions used by TEC-MAP, and presents a procedure for the specification of a concrete syntax. Semantics express the meaning of model elements and their relationships. Bork and Fill [6] and Höfferer [197] make a distinction between type semantics and inherent semantics. In the context of TEC-MAP, the focus lies on the evaluation of modelling languages and not the evaluation of models. Therefore, the pillar Semantics refers to the type semantics. The Modelling Procedure in the comparison framework by Bork and Fill [6] corresponds to the Modelling Guidelines pillar in TEC-MAP. Finally, the Mechanisms and Algorithms in Bork and Fill's framework [6] (e.g. verification, simulation or model transformation algorithms that can be executed on models) combine aspects of the syntax (e.g. intermediate states need both incoming and outgoing arrows), semantics (e.g. the firing rule of a Petri Net), procedures to support modelling guidelines (an algorithm to verify a model for dangling states and deadlocks), and tool support. In this sense, the Mechanisms and Algorithms is addressed by a combination of pillars.

7.4.4   Final taxonomy

Figure 7.5 provides a summary of the criteria grouped by characteristic within the populated taxonomy. The final populated taxonomy can be found online[1] as interactive map of all criteria, including different visualisation and filtering options. Clicking on a criterion displays some informative attributes: the origin framework, the original description and the proposed method of evaluation.

It immediately stands out that the design phase contains many more criteria than the two other phases, in particular for the Data Objects, Lifecycles, Microservices and Process viewpoints; There's a lack of criteria for the User viewpoint. The coordination viewpoints have very few criteria. This is to be expected for the trivial coordination viewpoints. However, the other coordination viewpoints would benefit from more detailed criteria.

In a meta-review of surveys on MDE practitioners [12], some of the main challenges that practitioners face are the following: visual notations at odds with the principles of Physics of Notation [31], the organization's culture as an inhibitor of the adoption of modelling practices, missing tool functionalities and tools being difficult to use. TEC-MAP provides the required criteria for evaluating tool functionalities. To fill the gap in the User viewpoint, the field of User Interface design could be investigated,

---

[1] https://charlotteverbruggen.notion.site/TEC-MAP-654d70294dd44d54bcc490b2025e733a

which has a tradition of user modelling [198]. However, for the other challenges, the criteria listed in TEC-MAP need further improvement. The Physics of Notation could be added as instrument to evaluate the Concrete Syntax. Complementing TEC-MAP with UTAUT2's "social norm" variable [185] could be used to analyse the cultural factors that might inhibit adoption, while also its "habit" variable could be relevant. Börstler et al. conducted a systematic literature review analysing thirty acceptance models and theories, and how they are applied in software development [199]. They discuss how each of these models and theories is evaluated within the individual context of a practitioner. One of the models that has been used more often and that is evaluated rationally instead of intuitively, is the Task-Technology Fit (TTF) model [199]. Complementing TEC-MAP with TTF would allow evaluating the tool usability and acceptance in more detail. Another interesting theory that they discuss is the Innovation Diffusion Theory which discusses the individual, organizational and external factors that impact the adoption of new technologies [199].

As stated in section 7.3.2, we conducted a qualitative analysis to identify which criteria from different origin frameworks are identical, or which criteria subsume criteria from other frameworks. We find mostly relations between the PHILharmonicFlows framework and its extensions, and between the PHILharmonicFlows framework and the Dalec framework. This is not surprising, given that all these frameworks share authors. Many of these criteria fall in the Design and implementation phases, and could account for the high number of criteria in these criteria groups.

| | PHASE DIMENSION | | | | | | | | |
	Design			Implementation & Execution			Diagnosis and Optimisation		
Users	AS: 1	CS: 1		AS: 1	CS: 0		AS: 0	CS: 0	
	MG: 3	T: 10	SE: 2	MG: 0	T: 6	SE: 2	MG: 0	T: 2	SE: 0
Data Objects	AS: 10	CS: 6		AS: 1	CS: 0		AS: 0	CS: 0	
	MG: 8	T: 10	SE: 9	MG: 0	T: 10	SE: 2	MG: 0	T: 3	SE: 0
Lifecycles	AS: 8	CS: 6		AS: 0	CS: 0		AS: 0	CS: 0	
	MG: 8	T: 10	SE: 10	MG: 0	T: 6	SE: 2	MG: 0	T: 3	SE: 0
Microservices	AS: 7	CS: 6		AS: 1	CS: 0		AS: 0	CS: 0	
	MG: 9	T: 10	SE: 9	MG: 0	T: 8	SE: 4	MG: 0	T: 3	SE: 0
Process	AS: 7	CS: 6		AS: 1	CS: 0		AS: 0	CS: 0	
	MG: 10	T: 13	SE: 12	MG: 0	T: 13	SE: 2	MG: 0	T: 3	SE: 0
Microservices - Lifecycles	AS: 1	CS: 1		AS: 0	CS: 0		AS: 0	CS: 0	
	MG: 3	T: 3	SE: 5	MG: 0	T: 3	SE: 2	MG: 0	T: 3	SE: 0
Microservices - Process	AS: 0	CS: 0		AS: 0	CS: 0		AS: 0	CS: 0	
	MG: 0	T: 0	SE: 2	MG: 0	T: 0	SE: 0	MG: 0	T: 1	SE: 0
Lifecycles - Process	AS: 0	CS: 1		AS: 0	CS: 0		AS: 0	CS: 0	
	MG: 3	T: 3	SE: 2	MG: 0	T: 2	SE: 1	MG: 0	T: 3	SE: 0
Data objects - Lifecycles	AS: 0	CS: 0		AS: 0	CS: 0		AS: 0	CS: 0	
	MG: 0	T: 0	SE: 3	MG: 0	T: 0	SE: 0	MG: 0	T: 1	SE: 0
Data objects - Microservices	AS: 0	CS: 1		AS: 0	CS: 0		AS: 0	CS: 0	
	MG: 3	T: 3	SE: 3	MG: 0	T: 3	SE: 4	MG: 0	T: 3	SE: 0
Data objects - Process	AS: 0	CS: 0		AS: 0	CS: 0		AS: 0	CS: 0	
	MG: 0	T: 0	SE: 2	MG: 0	T: 0	SE: 0	MG: 0	T: 1	SE: 0
Data objects - Users	AS: 1	CS: 1		AS: 0	CS: 0		AS: 0	CS: 0	
	MG: 3	T: 3	SE: 11	MG: 0	T: 3	SE: 5	MG: 0	T: 3	SE: 0
Microservices - Users	AS: 1	CS: 1		AS: 0	CS: 0		AS: 0	CS: 0	
	MG: 3	T: 3	SE: 6	MG: 0	T: 4	SE: 3	MG: 0	T: 3	SE: 0

Figure 7.5 Summary of criteria groups in TEC-MAP. The table shows the number of criteria per Pillar for each Phase-Viewpoint combination. Groups with more than 5 criteria are indicated. AS = Abstract Syntax, CS = Concrete Syntax, MG = Modelling Guidelines, T = Tool support, SE = Semantics

7.5 Applications

The populated taxonomy can be used in several ways. In this section, we present a set of general guidelines for the use of the populated taxonomy (Section 7.5.1) and we present example evaluations with the populated taxonomy (Section 7.5.2, 7.5.3 and 7.5.4). These example evaluations also serve the purpose of validating the utility of TEC-MAP, as a descriptive evaluation as defined by Hevner [10].

7.5.1 General guidelines

The framework can be used in several ways. Existing approaches can be evaluated using all criteria of the framework, in order to discover strengths and weaknesses of the approach or compare them to other approaches. This can help with determining future developments of a multi-modelling approach, or it can help researchers to select an approach for a specific project. On the other hand, when a multi-modelling approach is under development, the criteria groups that are relevant for the project can be selected for its evaluation.

An evaluator of a multi-modelling approach should first determine the objective of their evaluation. The objective could be a complete evaluation of the approach using all criteria of the populated taxonomy. However, the context of the evaluation (selecting, comparing or developing a multi-modelling approach for a certain modelling goal) will often result in the prioritization of certain characteristics. In that case, the evaluator should select the phase(s), viewpoint(s) and pillar(s) that fit the objective of the evaluation. Each criterion belongs to a viewpoint, a phase and a pillar. Therefore, at least one phase and one pillar should be selected for an evaluation. To know which viewpoint to select, the evaluator needs to consider the coordination between viewpoints. Therefore, the evaluation of a multi-modelling approach requires at least two regular viewpoints (Data Objects, Lifecycles, Microservices, Process or Users) and all the non-trivial coordination viewpoints related to the selected regular viewpoints. To further optimize the selection of criteria, the evaluator should consider the framework of origin of the criteria in order to filter further if necessary. The evaluator should have clear arguments for the selection or exclusion of a particular framework of origin. The objective of the evaluation can thus be defined as the selected viewpoint(s), phase(s), pillar(s) and framework(s) of origin.

7.5.2 Example of a TEC-MAP evaluation: identifying potential improvements of the Merode approach

In this section we will illustrate the use of TEC-MAP with a partial evaluation of the Merode approach [88] before the adaptions proposed in Part III of this dissertation. The evaluation objective is to evaluate which aspects of Merode can be improved upon for the design phase (Phase dimension) regarding the abstract syntax and semantics of the Data Objects viewpoint, the Lifecycles viewpoint and the Microservices viewpoint. The first step is to select all criteria that fall under these characteristics in TEC-MAP, which is visualized in Table 7.3.

Table 7.3 Selection of TEC-MAP criteria

	Abstract Syntax	Semantics
Data Objects (19)	*CMQF_K2a, CMQF_K3a, CMQF_K5a, CMQF_P2a, CMQF_P3a, CMQF_P5a,* D09a, PF01, PF02, PFbis4.1	*CMQF_K2e, CMQF_K5e, CMQF_K6a, CMQF_P2e, CMQF_P5e, CMQF_P6a,* D02, D06a, PFbis5.06a
Lifecycles (18)	*CMQF_K2b, CMQF_K3b, CMQF_K5b, CMQF_P2b, CMQF_P3b, CMPF_P5b,* PF04, PFbis4.6	*CMQF_K2f, CMQF_K5f, CMQF_K6b, CMQF_P2f, CMQF_P5f, CMQF_P6b,* D04, D06b, PFbis3.2, PFbis5.06b
Microservices (16)	*CMQF_K2c, CMQF_K3c, CMQF_K5c, CMQF_P2c, CMQF_P3c, CMQF_P5c,* PF14a	*CMQF_K2g, CMQF_K5g, CMQF_K6c, CMQF_P2g, CMQF_P5g, CMQF_P6c,* D06c, PFbis4.4a, PFbis5.06c
Data-Lifecycles (3)		D03, PFbis5.02a, PFbis5.03a
Data-Microservices (3)		PFbis4.3a, PFbis5.02b, PFbis5.03b
Lifecycles-Microservices (6)		PF15a, PF18a, PFbis4.3b, PFbis4.5, PFbis5.02d, PFbis5.03d

The 65 selected criteria all come from three origin frameworks: CMQF, Dalec and PHILharmonicFlows. More specifically 36 of the 65 criteria are very high-level and abstract (for example, CMQF_K2a is the perceived ontological quality of the abstract syntax of the data objects viewpoint for the design phase, and CMQF_P2a is the (actual) ontological quality of the abstract syntax of the data objects viewpoint for the design phase). These criteria are mostly useful when designing a new modelling approach, but less so when pinpointing potential improvements or comparing specific aspects of different existing modelling approaches, as we will do in this and the following sections, because they are formulated very generally and lack concrete evaluation metrics. Therefore, we decide to drop the CMQF criteria from our selection resulting in the remaining 29 criteria, listed in Table 7.3 (the dropped criteria are included in grey italics). The full description of these criteria can be found online[2]. The descriptions of the DALEC criteria contain conditions for a criterion to be partially or fully supported, as found in the original publications.

The next step is to evaluate Merode for each criterion. An example of a criterion as can be found in the online catalogue is depicted in Figure 7.6. A criterion is labelled '✓✓' when fully supported by the Merode approach; '✓' when partially supported, and with a 'X' when not supported. The evaluation of these criteria is based on their description in the Dalec framework [93].

- D02 – Specification DRCs ✓✓: the data representation constructs in Merode are fully formalized as object types with attributes. The connected structure of object types is formally represented in an Existence Dependency Graph.
- D03 – Specification of Behaviour ✓✓: the Merode approach imposes formal specification of the behaviour of object types by including Finite State Machines as the lifecycles of the object types.
- D04 – Specification of Interactions ✓✓: the Merode approach contains a fully formalized specification of interactions based on process algebra. In short, a Merode

---

[2] https://charlotteverbruggen.notion.site/TEC-MAP-654d70294dd44d54bcc490b2025e733a

model contains an Object Event Table that assigns event types to object types. If an object type participates in an event type, that event type should occur at least once in the finite state machine of that object as a transition. Multiple object types can participate in an event type. In that case, an instance of the event type can only occur if all participating instances of object types are in a correct state in their lifecycles. For a more detailed explanation, we refer the reader to [200].

- D05b – Support for Managed Process Granularity ✕: The approach allows the modeller to use a process modelling language of choice. In order to satisfy this criterion, the modeller should choose a process modelling language that addresses the issue of process granularity management.
- D06a – Support for Model Verification (viewpoint Data Objects, sub-criteria: D02) ✓✓: The Merode Existence Dependency Graph is accompanied by formally defined semantics detailing the correctness criteria for the Existence Dependency Graph [99], thus this criterion is fully supported.
- D06b – Support for Model Verification (viewpoint Lifecycles, sub-criteria: D03, D04) ✓✓: The Merode Finite State Machines and Object Event Table are accompanied by formally defined semantics detailing their correctness criteria [99], thus this criterion is fully supported.
- D06c – Support for Model Verification (viewpoint Microservices) ✓: The Merode approach contains input and output services that model the interaction between the process and the data. The syntax and semantics of these input and output services is described in detail, but only part of the description is formal. Other parts, such as the automatic verification of executability at runtime, are not yet formally defined [102].
- D06d – Support for Model Verification (viewpoint Processes, sub-criteria: D05b, D09b) ✕: For the Process viewpoint, Merode does not support model verification, due to the free choice in process modelling language. In order to satisfy this criterion, the modeller should choose a process modelling language that addresses the issue of model verification.
- D08 – Specification of Data access permissions ✕: the User viewpoint, and therefore the User-Data coordination Viewpoint, is not yet supported by the Merode approach.
- D09a – Support for Variants (viewpoint Data Objects) ✕: The Merode approach does not support the use of variants of object types.
- D09b – Support for Variants (viewpoint Processes) ✕ The Merode approach does not support the use of variants of process models, due to the free choice in process modelling language. In order to satisfy this criterion, the modeller should choose a process modelling languages that addresses the issue of process variants.
- PF01 – Data Integration, PF04 – Object Behaviour ✓✓: In a previous publication [115], Merode was already evaluated based on the PHILharmonicFlows criteria. These criteria were considered fully supported.
- PF02 – Cardinalities, PF14a – Black-box activities, PF15a – Form-based activities, PF18a – control-flow within user forms ✓: In a previous publication [115], Merode was already evaluated based on the PHILharmonicFlows criteria. These criteria were considered partially supported.
- PFbis3.2 – Hierarchical structuring ✕: this criterion deals with the hierarchical structuring of model variants. Since Merode does not support model variants, this criterion is not supported.

- PFbis4.1 – Data Integration ✓✓: this criterion corresponds to criterion PF01, and is thus supported.
- PFbis4.3a, PFbis4.3b – Support of form-based activities and control-flow within user forms ✓: These criteria are very similar to PF15a, and are partially supported by Merode through input and output services (which can be used to define the functionality of a user form).
- PFbis4.4a – Support of variable activity granularity ✓: This criterion requires support for instance-specific, context-specific and batch activities. The Merode approach partially supports this criterion as it includes composed and complex input services that combine atomic change operation to object instances. However, execution semantics and correctness criteria for these composed or complex input services are not yet formally defined.
- PFbis4.5 – Support of mandatory as well as optional activities ✓✓: Both at the level of FSMs, and at the level of the Business Processes, mandatory and optional events/activities can be defined.
- PFbis4.6 – Alignment of process execution with object behaviour ✓✓: This criterion requires dynamic process execution based on attribute value changes. In Merode, the alignment between object behaviour and process execution is supported implicitly, as attribute values are changed by triggering events, and these events are executed by tasks in a process via input services. These input services can be executed manually or triggered automatically, for example by the execution of another input service, thus reacting to a change of attribute values. Additional conditions on the value of the considered attributes can be included in the definition of the input service.
- PFbis5.02a – Cascading effects (viewpoint Data-Lifecycles) ✓✓: This criterion requires the identification of necessary concomitant changes to ensure consistency between models. Following the formal definition of the data model (Existence Dependency Graph), Object-Event Table and Finite State Machines, the Merode handbook [88] includes formal definitions of the necessary consistency rules between lifecycles and data object types. These consistency rules can be used to identify cascading changes in Merode, therefore, this criterion is fully supported for the Data-Lifecycles viewpoint.
- PFbis5.02b, PFbis5.02d – Cascading effects (viewpoints Data-Microservices, Lifecycles-Microservices) ✗: In Merode, there are no modelling guidelines or consistency rules yet that define cascading effects between Lifecycles and Microservices. The coordination between Data Objects and Microservices occurs indirectly through the Lifecycles. Therefore, both criteria are not yet supported.
- PFbis5.03a – Change operations and change patterns (viewpoint Data-Lifecycles) ✓✓: Following from criterion PFbis5.02a, several change patterns are defined in Merode to ensure consistency between models. For example, when a new event is linked to its owning object type in the Object Event Table, the propagation rule states that it is acquired by all the (direct and indirect) master object types of that owning object type. The rule groups several primitive changes (an object type acquiring an event) into one high-level change pattern.
- PFbis5.03b, PFbis5.03d – Change operations and change patterns (viewpoints Data-Microservices, Lifecycles-Microservices) ✗: As these criteria build upon criteria PFbis5.02b and PFbis5.02d, these criteria are not yet defined

- PFbis5.06a, PFbis5.06b – Correctness (viewpoint Data Objects, Lifecycles) ✓✓: The Merode approach includes formal definitions of the data model and lifecycles, as well as consistency rules for these viewpoints. These definitions and rules can be used as correctness criteria, both as soft checks during the modelling process and as a final correctness check before finalizing the model. Therefore, these criteria are supported.
- PFbis5.06c – Correctness (viewpoint Microservices) ✗: Merode does not yet provide formal definitions and consistency rules for microservices, therefore, this criterion is not yet supported.

Table 7.4 Summary of the TEC-MAP evaluation for Merode along the selected criteria

	Abstract Syntax	Semantics
Data Objects (19)	D09a: ✗ PF01: ✓✓ PF02: ✓✓ PFbis4.1: ✓✓	D02: ✓✓ D06a: ✓✓ PFbis5.06a: ✓✓
Lifecycles (18)	PF04: ✓✓ PFbis4.6: ✓✓	D04: ✓✓ D06b: ✓✓ PFbis3.2: ✗ PFbis5.06b: ✓✓
Microservices (16)	PF14a: ✓	D06c: ✓ PFbis4.4a: ✓ PFbis5.06c: ✗
Data-Lifecycles (3)		D03: ✓✓ PFbis5.02a: ✓✓ PFbis5.03a: ✓✓
Data-Microservices (3)		PFbis4.3a: ✓ PFbis5.02b: ✗ PFbis5.03b: ✗
Lifecycles-Microservices (6)		PF15a: ✓ PF18a: ✓ PFbis4.3b: ✓ PFbis4.5: ✓✓ PFbis5.02d: ✗ PFbis5.03d: ✗

As shown in Table 7.4, the criteria in the Data Objects viewpoint, the lifecycles viewpoint and the Data-Lifecycles coordination viewpoint are mostly covered. Criteria D09a and PFbis3.2 have to do with model variants, which is not yet supported by Merode. The main improvement that can be made to the Merode approach for these three viewpoints is thus the inclusion of model variants. On the other hand, most criteria in the Microservices viewpoint, and the Data-Microservices and Lifecycles-Microservices viewpoints are not or only partially supported. This is clearly another focus point for the further improvement of the Merode approach.

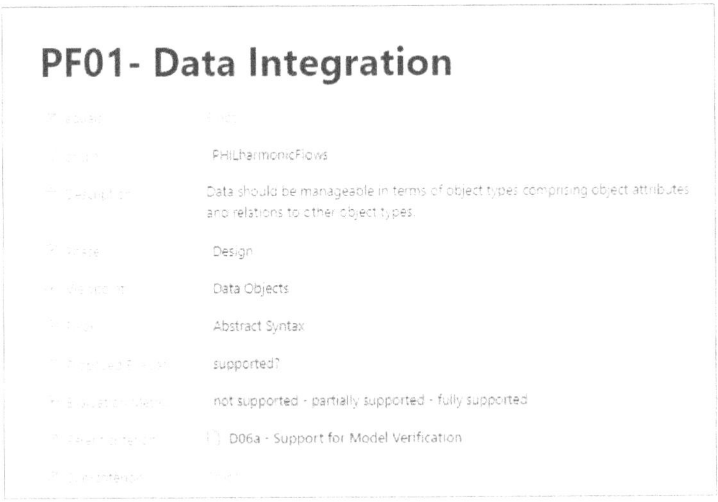

PF01- Data Integration

PHILharmonicFlows

Data should be manageable in terms of object types comprising object attributes
and relations to other object types.

Design

Data Objects

Abstract Syntax

supported?

not supported · partially supported · fully supported

D06a · Support for Model Verification

Figure 7.6. Example of a criterion

7.5.3 Example of a TEC-MAP evaluation: comparing the Merode approach to the BAUML and 4EM approaches

An alternative scenario is a teacher who wants to select an appropriate modelling approach for their new course, and wants to compare the Merode approach to The BAUML approach and 4EM approaches. For this comparison, we use the same selection of criteria as in section 7.5.2.

BAUML is short for BALSA UML and is a modelling approach that uses a subset of the UML diagram types in combination with OCL to cover the dimensions of the BALSA framework[135]. The subset of UML diagram types used are class diagrams (for Business Artefacts), state machine diagrams (for Lifecycles) and activity diagrams (for Associations, i.e., the sequence flow of microservices). The Microservices are defined with OCL operation contracts.

- D02 – Specification DRCs, PF01 – Data Integration, PFbis4.1 – Data Integration ✓✓: the data representation constructs in BAUML are fully formalized as object types with attributes. The connected structure of object types is formally represented in an UML class diagram.
- D03 – Specification of Behaviour ✓✓: the BAUML approach imposes formal specification of the behaviour of object types by including state machine diagrams as the lifecycles of the object types.
- D04 – Specification of Interactions ✓✓: The BAUML approach allows specifying interactions between lifecycles via the microservices.
- D06a, D06b, D06c – Support for Model Verification (viewpoint Data Objects, Lifecycles and Microservices, sub-criteria: D02, D03, D04) ✓✓: The BAUML approach is accompanied by formally defined semantics for all model types in the approach, as well as conditions to ensure that the models are verifiable [201], [202].
- D09a – Support for Variants (viewpoint Data Objects) ✗: The BAUML approach does not support variants of data object types.

- PF02 – Cardinalities ✓✓: The BAUML approach uses UML class diagrams for the data perspective. Therefore, the use of cardinalities is supported.
- PF04 – Object Behaviour ✓✓: The BAUML approach uses UML state machine diagrams for the modelling of behaviour of data objects. Therefore, this criterion is supported.
- PF14a – Black-box activities ✓: the BAUML approach uses OCL constraints to implement preconditions on services, however, to the best of our knowledge, the implementation of back-box activities is not included in the approach. Therefore, the criterion is partially supported.
- PF15a – Form-based activities ✗: To the best of our knowledge, user forms are not addressed by BAUML, and thus this criterion is not supported by the BAUML approach.
- PF18a – control-flow within user forms ✗: this criterion requires the possibility of adjusting the mandatory or optional character of an attribute ad-hoc while a user fills a form. This is not included in the BAUML approach, and therefore this criterion is not supported.
- PFbis3.2 – Hierarchical structuring ✗: this criterion deals with the hierarchical structuring of model variants. Since BAUML does not support model variants, this criterion is not supported.
- PFbis4.3a, PFbis4.3b – Support of form-based activities and control-flow within user forms ✗: To the best of our knowledge, user forms are not addressed by BAUML, and thus this criterion is not supported by the BAUML approach.
- PFbis4.4a – Support of variable activity granularity ✓✓: This criterion requires support for instance-specific, context-specific and batch activities. The BAUML approach partially supports this criterion as it includes the modelling of services with OCL that can affect multiple object instances.
- PFbis4.5 – Support of mandatory as well as optional activities ✓✓: The BAUML approach uses the OCL language to define microservices and UML activity diagrams for modelling the process (i.e., the allowed execution sequences of microservices). Therefore, optional and mandatory activities can be modelled in the activity diagrams.
- PFbis4.6 – Alignment of process execution with object behaviour ✓✓: This criterion requires dynamic process execution based on attribute value changes, more specifically, the criterion states that there should be a link between attribute values and states. In BAUML, The UML Class diagram is used to model business artefacts, where each business artefact has a superclass to represent the concept, and subclasses for each state the artefact can be in [202]. The instances of the business artefacts thus move from one subclass to another when the state of the business artefact changes. The sequence in which the states of the business artefact can occur, are modelled in an UML state machine diagram. Since each state is correlated with a subclass in the data model, it is possible to define which attributes are linked to each state, thus satisfying this requirement.
- PFbis5.02a, PFbis5.02b, PFbis5.02d – Cascading effects (viewpoints Data-Lifecycles, Data-Microservices, Lifecycles-Microservices) ✗: These criteria require the identification of necessary concomitant changes to ensure consistency between models. While the BAUML approach is supported with a transformation of the model to first order logic to test the correctness of a given BAUML model [202], to the best

of our knowledge, there are no explicit definitions of general consistency rules for the models. Therefore, cascading effects are not defined, and the criterion is not supported.

- PFbis5.03a, PFbis5.03b, PFbis5.03d – Change operations and change patterns (viewpoints Data-Lifecycles, Data-Microservices, Lifecycles-Microservices) ✗: As these criteria build upon criteria PFbis5.02a, PFbis5.02b and PFbis5.02d, these criteria are not yet defined.
- PFbis5.06a, PFbis5.06b, PFbis5.06c – Correctness (viewpoint Data Objects, Lifecycles, Microservices) ✓✓: The BAUML approach is supported with a transformation of the model to first order logic to test the correctness of a given BAUML model [202]. The test described in this publication be used as correctness criteria, both as soft checks during the modelling process and as a final correctness check before finalizing the model. Therefore, these criteria are supported.

The coverage of the BAUML approach on the selected criteria is very similar to that of the Merode approach (see Table 7.5, the criteria that differ from the Merode evaluation are highlighted in bold). Only criteria D06c and PFbis4.4a (both in on semantics of Microservices) are better supported in BAUML. On the other hand, criteria PFbis5.02a, PFbis5.03a, PFbis4.3a, PFbis4.3b, PF15a and PF18a (on the coordination viewpoints Data-Lifecycles, Data-Microservices and Lifecycles-Microservices) are better supported in Merode. We can thus conclude that both approaches are very similar in the selected dimensions, with a slight difference in the definitions of semantics. However, it is important to keep in mind that the approach can have specific characteristics that are not covered by the evaluation frameworks in TEC-MAP. For example, a major difference between Merode and BAUML is the added restriction in Merode that all relationships between object types should express existence dependency. This restriction leads to more complexity in the definition of data object types, but also has added benefits when it comes to defining object lifecycles and object interactions, and mathematical verification of the complete model. Also, the evaluation of criterion PFbis4.6 revealed that object instances can move from one sub-class to another in BAUML. In Merode this is prohibited because Merode adheres to the principle of strong typing not all programming languages allow objects to change type [88]. Therefore, we recommend that modelling language developers, modellers and tool buyers use TEC-MAP for an initial evaluation of a given modelling approach, and supplement this evaluation with a reflection on the aspects that are specific and unique to the modelling approach under evaluation.

Table 7.5 Summary of the TEC-MAP evaluation for BAUML along the selected criteria.

	Abstract Syntax	Semantics
Data Objects (19)	D09a: ✗ PF01: ✓✓ PF02: ✓✓ PFbis4.1: ✓✓	D02: ✓✓ D06a: ✓✓ PFbis5.06a: ✓✓
Lifecycles (18)	PF04: ✓✓ PFbis4.6: ✓✓	D04: ✓✓ D06b: ✓✓ PFbis3.2: ✗ PFbis5.06b: ✓✓
Microservices (16)	PF14a: ✓	D06c: ✓✓ **PFbis4.4a: ✓✓** PFbis5.06c: ✓✓
Data-Lifecycles (3)		D03: ✓✓ **PFbis5.02a: ✗** **PFbis5.03a: ✗**
Data-Microservices (3)		**PFbis4.3a: ✗** PFbis5.02b: ✗ PFbis5.03b: ✗
Lifecycles-Microservices (6)		**PF15a: ✗** **PF18a: ✗** **PFbis4.3b: ✗** PFbis4.5: ✓✓ PFbis5.02d: ✗ PFbis5.03d: ✗

4EM is a general purpose modelling language for enterprises that also takes into account the pragmatic considerations that come with stakeholder participation and project management. 4EM uses seven model types: the goals model, business rules model, concepts model, business process model, actors and resources model, product/service model and technical components model [163]. 4EM cannot be mapped exactly to the viewpoints of TEC-MAP, for example, lifecycles are not considered as a separate model type. On the other hand, TEC-MAP does not cover the perspective of enterprise goals. Still, 4EM is often used in university settings [203] to teach enterprise modelling, so it would be interesting to analyse how the method compares to the Merode approach and BAUML regarding the selected criteria.

- D02/PF01/PFbis4.1 – Specification DRCs ✓: the concept model of 4EM has a slightly wider scope than purely defining data representation constructs, as the concepts in this model can also include (intangible) concepts of other models, for example business rules. While the handbook states that the concepts model can be used as a basis for database design, it mentions that the concept model would need to be replaced by a formal data modelling language. However, the meta-model (abstract syntax) of the concept model of 4EM includes attributes and relationships between concepts, and the semantics are described informally. The concept model of 4EM thus provides partial support of this criterion.
- D03 – Specification of Behaviour ✗: 4EM does not specifically address the lifecycles of data objects in as a separate model type. Therefore, this criterion is not supported.

To address this issue, the modeller could decide to model lifecycles as business rules, however, to the best of our knowledge, there is no formal or informal description of this.

- D04 – Specification of Interactions ✓: Since 4EM does not support lifecycles, this criterion deals with the interactions between processes. Process interaction is addressed to a limited extend in the 4EM handbook, in the sense that processes can contain sub-processes. However, other interactions between processes are not addressed. Therefore, this criterion is partially addressed.
- D06a, D06b, D06c – Support for Model Verification (viewpoint Data Objects, Lifecycles and Microservices, sub-criteria: D02, D03, D04) ✗: Since 4EM does not provide fully formal specifications of the semantics of data objects lifecycles and microservices, there are no formal correctness criteria that can be used for the verification of these models. Thus, this criteria D06a, D06b and D06c are not supported.
- D09a – Support for Variants (viewpoint Data Objects) ✗: The 4EM method does not support variants of data objects.
- PF02 – Cardinalities ✓✓: The 4EM concepts model includes cardinalities on the relationships between concepts.
- PF04 – Object Behaviour ✗: 4EM does not specifically address the lifecycles of data objects in as a separate model type, or their interaction with the attribute values. Therefore, this criterion is not supported.
- PF14a – Black-box activities ✓: 4EM specifies information/material sets as input for activities in process models. These information/material sets refer to concepts in the concepts model, which can have attributes. The meta-model of activities thus allows the specification of pre-conditions on (black-box) process activities in the form of required information. However, there is only an informal specification of such information/material sets. The criterion is partially supported.
- PF15a – Form-based activities ✗: The most recent publication of 4EM contains the Product/service model, where forms could be considered services. However, the publication does not provide a detailed description of how these services and their features should be specified. Therefore, the criterion is not supported.
- PF18a – Control-flow within user forms ✗: Similar to criterion PF18a, 4EM does not support the specification of forms and thus this criterion is not supported.
- PFbis3.2 – Hierarchical structuring ✗: this criterion deals with the hierarchical structuring of model variants. Since 4EM does not support model variants, this criterion is not supported.
- PFbis4.3a, PFbis4.3b – Support of form-based activities and control-flow within user forms ✗: As form-based activities are not supported by 4EM (see criterion PF15a), this criterion is not supported by 4EM.
- PFbis4.4a – Support of variable activity granularity ✓: This criterion requires support for instance-specific, context-specific and batch activities. 4EM uses information sets in its process models to capture the output of an activity. This could include the changes that are made to one or more instances of data objects. However, as the database structure is not formally defined (see criteria D02/PF01/PFbis4.1), this relationship between data objects and activities is also not formally defined. The criterion is partially supported.

- PFbis4.5 – Support of mandatory as well as optional activities ✓✓: 4EM includes a Business Process Model for modelling the allowed execution sequences of tasks (microservices). Therefore, optional and mandatory activities can be modelled in this model.
- PFbis4.6 – Alignment of process execution with object behaviour ✗: This criterion requires dynamic process execution based on attribute value changes, more specifically, the criterion states that there should be a link between attribute values and states. As stated in criterion D03, 4EM does not specifically address the lifecycles of data objects in as a separate model type. Therefore, this criterion is not supported.
- PFbis5.02a, PFbis5.02b, PFbis5.02d – Cascading effects (viewpoints Data-Lifecycles, Data-Microservices, Lifecycles-Microservices) ✗: These criteria require the identification of necessary concomitant changes to ensure consistency between models. While the 4EM handbook does include an overview of how the different models interact with each other [204], to the best of our knowledge, there are no explicit definitions of general consistency rules between the models. Therefore, cascading effects are not defined, and the criterion is not supported.
- PFbis5.03a, PFbis5.03b, PFbis5.03d – Change operations and change patterns (viewpoints Data-Lifecycles, Data-Microservices, Lifecycles-Microservices) ✗: As these criteria build upon criteria PFbis5.02a, PFbis5.02b and PFbis5.02d, these criteria are not yet defined.
- PFbis5.06a, PFbis5.06b, PFbis5.06c – Correctness (viewpoint Data Objects, Lifecycles, Microservices) ✗: To the best of our knowledge, 4EM does not provide semantic checks or tests to verify the correctness of the models, besides verifying compliance with the abstract syntax provided in [163], [204]. Therefore, these criteria are not supported.

The evaluation of 4EM with TEC-MAP reveals that the abstract syntax and semantic aspects of 4EM are not as well defined as the semantic aspects of Merode (see Table 7.6, the criteria that differ from the Merode evaluation are highlighted in bold). This could be clarified by the fact that 4EM is not meant for MDE, and thus transformations of the models to executable code are not its main focus. Rather, one of the main objectives of 4EM is to provide a means for different stakeholders to model a business as-is from several different perspectives, and to model the changes, improvements and new developments they wish to implement [203]. Therefore, formal semantics are not as important as in a modelling approach for MDE. In that regard, the strengths of 4EM would have been reflected more prominently if our evaluation objective was not restricted to the abstract syntax and semantics, but rather focuses on modelling guidelines. In that scenario, the criteria from the MEM framework would have been included, which focus in more general terms on usability and usefulness of the method.

Table 7.6 Summary of the TEC-MAP evaluation for 4EM along the selected criteria

	Abstract Syntax	Semantics
Data Objects (19)	D09a: ✗ **PF01: ✓** PF02: ✓✓ **PFbis4.1: ✓**	**D02: ✓** **D06a: ✗** **PFbis5.06a: ✗**
Lifecycles (18)	**PF04: ✗** **PFbis4.6: ✗**	**D04: ✓** **D06b: ✗** PFbis3.2: ✗ **PFbis5.06b: ✗**
Microservices (16)	PF14a: ✓	**D06c: ✗** PFbis4.4a: ✓ PFbis5.06c: ✗
Data-Lifecycles (3)		**D03: ✗** **PFbis5.02a: ✗** **PFbis5.03a: ✗**
Data-Microservices (3)		**PFbis4.3a: ✗** PFbis5.02b: ✗ PFbis5.03b: ✗
Lifecycles-Microservices (6)		**PF15a: ✗** **PF18a: ✗** **PFbis4.3b: ✗** PFbis4.5: ✓✓ PFbis5.02d: ✗ PFbis5.03d: ✗

7.5.4 Evaluation of the adaption proposed in Part III

In this section we will evaluate how the adaptions proposed in Part III affect the evaluation of Merode based on the same criteria as used in section 7.5.2.

The criteria that are affected by the changes are the following:

- D05b – Support for Managed Process Granularity ✓✓: Using BPMN as a process modelling languages allows managing the process granularity.
- D06c – Support for Model Verification (viewpoint Microservices) ✓ → ✓: The Merode approach contains input and output services that model the interaction between the process and the data. The syntax and semantics of these input and output services is have been defined formally in Part III of this dissertation, providing a basis for formal verification. While the proposed adaptions improve the support for this criterion, full support requires additional correctness rules that can be used to verify whether the modelled microservices are consistent with the FSMs in the domain model.
- PF15a – Form-based activities ✓ → ✓✓: the adaptions proposed in Part III allow the modeler to describe input services very precisely, which can then be used to build forms.
- PFbis4.3a, PFbis4.3b – Support of form-based activities and control-flow within user forms ✓ → ✓✓: These criteria are very similar to PF15a, and are supported through

input and output services (which can be used to define the functionality of a user form).

- PFbis4.4a – Support of variable activity granularity ✓ → ✓✓: This criterion requires support for instance-specific, context-specific and batch activities. The proposed adaptions to the Merode approach support the precise definition of composed and complex input services that combine atomic change operation to object instances.
- PFbis5.02b, PFbis5.02d – Cascading effects (viewpoints Data-Microservices, Lifecycles-Microservices) ✗ → ✓✓: The adaptions proposed in Part III specify that microservices are composed of atomic events, therefore, the changes made to the definition of event types should automatically cascade to the services that use these event types. The interaction between data and services is now also defined by the functional model that was incorporated. Therefore, both criteria are now supported.
- PFbis5.03b, PFbis5.03d – Change operations and change patterns (viewpoints Data-Microservices, Lifecycles-Microservices) ✗ → ✓: As these criteria build upon criteria PFbis5.02b and PFbis5.02d, these criteria are now partially supported. The criterion requires the definition of empirically grounded change patterns for full support. Since the tool support is not yet fully developed and has not been used in practice yet, we only consider this criterion partially supported.
- PFbis5.06c – Correctness (viewpoint Microservices) ✗ → ✓: The proposed adaptions provide clear definitions for microservices, therefore, this criterion is considered partially supported. When the correctness rules required for full support of criterion D06a are defined, we can consider this criterion fully supported as well.

7.6   Discussion

Our first research question investigated the relevant evaluation frameworks for data-aware process modelling approaches, including general frameworks that can be applied to these approaches. The research question has been addressed with a systematic literature review, described in section 7.2, resulting in a selection of nine reference frameworks. The second research question investigates the minimal set of dimensions and characteristics required to classify and summarize the evaluation criteria from the different evaluation frameworks identified in RQ1. This research question is addressed in section 7.3 and 7.4 by the development of a taxonomy called TEC-MAP, and the classification of the evaluation criteria found in the systematic literature review.

TEC-MAP represents a taxonomy for evaluation criteria for the evaluation of data-aware process modelling approaches. TEC-MAP includes the most important general and seminal frameworks such as TAM and MEM but thanks to the systematic literature search, it also includes a number of more specific frameworks for multi-modelling approaches to data and process modelling. In total, it is based on nine evaluation frameworks and their corresponding criteria. It provides an extensive overview of these evaluation frameworks, and by classifying all the criteria into a taxonomy, it identifies important dimensions for the evaluation of multi-modelling approaches. To make the framework actionable, it has been implemented as an online catalogue with filtering capabilities. This allows users to distil relevant sets of criteria for their goal more easily. Section 7.4.4 contains a critical reflection on the populated taxonomy, concluding that the majority of the criteria fit in the Design phase and that especially the non-trivial coordination viewpoints lack evaluation criteria. Section 7.5 also presents scenarios demonstrating the utility of TEC-MAP. These evaluation scenarios serve as a descriptive evaluation as defined by Hevner in his MISQ paper: "Construct detailed scenarios around the artifact to demonstrate its utility" [10].

Despite these strengths, several limitations can be identified. A first set of limitations relate to the construction of the framework. While the currently identified papers seem to suggest that the taxonomy is sufficiently complete (as saturation was reached), we cannot exclude that future use and evaluation of the framework may nevertheless lead to the identification of missing dimensions. Another limitation is that the different levels of detail in the original publications leave room for interpretation. While we attempted to adhere as faithfully as possible to the intent of the original publications, the classification of certain criteria might be subject to discussion. Finally, the evaluation of the ending conditions is (partially) subjective by design of the methodology, something that is inevitable according to [191]. A second set of limitations relate to the practical use of TEC-MAP. While TEC-MAP can already be a useful tool for practitioners to identify relevant criteria, a certain level of knowledge on the different evaluation frameworks included is still required to be able to correctly interpret each criterion. We attempted to alleviate this requirement by providing an overview of the included frameworks in section 7.2 and by providing links to the corresponding publications for further reading on the website. The practical applicability is also hampered by the fact that most of the criteria are quite theoretical. Only the TAM and MEM criteria address the practitioner's perspectives of ease of use, efficiency and effectiveness. A more in-depth evaluation of approaches that potentially reveal other criteria can be achieved by interviewing practitioners. In section 7.4.4, the TEC-MAP framework is compared to some of the main challenges that practitioners face as found in [12]. A number of complementary frameworks and evaluation models are proposed to fill the gaps. A qualitative analysis was also conducted to identify subsuming and identical criteria from different frameworks. Finally, the evaluation was limited to the application to three cases. Future work is to setup an empirical meta-evaluation with practitioners and experts in method evaluation. The aim of this meta-evaluation should be two-fold: the dimensions and characteristics of the taxonomy itself should be evaluated, as well as the practical usefulness and ease of use of the populated taxonomy. In order to satisfy both aspects of the meta-evaluation, we would conduct interviews with method evaluation experts, as well as empirical experiments with practitioners and method evaluation experts. However, these interviews and experiments require a dedicated paper, and are therefore left as future work in this chapter.

On the other hand, the framework and its online availability offer a number of opportunities for modelling language evaluation. Provided some extra developments, it could facilitate making evaluations of existing modelling languages available online for use by researchers and practitioners, generating evaluation templates based on selected criteria, and generating heat-maps based on the evaluation of an approach in order to highlight the dimensions and/or characteristics that are missing.

7.7 Conclusion

This chapter analysed and combined a total of nine different frameworks and 13 supplementary publications in view of creating a more complete populated taxonomy of evaluation criteria for the evaluation of a multi-modelling approach to data and process modelling. The resulting populated taxonomy TEC-MAP collects evaluation criteria arranged in four foundational viewpoints and six coordination viewpoints, four phases and five pillars. While the design phase has the largest number of criteria, many categories within the populated taxonomy have currently a limited number of criteria and the user viewpoints lack criteria. Thus, the taxonomy itself might benefit from further population with additional criteria. However, this is typical for a taxonomy according to [191]. Despite this potential for adding criteria, we believe that in its current state, the dimensions and characteristics are saturated and the resulting populated taxonomy provides already a useful overview of evaluation criteria that can be adapted to the needs of researchers while providing a robust capstone for expanding it with additional sets of criteria. The utility of the taxonomy is demonstrated in Section 7.5 with three scenarios, including the evaluation of three different approaches against 29 criteria. Future work includes extending the online support for TEC-MAP with a more interactive tool to make, store and share evaluations of modelling approaches online. This online support can also include more options when it comes to visualizing the evaluations, for example with a heat map or spider diagrams. Another opportunity for future work is to provide a complete evaluation and comparison of several well-known modelling approaches. This would be beneficial both for researchers and practitioners when selecting a modelling approach.

Chapter 8
A Study on Evaluating the Usability
of a Multi-Modelling Tool

In the previous chapter, the abstract syntax and semantics proposed in Part III were evaluated using the criteria from TEC-MAP. However, TEC-MAP has zero criteria for the evaluation of Tool Support in the Design phase of the Microservices-Process viewpoint. Therefore, another approach is required for the evaluation of the tool extensions proposed in section 5.6.

8.1 Introduction

To address the concerns of different stakeholders, business architects need to model different viewpoints of the same system. For example, they need to create goal models, process models, data models, etc. Typically, the models that address different viewpoints make use of different modelling languages (e.g. GRL, BPMN, UML). Furthermore, as all these models represent a different viewpoint on the same system, they need to be coordinated, thus requiring the integration of models created in different languages. However, combining different modelling languages is not straightforward as the coordination between languages requires careful consideration.

Multi-modelling approaches are specifically developed to address this concern. Several frameworks for multi-modelling approaches exist, e.g. addressing specifically the combination of data and processes as is done in BALSA [135] and Dalec [93]. Some multi-modelling methods already exist (for example, Archimate [205], 4EM [206], PHILharmonicFlows [133] and Merode [88]), but they rarely fit into a model-driven engineering (MDE) process, where the bridge between different models is formalized in such a way that generation of the bridging code can be done without manual intervention. To the best of our knowledge, the multi-modelling approaches that allow for code generation for different aspects are rare. Data-aware process modelling approaches are not able to deal with "object-oriented" applications, and business logic (functions) that are defined as object operations as they typically go directly to the database level via SQL operations [207]. The OO-method is -in line with the OO paradigm- able to deal with data and business logic implemented as operations in the classes. It also integrates UI design, but is not able to link the generated application to a BP engine automatically. This also goes for the Merode approach.

Multi-modelling approaches that combine different independent languages require the definition of a mapping of concepts between the elements of the two languages. E.g. mapping between goals and processes, between processes and data, between tasks and user interfaces, etc. These mappings can be one-to-one (e.g., each task is mapped onto one user interface), one-to-many (e.g., a goal is achieved by multiple processes), or

© The Author(s), under exclusive license to Springer Nature Switzerland AG 2026
C. Verbruggen, *Advancing Multi-modelling in MDE for Integrated Domain
and Business Process Modelling*, Lecture Notes in Business Information Processing 576,
https://doi.org/10.1007/978-3-032-13876-7_8

many-to-many (e.g., a task in a process can execute multiple operations on data classes and an operation on a data class can be executed by multiple tasks). Once the mapping has been defined at the meta-model level, modelers that create models need to be able to instantiate these mappings for the models they create directly, in the modelling tool.

Two of the most important issues that practitioners face with model-driven engineering are a lack of tool functionalities and the high effort required to use these tools, i.e., the tools lack usability [12]. For multi-modelling tools in particular, this comes with added challenges as multi-modelling approaches themselves come with a steep learning curve and high complexity [12]. Therefore, multi-modelling tools should not only allow practitioners to create all models that are part of the multi-modelling approach, including the model mappings. They should pay a particular attention to usability. Ideally, the modelling tools can help practitioners learn and navigate the multi-modelling approach.

While the lack of tool functionalities can be solved by further implementing elements of modelling approaches that are still missing from the tools, improving the usability of modelling tools is less straightforward. Our research addresses the design of a tool for designing the mappings required to connect models created in different languages. We will investigate some existing, general design principles and how important they are when designing a UI for a multi-modelling tool, based on the results of a multi-modal experiment with 20 participants that are familiar with the multi-modelling approach Merode [208].

8.2 Related Research

Research on the usability of modelling tools is limited [209]. Therefore, there are no universal design recommendations or standards that modelling tool developers can take into account. This is confirmed by the findings of Reijers et al. [137], who argue that the Business process management community focusses on developing modelling notations and approaches, rather than the usability of these notations and approaches. They encourage researchers to focus more on the intended users of their end product.

Bobkowska et al. [210] performed an empirical study on the usability of six UML tools where Visual Paradigm was the tool with the highest usability. However, this analysis only measured the overall usability with the average duration of creating a model and the number of steps required. The study did not discuss specific UI design principles or how the relate to the measured usability.

Pietron et al. [211] argue that the lack of usability in MDE tools is the main factor limiting the adoption of MDE in industry. In order to improve usability of a specific tool, the usability issues of that tool first need to be uncovered. They therefore developed a study design for discovering usability issues in modelling tools. This study design takes into account several concerns such as the distinction between the usability of the tool and the usability of the modelling language itself, the characteristics of good participants, the complexity of the modelling task, and the manner of data collection.

Ruiz et al. [212] performed a systematic literature review on functional user interface design principles, using publications from 1982 to 2019. They selected 36 principles as the most cited principles in the field, with the three most important identified principles being "offer informative feedback", "strive for consistency" and "prevent errors".

8.3 Methodology

As practitioners place great importance on usability of tools, the goal of this chapter is investigating the impact of applying existing, general design principles for usability on a UI for a multi-modelling tool. In particular, we formulate the following research questions:

- **RQ1** – Is the perceived usability of the interface of a multi-modelling tool significantly affected by the application of UI design principles?
- **RQ2** – Which kind usability issues occur frequently in the use of a multi-modelling tool, before and after applying UI design principles?
- **RQ3** – Which kind of improvements to the interface are frequently suggested before and after applying UI design principles?

In order to answer these research questions, we developed the following methodology, based on the study design by Pietron et al. [211].

8.3.1 Selection of UI design principles

In order to select the UI design principles to apply in this experiment, we start from the systematic literature review by Ruiz et al. [212], using publications from 1982 to 2019. They selected 36 principles as the most cited principles in the field, with more than 500 citations each. The principles were ordered by the number of authors that identified each principle. Thus, the three most important identified principles are "offer informative feedback", "strive for consistency" and "prevent errors". While they performed an extensive analysis in order to identify the most important principles according to the research community, they did not analyse how these principles interact with each other, or perform an empirical validation of the principles. In further research [213], they linked 22 of the 36 selected principles to a corresponding ergonomic criterion. They state that the added benefit of this mapping is that the ergonomic criteria have been empirically validated, and have corresponding guidelines, which are more specific in the actions that need to be taken in order to implement the criteria and thus the principles. Of these 22 principles, they determined that eight principles are easy to implement in an MDE tool, while eight principles are difficult to implement in such a tool. The eight principles that receive a significant amount of citations, can be linked to an ergonomic criterion and are easy to implement in an MDE tool according to [213], are the following: "Offer informative feedback", "Strive for consistency", "Prevent errors", "Make things visible", "Structure the User's Interface", "Provide shortcuts for skilled users", "Provide good error messages" and "Provide visual cues". Since the principles are ordered by their importance, the five most important principles are Feedback, Consistency, Error Prevention, Visibility and Structure. Error Prevention is very broad and can be achieved through the implementation of other principles and is therefore not further considered independently. Visibility is a very broad principle, that can be interpreted in several different ways and is therefore replaced with the more concrete subprinciple Affordance. Affordance is defined by Norman as "fundamental properties that determine just how the thing could possibly be used" [214]. In other words, the Affordance UI Design principle ensures that the design of each feature of the UI clearly shows what the feature can be used for, at which point in the user's process. The final set of UI Design principles that is applied to the UI in this experiment thus consists of Feedback, Consistency, Affordance and Structure.

8.3.2   UI design

Since a complete modelling tool for a multi-modelling approach can become very extensive requiring multiple different views and complex backend logic, we will focus on a specific aspect that deals with the complexity of modelling the interaction between different model types. More specifically, we developed a prototype of an extension on the online Merode modelling tool.

In Chapter 5, we developed an extension to the Merode tools that allows modellers to create a bridging model that link tasks from a BPMN model (BPL) to input services (ISSL) via a mapping table. Since a single task in a business process could trigger multiple events, for multiple objects, we also included the modelling of complex input services in this extension of the tool. In order to achieve this, the extension prototype allows the modeller to import a Merode model (created in Merlin) and a BPMN model (created in Camunda). The prototype will then visualize the EDG of the Merode model. When initially developing this prototype, we focussed on the implementation of the backend logic, and not on the usability of the tool. This prototype will further be referred to as 'Interface A' and is shown in Figure 8.1.

In order to analyse the importance of the selected UI design principles, we design a new UI for the extension using Figma. This UI will further be referred to as 'Interface B' and is shown in Figure 8.2. The selected design principles are implemented in Interface B as follows: Affordance is implemented by fading out the inactive features of the tool and by reducing the number of features for the modelling of complex input services. Specifically, the "navigate to related object type" was dropped since this feature simplifies the logic to be implemented in the backend of the tool, but overcomplicates the steps that the user needs to take in order to define a complex input service. Feedback is implemented by changing the colours of the upload buttons to green after upload, and by unfading features as they become active. Figure 8.3 shows Interface B after uploading the Merode and BPMN models. Structure is implemented by grouping the features related to the same flow together (creating complex input services on the left, and uploading models and mapping the ISSL to the BPL on the right). Finally, Consistency is implemented by adding placeholders for the to-be visualized EDG and ISSL-BPL mapping table, avoiding the shifting of the UI elements as in Interface A.

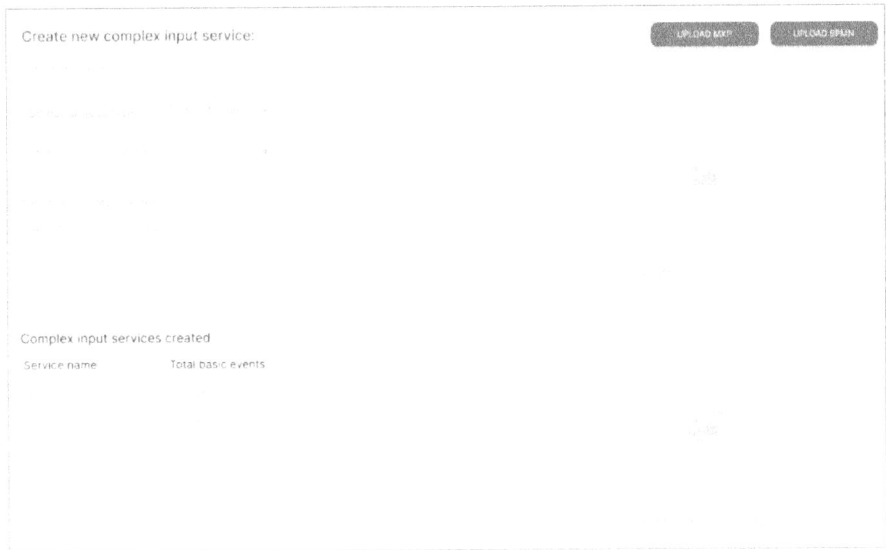

Figure 8.1 Initial layout of Interface A

Figure 8.2 Initial layout of Interface B

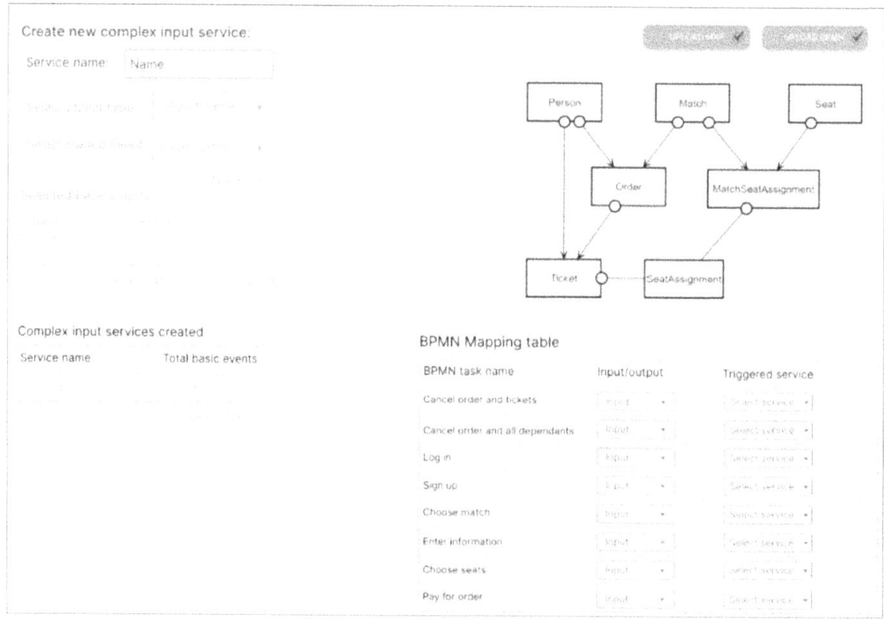

Figure 8.3 Interface B after uploading the Merode and BPMN models

8.3.3   Experiment Setup

As knowledge of the Merode Approach is essential to accurately assess the usability of both interfaces, the participants are selected from a group of students that followed the course 'Architecture and Modelling of Management Information Systems'[1] in 2021 or 2022. This course teaches the Merode Approach following the handbook 'Enterprise Information Systems Engineering' [88] and focusing on practical exercises using the existing tools. In total, 20 students participated.

Since we aim to measure the usability of the interface before and after applying design principles, we should make sure that the user experience is not affected negatively by the knowledge gaps participants have on the Merode Approach. Therefore, all participants receive a brief refresher of the main principles of Merode and their level of knowledge was verified by means of a short quiz.

Regardless of their understanding of the main concepts of the modelling approach, the participants could have varying skills when it comes to actually creating a model based on a given case description. These variations in skill should also not affect the measurements of the usability of the tool. Therefore, participants are not asked to create a Merode model themselves, but are given a completed model for a provided case description and are asked to input aspects of the model in the tool. The full case description and the corresponding model can be found in [208]. More specifically, the participants are asked to input two complex input services and map them to tasks in the BPMN model. Before getting started, the participants were asked about their first impressions after a "five second test" [215]. Throughout the experiment, participants are questioned on

---

[1] https://onderwijsaanbod.kuleuven.be/syllabi/e/D0I71AE.htm

their internal modelling process, their understanding of the interface's functionalities, any issues they might face, or which improvements to the interface they would suggest. Half of the participants (Group A) completed this task using Interface A, the other half (Group B) completed the task using Interface B.

After completing the task, the participants were asked to fill in an adapted System Usability Scale (SUS) questionnaire [216], to measure the perceived usability of the interface they used. The SUS questionnaire is a standardized form that can be used to calculate a composite measure of the overall usability of a system (the SUS score). While SUS scores lie between 0 and 100, they are not comparable to percentages because participants don't usually give extreme answers to survey questions. However, a SUS score can be transformed to a SUS norm which is a grade from A to F [217]. These norms can be used to compare the usability of both interfaces.

To measure the usability of the interface, we need to measure the effect of the UI design choices on the cognitive process of the participants. Since this is not directly observable, this effect is approximated based on several observable aspects as proposed by Rosenthal et al. [218]. The used modes of observation are the SUS questionnaire to address RQ1, and audio and screen recordings to address RQ2 and RQ3.

8.4 Results

Participants of both groups demonstrated a thorough understanding of Merode in the pre-experiment quiz (90% on average for both groups). The median for the A-participants is 94%, while the median for the B-participants is 88%. The participants with the lowest score (63%) still demonstrated a decent understanding of the basic principles of the approach. Since there is no significant difference in understanding between both groups, we can assume that any differences in perceived usability be-tween groups will not be caused by a lack of understanding of the Merode method.

8.4.1 Results for RQ1

Regarding the first impressions, there was a clear difference between the groups. A-participants mostly mentioned negative impressions such as the lack of structure (6 out of 10 participants), the unclear flow (5), and the busy look (5). While two A-participants considered the interface as structured, in contrast to their peers, all other positive impressions can be ascribed to a single A-participant. B-participants experienced fewer negative impressions and more positive impressions, however, each impression was observed with at most three of the ten B-participants. After their first impressions were recorded, all participants evaluated the structure of the inter-face on a scale from 1 (chaotic) to 5 (well-structured). Interface B (3.84) clearly yielded a higher score than Interface A (2.12), showing that the changes made with regard to the Structure Principle result in an improvement the perceived structure of the interface.

At the end of the experiment, participants were asked to rate the difficulty of the given assignments on a scale from one (effortless) to five (difficult). A-participants had a neutral experience with an average score of 3.03. They clarified that the tool requires a steep learning curve and they felt that they needed some guidance. How-ever, once they had grasped the basics of the tool, using it became easier. By contrast, the experience of B-participants seemed to be rather effortless, with an average score of 1.87. Participants were also asked to rate their general experience using the tool on a scale from one (bad) to five (good). Again, A-participants reported a rather neutral experience with an average score of 2.72. They further clarified that the structure and looks of the interface need improvement, maintaining the concerns they expressed after their first impression of the tool. B-participants reported a better overall experience with an average score of 3.65. They reported that after a certain learning curve, the tool is quite intuitive and easy to work with. Thus, the ap-plied UI Design Principles seem to have a positive impact on the overall user experience of the tool.

Finally, the results of the SUS questionnaire confirm that the combination of de-sign changes in Interface B has a major positive impact on the perceived usability of the interface, given that Interface A received an average aggregated SUS-score of 45.06 while Interface B obtained an average aggregated SUS-score of 80.28. These scores result in a SUS norm of F and A-, respectively. Since the industry considers a SUS-score of 80 or more as an indication of above-average user experience [21], the application of the four selected UI Design Principles in Interface B already results in an acceptable level of usability.

8.4.2   Results for RQ2

All distinct issues that participants ran into when interacting with both interfaces were identified. A small minority of the issues pertains to bugs that participants discovered in both interfaces. These issues were discarded from the analysis as they do not provide information on the effect of UI design choices. Each of the remaining issues was linked to the UI Design Principle that it is related to (Affordance, Feedback, Structure or Consistency). Table 8.1 summarizes the number of issues that occur per UI Design Principle for both interfaces. There were no issues related to Consistency. The improvements made to Interface B compared to Interface A, result in a strong decrease of issues related to Affordance. The decrease in issues related to Feedback is even stronger. Despite Interface B scoring higher on the structure after the first impressions, B-participants mentioned a larger number of structure issues after using the tool.

Table 8.2 visualizes the issues in interface A and B, in order of their occurrence in the modelling flow. If a certain issue can only occur in one interface, the cell of the other interface is greyed out. If a problem occurs four times or more, we consider it to be a frequent problem. Interface A had 17 distinct issues of which seven were frequent, while Interface had 15 distinct issues of which five were frequent. We will discuss the findings related to the most frequent occurring issues in the following paragraphs.

Table 8.1 Number of issues per UI Design Principle for both interfaces

	A	B	Total
Affordance	30	16	46

(continued)

Table 8.1 (*continued*)

	A	B	Total
Feedback	26	8	34
Structure	17	21	43
Total	73	45	118

The first frequent issue related to Affordance is that participants from both groups forget to upload the mxp-file and BPMN models (three A-participants and four B-participants). Putting the upload buttons on the right side of Interface B had therefore a very small negative impact on the usability. The second frequent Affordance issue only occurs for Interface A, namely that seven participants are confused by the "Navigate to related" button, not understanding what its purpose was and whether they were supposed to use it. Additionally, five A-participants did not use the button throughout the experiment. While three of these participants did not understand the button's functionality, the other two seemed to have a good understanding of the purpose of the tool. They explained that the button seemed unnecessary and that they did not feel like going through the trouble of getting to know a new functionality when they assumed they could easily perform their tasks with the other features of the tool. While this was not the intended path, Interface A indeed allows this. These two issues did not occur in Interface B, since the 'navigate to related object type' button was removed. The final two frequent issues related to Affordance relate to the "Add event" and "Add owned event" buttons. In Interface A, five participants were confused about the difference between these two buttons. On the other hand, in Interface B, five participants assumed that the "Add Event" button is a final step instead of an intermediate step. By contrast, only two A-participants encountered this issue. This is probably because the button for the final step in the flow of Interface B ('save complex input service') is still faded.

Regarding Feedback, there were two issues that were encountered by every single A-participant. On the one hand, there were no visual changes to the interface after uploading the BPMN model. This gave the impression that the model was not uploaded successfully. On the other hand, all A-participants experienced a lack of feedback when clicking the buttons 'add owned event' and 'navigate to related object type'. Therefore, they did not realize how clicking these buttons affected the next step in their modelling process. Finally, for both interfaces, the feedback upon uploading the BPMN file did not match the feedback expected by the participants: while the participants expected a visualization of the BPMN diagram, both interfaces visualize the mapping table. The inclusion of placeholders in Interface B adds to the confusion since due to the image icon and the small text inside the placeholders.

Regarding Structure, both interfaces seem to lack an intuitive starting point since three A-participants and four B-participants, tried to start creating complex input services within the mapping table. Further in the modelling process, issues related to flow mostly occurred in Group A. Nine of the ten A-participants were confused about which feature to use next at some point in the process. Only two B-participants encountered this issue. Thus, the changes made in Interface B had a major positive impact on the perceived flow. However, an issue only occurring for Interface B is that five B-participants felt they should be able to select all events simultaneously before pressing the "Add event" button. As the order of execution of the events in a complex input service should be compatible with the lifecycle definitions, this option is not viable. This indicates that the complex functionality of defining transactions constituted of a series of event invocations requires further thought to obtain an easy-to-use design.

Table 8.2 Most Frequent Recorded Usability Issues in Interface A and Interface B

	Modelling task	Issue	A	B
Affordance	upload MXP and BPMN	forgets to upload models before starting modelling process	3	4
	navigate to related	gets confused by the navigate to related object type button	7	
	navigate to related	completely ignores the navigate to related object type button	5	
	add event	does not know whether add event is an intermediary or finalizing step	2	5
	add owned event vs add event	does not intuitively understand the difference between the two options	5	
Feedback	upload BPMN	does not see any changes upon uploading BPMN	10	
	upload BPMN	expected a BPMN visualization	4	8
	both blue buttons	gets confused at the lack of feedback upon clicking the buttons	10	
	add event	wants to add multiple events at once instead of adding them one by one		5
	mapping table	tries to start the modelling process in the mapping table	3	3
	mapping table	takes a while to find complex services since they are on bottom of list		5
	general	does not know which feature to use next since the flow is unclear	9	2

8.4.3   Results for RQ3

During the experiments, participants were asked to suggest improvements to the interface. We were able to relate 64 suggestions to one of the selected UI Design Principles (see Table 8.3, left). Most of these suggestions related to Structure or Affordance. Most of these suggestions were given for Interface A. The remaining 31 suggestions were classified into the categories Cosmetic, Documentation, Functional Interaction or Model Visualization (see Table 8.3, right). The suggestions related to Model Visualization are noticeably the most frequent in this group and spread fairly equally over both interfaces. The observed frequencies of distinct suggestions (Table 8.4) are quite low. Thus, suggestions made by three or more participants are considered frequent. This results in seven frequent suggestions for Interface A and two for Interface B.

Table 8.3 Improvement suggestions related to the selected UI Design Principles

Related to selected UI Design Principles	A	B	Total	Not related to selected UI Design Principles	A	B	Total
Affordance	9	11	20	Cosmetic	3	2	5
Consistency	1	0	1	Documentation	4	1	5
Feedback	15	0	15	Functional	0	2	2
Structure	21	8	29	Interaction	1	2	3
				Model Visualization	9	8	17
Total	26	19	65	Grand Total	17	14	31

Regarding Affordance, a frequent suggestion is to give the buttons clearer labels, especially the "Add event", "Add owned event" and "Navigate to related object type" buttons. Also, in both interfaces, participants suggested the use of colour to guide the user.

Regarding Feedback, A-participants suggest a visual indication of successful uploading of the models. There were no suggestions made by B-participants regarding feedback.

Regarding Structure, four A-participants suggested that the intuitive flow should be improved by presenting the sequence of steps more clearly. Some A-participants also got confused by the placement of the "Add owned event" and "Navigate to related object type" buttons.

Table 8.4 Most frequent suggestions for improvement

	Suggestion	A	B
Affordance	Make the button names more self-explanatory	3	2
	Use colour to guide the user	2	2
Feedback	Visual indicators to show upload was successful	4	
	Visual indicators to show results of modelling actions	3	
Structure	Make the website flow structurally: clear sequence of steps to perform	4	
	Add…/Navigate… buttons next to each other with respective dropdowns close by	3	
	Provide more structure in the event list (additional dropdowns to choose subsets of events to narrow down the event list)		3
Doc.	Onboarding flow	2	1
Model Visualization	Include the BPMN diagram	3	3
	Showcase which events are part of the exported complex events (or option to do so)	3	

Of the suggestions that are not related to one of the selected UI Design Principles, three participants (two in Group A and two in Group B) suggested the inclusion of an onboarding flow. Across groups, participants also agree that the interface should visualize the uploaded BPMN diagram. They mainly requested this visualization to distinguish between tasks with similar names. Participants also suggested a way of showing the events that a complex input service consists of after it has been created as this is not yet implemented in either Interface.

Interestingly, there are three separate Model Visualization suggestions that come down to adding the OET as a model visualization. These are not pictured in Table 8.4 as they do not occur frequently as individual suggestions. This is also supported by the observation that all participants consulted the OET several times throughout the modelling process. One participant suggested that the interface should allow the modeler to decide which models to visualize, to deal with the limited space provided by a computer screen.

8.5   Discussion

Overall, the changes made in Interface B in order to apply the selected UI Design Principles significantly increased the overall usability from SUS norm F (Interface A) to SUS norm A- (Interface B). This is especially reflected in the sharp reduction in the number of issues related to the Feedback and Affordance principles in Interface B. The changes made to implement these principles therefore had a high pay-off in the overall usability of the tool. We can conclude that these principles were relatively straightforward to implement in an existing interface. The changes made to implement the Structure principle did not reduce the number of issues, but rather shifted the issues. This could be the case because the changes made for this principle were more limited that the changes for the Affordance and Feedback principle. However, we feel that this principle is still very important to consider for multi-modelling tools specifically, as multi-modelling is a very complex process that can have different starting points and flows. The structure of the modelling tool can therefore play a crucial role in the learning curve of the modeller. Our results illustrate that the Structure needs to be considered on a higher level than simply grouping features related to the same flow. The results suggest that the structure of a multi-modelling tool should guide the user through these flows with additional visual indicators like colours and dividers. An onboarding flow, as suggested by our participants, could also help with this. Implementing Consistency seems less important as it did not generate any issues or any frequent suggestions. Therefore, both interfaces can be considered to have good Consistency.

The results of RQ3 show that the selected UI Design principles are not sufficient for multi-modelling tools; the UI designer should pay special attention to Model Visualizations, which is reflected in the suggestions of our participants. We propose "Complete and Flexible Model Visualizations" as a new UI Design Principle specifically for multi-modelling tools. The modeler should be able to choose which models they visualize while using the multi-modelling tool.

A first limitation of this study is that only a reduced set of four principles is investigated. However, this ensures that the measured increase in usability can be ascribed to these four principles, and especially the Feedback and Affordance principles. Additionally, all encountered issues and the majority of the participants' suggestions could be mapped on these principles. A second limitation is that, despite the high scores on the Merode knowledge quiz, some participants seemed to have some gaps in their recollection of the Merode approach while modelling. However, a good multi-modelling tool should be able to guide this type of modeler as well. Additionally, we gave some extra explanations where necessary to avoid a large negative impact of the lack of knowledge on the evaluation of the usability of the tool. A third limitation is that both interfaces were implemented differently; Interface A as an online tool and Interface B as a Figma prototype. Therefore, Interface B had limited functionality compared to Interface A. This was mediated by always asking the participants upfront which action they wanted to perform next. This way, we were able to deduce our results from their intended solution path, rather than the solution path dictated by the Interface. Finally, four participants had less time to finish the experiment. For these participants, we dropped a repeat task to make sure they still experienced all aspects of the tool. However, this also means that they are slightly less familiar with the Interface. Since the SUS norms for both interfaces are so different, we don't believe this had a major impact on the results.

8.6 Conclusion

In conclusion, the application of the UI Design principles Feedback and Affordance have a major impact on the usability of a multi-modelling tool that allows modellers to define the interactions between different model types. Structure can also be considered as an important principle for these tools, but requires further research. Additionally, we propose a new principle specifically for multi-modelling tools called "Complete and Flexible Model Visualizations" as it is important that modellers can visualize the models relevant to their current modelling task.

Part V
Epilogue

Chapter 9
Conclusions & Future work

9.1 Summary & Conclusions

This dissertation aimed to advancing multi-modelling in MDE for integrated domain and business process modelling by proposing an integration of Merode, a domain modelling approach, and BPMN, a business process modelling language. More specifically, the three research objectives were formulated as formalizing the abstract syntax (RO1), the concrete syntax (RO2) and the semantics (RO3) of the integration between Merode and BPMN.

The dissertation followed a design science approach. First, the problem was identified and motivated in Part II of the dissertation with an in-dept look at the domains of MDE and multi-perspective modelling, and the challenges that practitioners and students face in these domains. The problem was approached from two sides: the knowledge base (existing literature) and the environment (empirical research). The knowledge base consists of a literature review on the use of model-driven engineering by practitioners. The general challenge that was found in this literature review is the integration of modelling languages and tools for multi-perspective modelling. Researching the environment was conducted by means of two case studies on students' understanding of multi-perspective modelling. The main findings were that students often struggle with the creation of multiple models for the same case description, but students who have a good understanding of multi-perspective modelling (in this case data and process modelling) seemed to produce models of higher quality. This shows that overcoming the problems of multi-modelling is feasible, provided good support and training are provided.

Part III presented and demonstrated the designed artefacts. In this part, RO1 was addressed by the development of an integrated MERODExBPMN meta-model that represents the abstract syntax. RO2 and RO3 were addressed jointly with a proof of concept for the integration of the concrete syntax and semantics. The missing components and possible sources for filling the gaps were identified and addressed. The use of these artefacts was demonstrated by defining a common terminology for object-centric event logging and data-centric process modelling.

Part IV presented the final part of the design science approach: the evaluation. First, an evaluation framework for multi-perspective modelling approaches was developed. The framework was applied to the Merode approach as documented in [88] and on the artefacts presented in part III, showing that the coverage of evaluation criteria for the Merode approach has improved by including these artefacts. While concrete evaluation criteria have already been defined for many parts of the framework, some of them still lack criteria. The last part of the thesis addresses one of these gaps by identifying criteria

C. Verbruggen, *Advancing Multi-modelling in MDE for Integrated Domain and Business Process Modelling*, Lecture Notes in Business Information Processing 576, https://doi.org/10.1007/978-3-032-13876-7_9

and evaluating the usability of the tool support that was developed as part of the artefacts with students.

9.2 Lessons learned for adapting multi-perspective modelling approaches for code generation

While this dissertation focused specifically on the integration of Merode and BPMN from Part IV onwards, we can deduce some general lessons learned for the integration of modelling languages/approaches for the purpose of MDE and code generation.

The first lesson concerns the selection of modelling languages/approaches. If custom integration of separate modelling languages is required to address a modelling need, the first step should be to identify modelling languages that cover the required perspectives as much as possible. The TEC-MAP framework presented in Chapter 7 can be used as a tool for this step. The modeler can identify which dimensions of the TEC-MAP framework are relevant to their project, and select the criteria that address these dimensions. These criteria can then be used for the comparison of candidate modelling languages.

Once candidate modelling languages have been identified, their compatibility should be analysed. The second lesson learned from this dissertation is that determining the compatibility of modelling languages is a task that should be executed carefully. Different modelling languages might use the same or similar terms, while the underlying concepts can be different. Therefore, this analysis should always be done based on the semantic definitions of the concepts of a modelling language, rather than using the terms as is. An example is the slight difference in the semantic definitions of a service in the OO-method and an information system service in the Merode approach. This lesson goes further than only the comparison of modelling languages. We also encountered the challenge of terminology alignment between two different research domains in Chapter 6. The alignment of the domains seemed straight-forward at first, given that 'events' are core concepts in both domains, but proved to be rather complex as they capture different semantics in each domain.

The integration between Merode and BPMN in this dissertation can be taken as a starting point for the integration of other domain modelling and process modelling approaches, by mapping the domain modelling approach on Merode. If the constructs of the chosen process modelling approach have similar properties to BPMN (i.e. tasks/activities trigger events), the chosen process modelling approach can be mapped on BPMN. Otherwise, we recommend repeating the process described in this dissertation to plug the process modelling languages into the Business Process Layer of Merode.

9.3 Limitations

The research developed in this thesis also presents some limitations. The first limitation is that the artefacts presented in Chapter 5, are a proof of concept to demonstrate the feasibility of complete the integration of Merode and BPMN. However, a fully formalized definition and proof of completeness is still missing. This is considered future work.

A second limiation is that the work is focused on automated processes, and that human processes, knowledge intensive processes and cross-system processes are not yet addressed. For human processes (meaning processes that are executed outside the context of an information system), the formal integration of the domain and process models is less essential. Humans will be able to complete a process even if instructions are given in a more informal manner. This is not the case for automated processes. For knowledge intensive processes, declarative process modelling languages are the better choice, meaning that the results of this dissertation need to be generalized as described in the previous section. Regarding cross-system processes, the layered architecture of Merode mostly supports this. Processes on different systems can each interact with the enterprise layer on a shared server. In that case, the FSMs in the shared Merode model should support all the different processes. The event handler will ensure that events are only invoked when allowed by the shared Merode model. The feasibility of this setup is demonstrated in [219], where Merode is used to setup cross-organisational processes with Blockchain. Of course, some implementation concerns specific to cross-system processes need to be considered, such as synchronous and asynchronous executions.

The third limitation is the choice for BPMN, as it has several drawbacks. BPMN is a very complex language and does not score well on the principles of Physics of Notations [31]. However, this is one of the pragmatic choices made in this dissertation, given that it is very well known by practitioners, researchers and students. To manage complexity, we focused on a set of core symbols in this dissertation, both in the experiments with students as in the integration with Merode.

A final reflection is that the research goal set a the beginning of this research project (i.e. advancing the adoption of MDE in industry through the integration of domain and process modelling), might no longer be perceived as necessary due to the arrival of LLMs. Nowadays, citizen developers can easily ask an LLM to generate code based on their requirements. However, we want to argue that full understanding of the logic to be captured by the code is still required to accurately describe the requirements for the system under design and for thouroughly testing the generated solutions. The exercise of creating a model for a system is still just as relevant, as the models represent this logic without writing code (models-as-code). Thus the need for the integration of modelling languages across different viewpoints of a system is still present and may even grow in relative importance compared to the need for understanding code or programming capabililties.

9.4   Future work

The main task for future work is the complete formalization of the integration and the implementation of a modelling and code generation tool for the elements proposed in this dissertation. While the prototype already demonstrated some functionalities, a complete implementation will allow empirical tests of the usability of the integration proposed in this dissertation, next to the theoretical evaluation presented in Chapter 10.

Another aspect that could be researched further is the understanding that students have of multi-perspective modelling when they have only been taught modelling lan-guages in isolation. The studies presented in Part II provide insights in the issues students might face and potential causes of these issues, but further research could investigate how multi-perspective modelling should be incorporated in modelling courses to mitigate these issues. Having a completely implemented tool as described above can be an aid in this research.

Another different research topic for future work could be the role LLMs play in the design process of an information system. Transformations from model to code via templates are more and more replaced by code generated by LLM based on textual descriptions. However, in section 3.4, we observed a strong difference in how students model two very similar requirements that were worded differently. It would be interesting to investigate how the wording of requirements affects the end result of the generated code, and how this differs between humans and LLM.

Finally, it would be interesting to research how it can be leveraged for the creation of organisational digital twins of businesses. As the data and process perspectives are the key perspectives of organisations, once the extensions to the modelling and code generation tools have been fully implemented, it will be possible to genertate applications that can be used as digital twins. Digital twins provide a virtual representation of the company and can be used to estimate the usefulness of applying certain advanced data analysis techniques, as well as their costs and required inputs by means of simulation. Companies that want to apply these techniques to obtain a competitive advantage, often lack the required volumes of data for these techniques. This could be due to the specific design and implementation of their information systems, or due to privacy regulations that restrict the use of customer data. The prototypes generated with Merode and BPMN can serve to simulate artificial data that is representative of reality.

Appendix A. Case Description and Model Solution for the Experiment in Section 3.3

Case Description

The KU Leuven wants to develop a web application for the recruitment of new PhD candidates. In this exercise, you will model the part of the system that deals with entering and reviewing new applications. The creation of a new vacancy and deciding which candidate to hire are out of scope for this exercise. The requirements are stated below:

In order to apply for a job vacancy, candidates have to fill in a form where they specify their personal information (name, surname, e-mail address, birthday, nationality) and they upload their grades transcript and motivation letter. The application can be saved and submitted when the applicant is ready. The application should be submitted before the deadline specified in the vacancy. Once the application is submitted, the HR department is notified and the application is assigned to an HR officer. After submission, the candidate can no longer make changes to the application.

The HR department will then make a first assessment of the application. They decide whether or not an application is eligible based on the obtained degree, grades transcript, university ranking, language certificates, and GMAT or GRE-score. If an application is ineligible, the candidate is immediately rejected. If an application is eligible, it must be reviewed by several people. First, international candidates will be reviewed by the international office. Once the international office has written a review, the HR department will then contact three professors with the request to write a review of the application. All reviews, both from the international office and from professors, should be filed within four weeks of being requested. Each review concludes with a proposal for the next step in the recruitment process: rejection, or an interview. When the deadline of the vacancy is passed, the HR office will decide which candidates to invite for an interview based on the reviews. Once a date has been set, interviews are registered in the system. The interviewers will fill in a form with their comments & conclusions.

Model Solution

The model solution consists of a UML class diagram (Fig. A.1) and a BPMN process model (Fig. A.2).

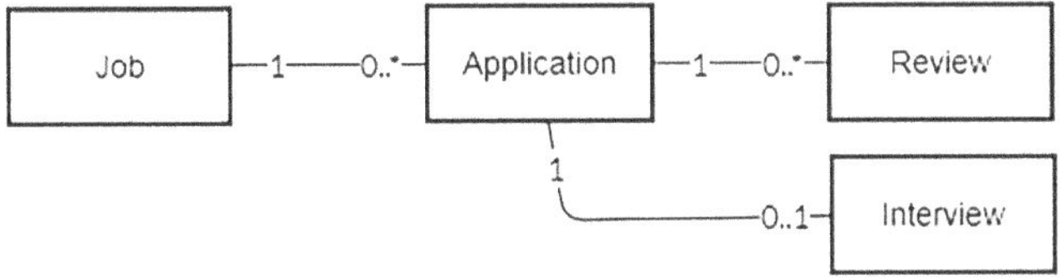

Figure A.1 UML class diagram - model solution

C. Verbruggen, *Advancing Multi-modelling in MDE for Integrated Domain and Business Process Modelling*, Lecture Notes in Business Information Processing 576,
https://doi.org/10.1007/978-3-032-13876-7

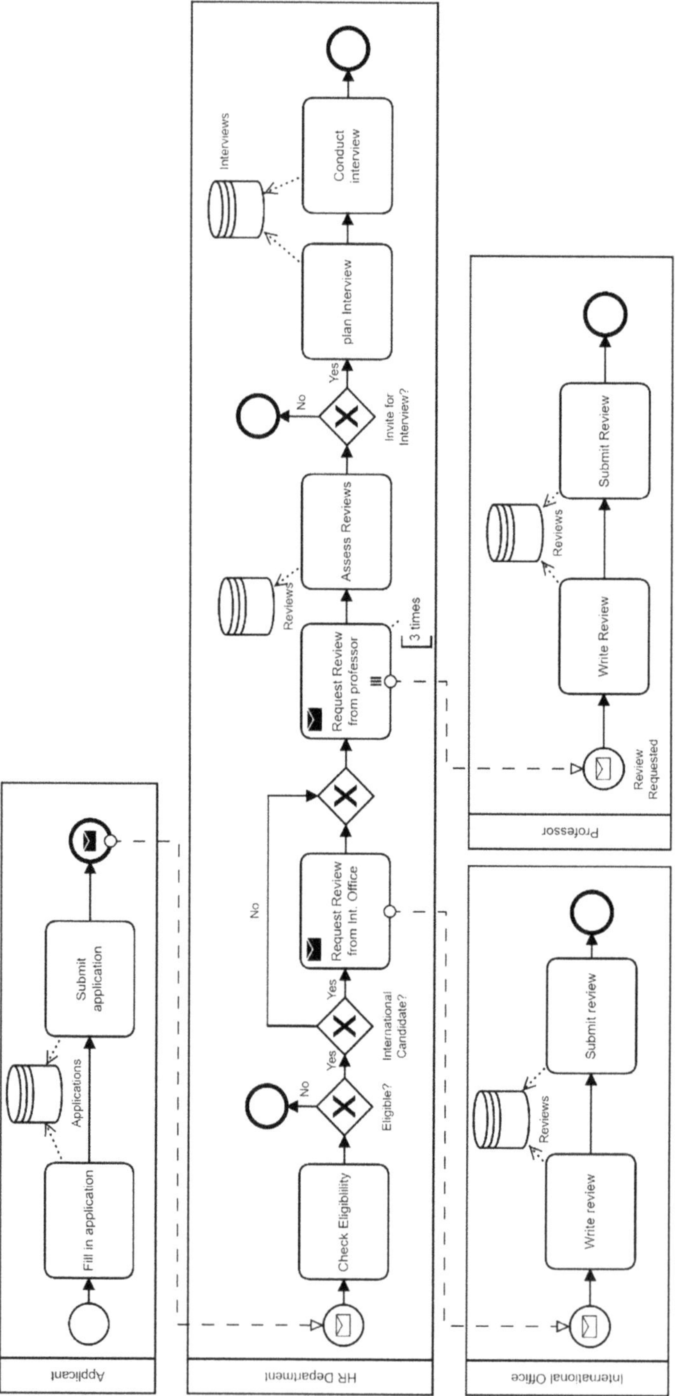

Figure A.2 BPMN process model - model solution

Appendix B. Complete error typology for Section 3.4

See Table B.1.

C. Verbruggen, *Advancing Multi-modelling in MDE for Integrated Domain
and Business Process Modelling*, Lecture Notes in Business Information Processing 576,
https://doi.org/10.1007/978-3-032-13876-7

Table B.1. Complete error typology for section 3.4

| CONCEPT | ERROR TYPES | UML CLASS DIAGRAM ERRORS | | BPMN PROCESS MODEL ERRORS | |
		CLASS ERRORS	ASSOCIATION ERRORS	TASK ERRORS	FLOW ERRORS
Syntactic quality	**Morphological errors**	Morphological error			
	Syntactic incompleteness	Missing class name	Missing association name	Missing task name	Missing start/end event
		Missing attribute name	Missing multiplicities		Missing gateway conditions
		Missing attribute data type			
Semantic quality	**Invalidity**	Superfluous class	Superfluous association	Superfluous task	Superfluous sequence flow
		Superfluous(/duplicate) attribute	Wrong multiplicity		Superfluous gateway
		Attribute in wrong class			Wrong gateway / gateways do not come in split-merge pairs of equal types
		Wrong attribute data type			Wrongly linked sequence flow
		Name-concept mismatch			Wrong gateway conditions
		Unnecessary reification			
			Role inversion		
			Wrongly linked association		
	Incompleteness	Missing class	Missing association	Missing task	Missing sequence flow
		Missing attribute			Missing gateway
Pragmatic quality	**Incomprehension**	No meaningful name for class	No meaningful name for association	No meaningful name for task	Implicit gateways
		No meaningful name for attribute			Split and merge in a single gateway
					Assign task to a different actor

Appendix C. Case Description for the Experiment in Section 3.4

The university wants to develop a web application for the recruitment of new PhD candidates. In this exercise, you will **model the part of the system that supports the HR department for reviewing applications**. *The creation of a new vacancy (= job for which candidates can apply), candidates filling in their applications and deciding which candidate to hire are out of scope for this exercise. The requirements are stated below:*

Each vacancy in the system contains information on its project title, project description, and application deadline. In order to apply for a job vacancy, candidates have to fill in an application where they specify their personal information (name, surname, e-mail address, birthday, nationality, degree, grades transcript and motivation letter). Once the application deadline has passed, the HR department starts reviewing each application. The HR department will make a first assessment of the application. They decide whether or not an application is eligible based on the obtained degree, grades transcript, university ranking, language certificates, and GMAT or GRE-score. If an application is ineligible, the candidate is immediately rejected. If an application is eligible, it must be reviewed by several people. If the candidate is international, they will first be reviewed by the international office. Once the international office has written a review, the HR department will then contact a professor with the request to write a review of the application. Professors can either accept or reject writing a review. If a professor rejects writing the review, the HR department will contact another professor, until one professor agrees to write the review. Each review concludes with a proposal for the next step in the recruitment process: rejection, or an interview. Based on the reviews, the HR office will decide to invite the candidate for an interview or to reject the candidate. If a candidate is invited for an interview, the interview and its date are registered in the system. The interviewers will add their comments and conclusions to the record of the interview.

C. Verbruggen, *Advancing Multi-modelling in MDE for Integrated Domain
and Business Process Modelling*, Lecture Notes in Business Information Processing 576,
https://doi.org/10.1007/978-3-032-13876-7

List of Figures

(*continued*)

© The Editor(s) (if applicable) and The Author(s), under exclusive license to Springer Nature Switzerland AG 2026
C. Verbruggen, *Advancing Multi-modelling in MDE for Integrated Domain and Business Process Modelling*, Lecture Notes in Business Information Processing 576, https://doi.org/10.1007/978-3-032-13876-7

(continued)

(continued)

(*continued*)

List of Tables

(continued)

© The Editor(s) (if applicable) and The Author(s), under exclusive license
to Springer Nature Switzerland AG 2026
C. Verbruggen, *Advancing Multi-modelling in MDE for Integrated Domain
and Business Process Modelling*, Lecture Notes in Business Information Processing 576,
https://doi.org/10.1007/978-3-032-13876-7

(continued)

Bibliography

1. R. Soley, "Model Driven Architecture," *OMG white paper*, Art. no. 308, 2000.
2. A. Bucchiarone, J. Cabot, R. F. Paige, and A. Pierantonio, "Grand challenges in model-driven engineering: an analysis of the state of the research," *Softw Syst Model*, vol. 19, no. 1, pp. 5–13, Jan. 2020, https://doi.org/10.1007/S10270-019-00773-6.
3. G. Liebel *et al.*, "Human factors in model-driven engineering: future research goals and initiatives for MDE," *Softw Syst Model*, 2024, https://doi.org/10.1007/s10270-024-01188-8.
4. M. Erwig, "Abstract Syntax and Semantics of Visual Languages," *J Vis Lang Comput*, vol. 9, no. 5, pp. 461–483, 1998, https://doi.org/10.1006/jvlc.1998.0098.
5. F. Fondement and T. Baar, "Making Metamodels Aware of Concrete Syntax," in *European Conference on Model Driven Architecture-Foundations and Applications*, 2005, pp. 190–204.
6. D. Bork and H.-G. Fill, "Formal Aspects of Enterprise Modeling Methods: A Comparison Framework," in *2014 47th Hawaii International Conference on System Sciences*, 2014, pp. 3400–3409. https://doi.org/10.1109/HICSS.2014.422.
7. OMG, *Business Process Model and Notation (BPMN), Version 2.0.2.* 2013.
8. D. van der Linden, I. Hadar, and A. Zamansky, "What practitioners really want: requirements for visual notations in conceptual modeling," *Softw Syst Model*, vol. 18, no. 3, pp. 1813–1831, Jun. 2019, https://doi.org/10.1007/s10270-018-0667-4.
9. K. Peffers, T. Tuunanen, M. A. Rothenberger, and S. Chatterjee, "A design science research methodology for information systems research," *Journal of Management Information Systems*, vol. 24, no. 3, pp. 45–77, Dec. 2007, https://doi.org/10.2753/MIS0742-1222240302.
10. A. R. Hevner, S. T. March, J. Park, and S. Ram, "Design science in information systems research," *MIS Q*, vol. 28, no. 1, 2004, https://doi.org/10.2307/25148625.
11. C. Verbruggen and M. Snoeck, *Model-Driven Engineering: A State of Affairs and Research Agenda*, vol. 421. 2021. https://doi.org/10.1007/978-3-030-79186-5_22.
12. C. Verbruggen and M. Snoeck, "Practitioners' experiences with model-driven engineering: a meta-review," *Softw Syst Model*, vol. 22, no. 1, pp. 111–129, 2023, https://doi.org/10.1007/s10270-022-01020-1.
13. O. Badreddin, R. Khandoker, A. Forward, O. Masmali, and T. C. Lethbridge, "A decade of software design and modeling: A survey to uncover trends of the practice," in *Proceedings - 21st ACM/IEEE International Conference on Model Driven Engineering Languages and Systems, MODELS 2018*, Association for Computing Machinery, Inc, Oct. 2018, pp. 245–256. https://doi.org/10.1145/3239372.3239389.
14. T. Ho-Quang, R. Hebig, G. Robles, M. R. V. Chaudron, and M. A. Fernandez, "Practices and perceptions of UML use in open source projects," in *Proceedings - 2017 IEEE/ACM 39th International Conference on Software Engineering: Software Engineering in Practice Track, ICSE-SEIP 2017*, Institute of Electrical and Electronics Engineers Inc., Jun. 2017, pp. 203–212. https://doi.org/10.1109/ICSE-SEIP.2017.28.
15. S. Group, "Chaos Reports." Accessed: Jan. 17, 2021. [Online]. Available: https://www.standishgroup.com/chaosReport/index
16. D. Jackson, *The Essence of Software: Why Concepts Matter for Great Design.* Princeton University Press, 2021. [Online]. Available: https://press.princeton.edu/books/hardcover/9780691225388/the-essence-of-software

C. Verbruggen, *Advancing Multi-modelling in MDE for Integrated Domain
and Business Process Modelling*, Lecture Notes in Business Information Processing 576,
https://doi.org/10.1007/978-3-032-13876-7

17. M. Grossman, J. E. Aronson, and R. V. McCarthy, "Does UML make the grade? Insights from the software development community," *Inf Softw Technol*, vol. 47, no. 6, pp. 383–397, Apr. 2005, https://doi.org/10.1016/J.INFSOF.2004.09.005.

18. M. Fowler, *UML distilled: a brief guide to the standard object modeling language*. Addison-Wesley Professional, 2004.

19. B. Dobing and J. Parsons, "Dimensions of UML diagram use: A survey of practitioners," *Journal of Database Management*, vol. 19, no. 1, pp. 1–18, 2008, https://doi.org/10.4018/JDM.2008010101.

20. A. Nugroho and M. R. V. Chaudron, "A Survey into the Rigor of UML Use and its Perceived Impact on Quality and Productivity," in *Proceedings of the Second ACM-IEEE International Symposium on Empirical Software Engineering and Measurement*, in ESEM '08. ACM, 2008, pp. 90–99. Accessed: Sep. 17, 2021. [Online]. Available: http://doi.acm.org/https://doi.org/10.1145/3247190

21. M. Petre, "'No shit' or 'Oh, shit!': responses to observations on the use of UML in professional practice," *Softw Syst Model*, vol. 13, no. 4, pp. 1225–1235, Oct. 2014, https://doi.org/10.1007/s10270-014-0430-4.

22. P. Fettke, "How Conceptual Modeling Is Used," *COMMUNICATIONS OF THE ASSOCIATION FOR INFORMATION SYSTEMS*, vol. 25, pp. 571–592, 2009, Accessed: Sep. 17, 2021. [Online]. Available: https://www.webofscience.com/wos/alldb/full-record/WOS:000414839300043

23. I. Malavolta, P. Lago, H. Muccini, P. Pelliccione, and A. Tang, "What industry needs from architectural languages: A survey," *IEEE Transactions on Software Engineering*, vol. 39, no. 6, pp. 869–891, 2013, https://doi.org/10.1109/TSE.2012.74.

24. J. Whittle, J. Hutchinson, M. Rouncefield, H. Burden, and R. Heldal, "A taxonomy of tool-related issues affecting the adoption of model-driven engineering," *Softw Syst Model*, vol. 16, no. 2, pp. 313–331, May 2017, https://doi.org/10.1007/S10270-015-0487-8.

25. B. Selic, "The Theory and Practice of Modeling Language Design for Model-Based Software Engineering-A Personal Perspective," in *Lecture Notes in Computer Science (including subseries Lecture Notes in Artificial Intelligence and Lecture Notes in Bioinformatics)*, 2011, pp. 222–289.

26. B. Selic, "What will it take? A view on adoption of model-based methods in practice," *Softw Syst Model*, vol. 11, no. 4, pp. 513–526, Oct. 2012, https://doi.org/10.1007/S10270-012-0261-0.

27. Y. Zheng and R. N. Taylor, "A classification and rationalization of model-based software development," *Softw Syst Model*, vol. 12, no. 4, pp. 669–678, Oct. 2013, https://doi.org/10.1007/S10270-013-0355-3.

28. F. D. Giraldo, S. España, W. J. Giraldo, and O. Pastor, "Modelling language quality evaluation in model-driven information systems engineering: A roadmap," in *International Conference on Research Challenges in Information Science*, C. Rolland, D. Anagnostopoulos, P. Loucopoulos, and C. Gonzales-Perez, Eds., Athens, Greece: IEEE Computer Society, May 2015, pp. 64–69.

29. D. Dermeval *et al.*, "Applications of ontologies in requirements engineering: a systematic review of the literature," *Requir Eng*, vol. 21, no. 4, pp. 405–437, Nov. 2016, https://doi.org/10.1007/s00766-015-0222-6.

30. A. Wortmann, O. Barais, B. Combemale, and M. Wimmer, "Modeling languages in Industry 4.0: an extended systematic mapping study," *Softw Syst Model*, vol. 19, no. 1, pp. 67–94, Jan. 2020, https://doi.org/10.1007/S10270-019-00757-6.

31. D. Moody, "The physics of notations: Toward a scientific basis for constructing visual notations in software engineering," *IEEE Transactions on Software Engineering*, vol. 35, no. 6, 2009, https://doi.org/10.1109/TSE.2009.67.

32. S. Kitchenham, B. and Charters, "Guidelines for performing systematic literature reviews in software engineering," *Technical report, Ver. 2.3 EBSE Technical Report. EBSE*, vol. EBSE-2007-, no. School of Computer Science and Mathematics, p. 65, 2007, [Online]. Available: https://www.elsevier.com/__data/promis_misc/525444systematicreviewsguide.pdf

33. S. Baltes and S. Diehl, "Sketches and diagrams in practice," in *Proceedings of the ACM SIGSOFT Symposium on the Foundations of Software Engineering*, Association for Computing Machinery, Nov. 2014, pp. 530–541. https://doi.org/10.1145/2635868.2635891.

34. M. Ozkaya and F. Erata, "A survey on the practical use of UML for different software architecture viewpoints," *Inf Softw Technol*, vol. 121, May 2020, https://doi.org/10.1016/j.infsof.2020.106275.

35. O. Badreddin, K. Rahad, A. Forward, and T. Lethbridge, "The Evolution of Software Design Practices Over a Decade: A Long Term Study of Practitioners," *Journal of Object Technology*, vol. 20, no. 2, pp. 1:1-19, 2021, https://doi.org/10.5381/jot.2021.20.2.a1.

36. I. Routis, C. Bardaki, G. Dede, M. Nikolaidou, T. Kamalakis, and D. Anagnostopoulos, "CMMN evaluation: the modelers' perceptions of the main notation elements," *Softw Syst Model*, 2021, https://doi.org/10.1007/s10270-021-00880-3.

37. A. Albaghajati and J. Hassine, "A use case driven approach to game modeling," *Requir Eng*, 2021, https://doi.org/10.1007/s00766-021-00362-4.

38. M. Ozkaya, "Do the informal & formal software modeling notations satisfy practitioners for software architecture modeling?," *Inf Softw Technol*, vol. 95, pp. 15–33, Mar. 2018, https://doi.org/10.1016/j.infsof.2017.10.008.

39. G. Liebel, N. Marko, M. Tichy, A. Leitner, and J. Hansson, "Model-based engineering in the embedded systems domain: an industrial survey on the state-of-practice," *Softw Syst Model*, vol. 17, no. 1, pp. 91–113, Feb. 2018, https://doi.org/10.1007/s10270-016-0523-3.

40. M. Ozkaya, "What is software architecture to practitioners: A survey," in *MODELSWARD 2016 - Proceedings of the 4th International Conference on Model-Driven Engineering and Software Development*, SciTePress, 2016, pp. 677–686. https://doi.org/10.5220/0005826006770686.

41. F. Saleh and M. El-Attar, "A scientific evaluation of the misuse case diagrams visual syntax," *Inf Softw Technol*, vol. 66, pp. 73–96, Oct. 2015, https://doi.org/10.1016/j.infsof.2015.05.002.

42. T. Huldt and I. Stenius, "State-of-practice survey of model-based systems engineering," *Systems Engineering*, vol. 22, no. 2, pp. 134–145, Mar. 2019, https://doi.org/10.1002/sys.21466.

43. D. Akdur, V. Garousi, and O. Demirörs, "A survey on modeling and model-driven engineering practices in the embedded software industry," *Journal of Systems Architecture*, vol. 91, pp. 62–82, Nov. 2018, https://doi.org/10.1016/j.sysarc.2018.09.007.

44. K. Farias, L. Gonçales, V. Bischoff, B. Da Silval, E. Guimarães, and J. Nogle, "On the UML use in the brazilian industry: A state of the practice survey," in *Proceedings of the International Conference on Software Engineering and Knowledge Engineering, SEKE*, Knowledge Systems Institute Graduate School, 2018, pp. 372–375. https://doi.org/10.18293/SEKE2018-183.

45. H. Störrle, "How are conceptual models used in industrial software development? A descriptive survey," in *ACM International Conference Proceeding Series*, Association for Computing Machinery, Jun. 2017, pp. 160–169. https://doi.org/10.1145/3084226.3084256.

46. A. M. Fernández-Sáez, D. Caivano, M. Genero, and M. R. V. Chaudron, "On the Use of UML Documentation in Software Maintenance: Results from a Survey in Industry," in *MODELS*, Ottawa, ON, Canada, 2015, pp. 292–301.

47. C. Monsalve, A. April, and A. Abran, "Business Process Modeling with Levels of Abstraction," in *IEEE COLCOM*, 2015.

48. M. Ozkaya, "Are the UML modelling tools powerful enough for practitioners? A literature review," Oct. 01, 2019, *Institution of Engineering and Technology*. https://doi.org/10.1049/iet-sen.2018.5409.

49. A. Awadid, S. Nurcan, and S. Ayachi Ghannouchi, "On leveraging the fruits of research efforts in the arena of business process modeling formalisms: a map-driven approach for decision making," *Softw Syst Model*, vol. 18, no. 3, pp. 1905–1930, Jun. 2019, https://doi.org/10.1007/s10270-018-0689-y.

50. M. Ozkaya, "The analysis of architectural languages for the needs of practitioners," *Softw Pract Exp*, vol. 48, no. 5, pp. 985–1018, May 2018, https://doi.org/10.1002/spe.2561.

51. M. Kocbek, G. Jošt, M. Heričko, and G. Polančič, "Business process model and notation: The current state of affairs," *Computer Science and Information Systems*, vol. 12, no. 2, pp. 509–539, Jul. 2015, https://doi.org/10.2298/CSIS140610006K.

52. N. Rozanski and E. Woods, "Software Systems Architecture." Accessed: Mar. 16, 2021. [Online]. Available: https://www.viewpoints-and-perspectives.info/home/viewpoints/

53. P. Kruchten, *The Rational Unified Process: An Introduction*, 3rd ed. Addison-Wesley, 2000.

54. K. Pohl, *The Requirements Engineering Framework*. Berlin, Heidelberg: Springer Berlin Heidelberg, 2010. https://doi.org/10.1007/978-3-642-12578-2_4.

55. K. Pohl, "The three dimensions of requirements engineering: A framework and its applications," *Inf Syst*, vol. 19, no. 3, pp. 243–258, 1994, https://doi.org/10.1016/0306-4379(94)900 44-2.

56. F. Härer and H.-G. Fill, "Past Trends and Future Prospects in Conceptual Modeling - A Bibliometric Analysis," in *Conceptual Modeling*, G. Dobbie, U. Frank, G. Kappel, S. W. Liddle, and H. C. Mayr, Eds., Cham: Springer International Publishing, 2020, pp. 34–47.

57. P. Lago, I. Malavolta, H. Muccini, P. Pelliccione, and A. Tang, "The Road Ahead for Architectural Languages," *IEEE Softw*, vol. 32, no. 1, pp. 98–105, 2015.

58. D. Naranjo, M. Sánchez, and J. Villalobos, "Evaluating the capabilities of Enterprise Architecture modeling tools for Visual Analysis," *Journal of Object Technology*, vol. 14, no. 1, pp. 3:1-32, Apr. 2015, https://doi.org/10.5381/jot.2015.14.1.a3.

59. P. Pourali and J. M. Atlee, "An Empirical Investigation to Understand the Difficulties and Challenges of Software Modellers When Using Modelling Tools," in *Proceedings of the 21th ACM/IEEE International Conference on Model Driven Engineering Languages and Systems*, in MODELS '18. New York, NY, USA: Association for Computing Machinery, 2018, pp. 224–234. https://doi.org/10.1145/3239372.3239400.

60. P. Pourali and J. M. Atlee, "UCAnDoModels: A Context-Based Model Editor for Editing and Debugging UML Class and State-Machine Diagrams," in *2019 ACM/IEEE 22nd International Conference on Model Driven Engineering Languages and Systems Companion (MODELS-C)*, 2019, pp. 779–783. https://doi.org/10.1109/MODELS-C.2019.00122.

61. P. Pourali and J. M. Atlee, "A Focus+Context Approach to Alleviate Cognitive Challenges of Editing and Debugging UML Models," in *2019 ACM/IEEE 22nd International Conference on Model Driven Engineering Languages and Systems (MODELS)*, 2019, pp. 183–193. https://doi.org/10.1109/MODELS.2019.000-3.

62. D. Bork, D. Karagiannis, and B. Pittl, "Systematic Analysis and Evaluation of Visual Conceptual Modeling Language Notations," in *12th International Conference on Research Challenges in Information Science (RCIS)*, Nantes, FRANCE: IEEE, 2018.

63. S. Liaskos, J. Mylopoulos, and S. M. Khan, "Empirically Evaluating the Semantic Qualities of Language Vocabularies," in *Conceptual Modeling*, A. Ghose, J. Horkoff, V. E. Silva Souza, J. Parsons, and J. Evermann, Eds., Cham: Springer International Publishing, 2021, pp. 330–344.

64. D. Bork and B. Roelens, "A technique for evaluating and improving the semantic transparency of modeling language notations," *Softw Syst Model*, vol. 20, no. 4, pp. 939–963, 2021, https://doi.org/10.1007/s10270-021-00895-w.

65. J. Ruiz, E. S. Asensio, and M. Snoeck, "Learning UI Functional Design Principles Through Simulation With Feedback," *IEEE Transactions on Learning Technologies*, vol. 13, no. 4, pp. 833–846, 2020, https://doi.org/10.1109/TLT.2020.3028596.

66. G. Sedrakyan, M. Snoeck, and S. Poelmans, "Assessing the effectiveness of feedback enabled simulation in teaching conceptual modeling," *Comput Educ*, vol. 78, pp. 367–382, 2014, https://doi.org/10.1016/j.compedu.2014.06.014.

67. D. Bogdanova and M. Snoeck, "Learning from Errors: Error-based Exercises in Domain Modelling Pedagogy," in *The Practice of Enterprise Modeling*, R. A. Buchmann, D. Karagiannis, and M. Kirikova, Eds., Cham: Springer International Publishing, 2018, pp. 321–334.

68. D. Bogdanova and M. Snoeck, "CaMeLOT: An educational framework for conceptual data modelling," *International Journal of Applied Earth Observation and Geoinformation*, 2019, https://doi.org/10.1016/j.infsof.2019.02.006.

69. C. Soyka, M. Striewe, M. Ullrich, and N. Schaper, "Comparison of required competences and task material in modeling education," *Enterprise Modelling and Information Systems Architectures (EMISAJ)*, vol. 18, pp. 1–7, 2023.

70. K. Rosenthal, B. Ternes, and S. Strecker, "Learning Conceptual Modeling: Structuring Overview, Research Themes And Paths For Future Research," in *Proceedings of the 27th European Conference on Information Systems (ECIS)*, Jun. 2019. [Online]. Available: https://aisel.aisnet.org/ecis2019_rp/137

71. K. Rosenthal and S. Strecker, "Toward a Taxonomy of Modeling Difficulties: A Multi-Modal Study on Individual Modeling Processes," in *ICIS 2019 Proceedings*, 2019.

72. K. Rosenthal, S. Strecker, and O. Pastor, "Modeling Difficulties in Data Modeling: Similarities and Differences Between Experienced and Non-experienced Modelers," *Lecture Notes in Computer Science (including subseries Lecture Notes in Artificial Intelligence and Lecture Notes in Bioinformatics)*, vol. 12400 LNCS, pp. 501–511, 2020, https://doi.org/10.1007/978-3-030-62522-1_37/TABLES/1.

73. K. Rosenthal, S. Strecker, and M. Snoeck, "Modeling difficulties in creating conceptual data models," *Softw Syst Model*, vol. 22, no. 3, pp. 1005–1030, 2023, https://doi.org/10.1007/s10270-022-01051-8.

74. D. Bogdanova and M. Snoeck, "Use of Personalized Feedback Reports in a Blended Conceptual Modelling Course," in *2019 ACM/IEEE 22nd International Conference on Model Driven Engineering Languages and Systems Companion (MODELS-C)*, 2019, pp. 672–679. https://doi.org/10.1109/MODELS-C.2019.00103.

75. D. Bogdanova, "Towards Personalized Feedback in a Smart Learning Environment For Teaching Conceptual Modelling," in *2019 13th International Conference on Research Challenges in Information Science (RCIS)*, 2019, pp. 1–5. https://doi.org/10.1109/RCIS.2019.8876983.

76. G. Sedrakyan, S. Poelmans, and M. Snoeck, "Assessing the influence of feedback-inclusive rapid prototyping on understanding the semantics of parallel UML statecharts by novice modellers," *Inf Softw Technol*, vol. 82, pp. 159–172, 2017, https://doi.org/10.1016/j.infsof.2016.11.001.

77. J. Ruiz., E. Serral., and M. Snoeck., "A Fully Implemented Didactic Tool for the Teaching of Interactive Software Systems," in *Proceedings of the 6th International Conference on Model-Driven Engi-neering and Software Development - MODELSWARD*, SciTePress, 2018, pp. 95–105. https://doi.org/10.5220/0006579600950105.

78. K. Figl, J. Mendling, and M. Strembeck, "The Influence of Notational Deficiencies on Process Model Comprehension," *J Assoc Inf Syst*, vol. 14, no. 6, pp. 312–338, Jun. 2013, [Online]. Available: https://www.proquest.com/scholarly-journals/influence-notational-deficiencies-on-process/docview/1470423062/se-2?accountid=17215

79. K. Figl and R. Laue, "Cognitive Complexity in Business Process Modeling," in *Advanced Information Systems Engineering*, H. Mouratidis and C. Rolland, Eds., Berlin, Heidelberg: Springer Berlin Heidelberg, 2011, pp. 452–466.

80. K. Figl, P. Soffer, and B. Weber, "Guiding attention in flow-based conceptual models through consistent flow and pattern visibility," *Decis Support Syst*, vol. 185, p. 114292, 2024, https://doi.org/10.1016/j.dss.2024.114292.

81. A. Burattin, M. Kaiser, M. Neurauter, and B. Weber, "Learning process modeling phases from modeling interactions and eye tracking data," *Data Knowl Eng*, vol. 121, pp. 1–17, 2019, https://doi.org/10.1016/j.datak.2019.04.001.

82. T. Sorg, A. Abbad-Andaloussi, and B. Weber, "Towards a Fine-grained Analysis of Cognitive Load During Program Comprehension," in *2022 IEEE International Conference on Software Analysis, Evolution and Reengineering (SANER)*, 2022, pp. 748–752. https://doi.org/10.1109/SANER53432.2022.00092.

83. S. Chakraborty and G. Liebel, "We do not understand what it says – studying student perceptions of software modelling," *Empir Softw Eng*, vol. 28, no. 6, p. 149, 2023, https://doi.org/10.1007/s10664-023-10404-w.

84. J. I. Panach and Ó. Pastor, "A Practical Experience of How to Teach Model-Driven Development to Manual Programming Students," *Enterprise Modelling and Information Systems Architectures (EMISAJ)*, vol. 18, pp. 1–6, 2023.

85. M. Manjunath, J. J. Raja, and M. Daun, "How teaching conceptual modeling to robotics students changes their perception of software engineering," 2023.

86. C. Verbruggen and M. Snoeck, "Exploratory Study on Students' Understanding of Multiperspective Modelling," in *Enterprise, Business-Process and Information Systems Modeling*, A. Augusto, A. Gill, D. Bork, S. Nurcan, I. Reinhartz-Berger, and R. Schmidt, Eds., Cham: Springer International Publishing, 2022, pp. 321–335.

87. V. Künzle, B. Weber, and M. Reichert, "Object-aware Business Processes: Fundamental Requirements and their Support in Existing Approaches," 2011.

88. M. Snoeck, *Enterprise Information Systems Engineering*. Springer, 2014. [Online]. Available: http://www.springer.com/series/8371

89. M. Snoeck, J. De Smedt, and J. De Weerdt, "Supporting Data-Aware Processes with MERODE," in *Enterprise, Business-Process and Information Systems Modeling*, A. Augusto, A. Gill, S. Nurcan, I. Reinhartz-Berger, R. Schmidt, and J. Zdravkovic, Eds., Cham: Springer International Publishing, 2021, pp. 131–146.

90. D. Bogdanova and M. Snoeck, "Academic and Industry Training for Data Modelling: Ideas for Mutual Benefit," in *Proceedings of the ACM/IEEE 44th International Conference on Software Engineering: Software Engineering Education and Training*, in ICSE-SEET '22. New York, NY, USA: Association for Computing Machinery, 2022, pp. 25–28. https://doi.org/10.1145/3510456.3514167.

91. O. I. Lindland, G. Sindre, and A. Solvberg, "Understanding quality in conceptual modeling," *IEEE Softw*, vol. 11, no. 2, pp. 42–49, 1994, https://doi.org/10.1109/52.268955.

92. D. L. Moody, "The Method Evaluation Model: A Theoretical Model for Validating Information Systems Design Methods," in *ECIS 2003 Proceedings*, 2003, p. 79. [Online]. Available: https://aisel.aisnet.org/ecis2003/79

93. S. Steinau, A. Marrella, K. Andrews, F. Leotta, M. Mecella, and M. Reichert, "DALEC: a framework for the systematic evaluation of data-centric approaches to process management software," *Softw Syst Model*, vol. 18, no. 4, pp. 2679–2716, 2019, https://doi.org/10.1007/s10270-018-0695-0.

94. J. Hunt, *Agile software construction*, vol. 16. Springer, 2006.

95. A. C. Bock and U. Frank, "Low-Code Platform," *Business & Information Systems Engineering*, vol. 63, no. 6, pp. 733–740, 2021, https://doi.org/10.1007/s12599-021-00726-8.

96. "The ADOxx Metamodelling Platform - Welcome to ADOxx.org - ADOxx.org." Accessed: Nov. 26, 2021. [Online]. Available: https://www.adoxx.org/live/home

97. C. Verbruggen, "MERODExBPMN." Accessed: Nov. 26, 2021. [Online]. Available: http://merode.econ.kuleuven.ac.be/MERODExBPMN.html

98. M. Snoeck, "Object Interaction," in *Enterprise Information Systems Engineering: The MERODE Approach*, M. Snoeck, Ed., Cham: Springer International Publishing, 2014, pp. 107–125. https://doi.org/10.1007/978-3-319-10145-3_5.

99. M. Snoeck and G. Dedene, "Existence dependency: The key to semantic integrity between structural and behavioral aspects of object types," *IEEE Transactions on Software Engineering*, vol. 24, no. 4, pp. 233–251, 1998, https://doi.org/10.1109/32.677182.

100. G. Dedene and M. Snoeck, "Formal deadlock elimination in an object oriented conceptual schema," *Data Knowl Eng*, vol. 15, no. 1, pp. 1–30, 1995, https://doi.org/10.1016/0169-023X(94)00031-9.

101. M. Snoeck, "The Existence-Dependency Graph," in *Enterprise Information Systems Engineering: The MERODE Approach*, M. Snoeck, Ed., Cham: Springer International Publishing, 2014, pp. 79–105. https://doi.org/10.1007/978-3-319-10145-3_4.

102. M. Snoeck, "The Information System Service Layer," in *Enterprise Information Systems Engineering: The MERODE Approach*, M. Snoeck, Ed., Cham: Springer International Publishing, 2014, pp. 205–222. https://doi.org/10.1007/978-3-319-10145-3_9.

103. M. Snoeck, J. de Smedt, and J. de Weerdt, "Supporting Data-Aware Processes with MERODE," in *Enterprise, Business-Process and Information Systems Modeling*, A. Augusto, A. Gill, S. Nurcan, I. Reinhartz-Berger, R. Schmidt, and J. Zdravkovic, Eds., Cham: Springer International Publishing, 2021, pp. 131–146.

104. N. Deehan, "Camunda Tutorial for Java Developers (Video 2) [Youtube video]." [Online]. Available: https://www.youtube.com/watch?v=HxtZf5VD6lQ&t=184s

105. M. De Backer, M. Snoeck, G. Monsieur, W. Lemahieu, and G. Dedene, "A scenario-based verification technique to assess the compatibility of collaborative business processes," *Data Knowl Eng*, vol. 68, no. 6, pp. 531–551, 2009, https://doi.org/10.1016/j.datak.2008.12.002.

106. M. Estañol, J. Munoz-Gama, J. Carmona, and E. Teniente, "Conformance checking in UML artifact-centric business process models," *Softw Syst Model*, vol. 18, no. 4, pp. 2531–2555, 2019, https://doi.org/10.1007/s10270-018-0681-6.

107. J. Ruiz, "Exploring the effectiveness of learning UI design by feedback ENable user interface simulation: the FENIkS approach.," KU Leuven, Leuven, 2018. [Online]. Available: Uhttps://lirias.kuleuven.be/retrieve/520252D18

108. J. Ruiz, E. Serral, and M. Snoeck, "UI-GEAR: User interface generation preview capable to adapt in real-time," in *MODELSWARD 2017 - Proceedings of the 5th International Conference on Model-Driven Engineering and Software Development*, SciTePress, 2017, pp. 277–284. https://doi.org/10.5220/0006115402770284.

109. O. Pastor and J. C. Molina, *Model-driven architecture in practice: a software production environment based on conceptual modeling*, vol. 1. Springer, 2007.

110. O. Pastor and J. C. Molina, "Object Model," in *Model-Driven Architecture in Practice: A Software Production Environment Based on Conceptual Modeling*, O. Pastor and J. C. Molina, Eds., Berlin, Heidelberg: Springer Berlin Heidelberg, 2007, pp. 55–114. https://doi.org/10.1007/978-3-540-71868-0_7.

111. O. Pastor and J. C. Molina, "Dynamic Model," in *Model-Driven Architecture in Practice: A Software Production Environment Based on Conceptual Modeling*, O. Pastor and J. C. Molina, Eds., Berlin, Heidelberg: Springer Berlin Heidelberg, 2007, pp. 115–135. https://doi.org/10.1007/978-3-540-71868-0_8.

112. O. Pastor and J. C. Molina, "Functional Model," in *Model-Driven Architecture in Practice: A Software Production Environment Based on Conceptual Modeling*, O. Pastor and J. C.

Molina, Eds., Berlin, Heidelberg: Springer Berlin Heidelberg, 2007, pp. 137–146. https://doi.org/10.1007/978-3-540-71868-0_9.

113. O. Pastor and J. C. Molina, "Presentation Model," in *Model-Driven Architecture in Practice: A Software Production Environment Based on Conceptual Modeling*, O. Pastor and J. C. Molina, Eds., Berlin, Heidelberg: Springer Berlin Heidelberg, 2007, pp. 147–189. https://doi.org/10.1007/978-3-540-71868-0_10.

114. J. Ruiz, G. Sedrakyan, and M. Snoeck, "Generating User Interface from Conceptual, Presentation and User models with JMermaid in a learning approach," in *Proceedings of the XVI International Conference on Human Computer Interaction*, in Interacción '15. New York, NY, USA: Association for Computing Machinery, 2015. https://doi.org/10.1145/2829875.2829893.

115. M. Snoeck, C. Verbruggen, J. De Smedt, and J. De Weerdt, "Supporting data-aware processes with MERODE," *Softw Syst Model*, 2023, https://doi.org/10.1007/s10270-023-01095-4.

116. OMG, "Case Management Model and Notation (CMMN)," 2016.

117. M. Snoeck, "The Information System Service Layer," in *Enterprise Information Systems Engineering: The MERODE Approach*, M. Snoeck, Ed., Cham: Springer International Publishing, 2014, pp. 205–222. https://doi.org/10.1007/978-3-319-10145-3_9.

118. A. Goossens, C. Verbruggen, M. Snoeck, J. De Smedt, and J. Vanthienen, "Aligning Object-Centric Event Logs with Data-Centric Conceptual Models," in *Enterprise, Business-Process and Information Systems Modeling*, H. van der Aa, D. Bork, H. A. Proper, and R. Schmidt, Eds., Cham: Springer Nature Switzerland, 2023, pp. 44–59.

119. C. Verbruggen, A. Goossens, J. De Smedt, J. Vanthienen, and M. Snoeck, "iDOCEM: defining a common terminology for object-centric event logging and data-centric process modelling," *Softw Syst Model*, 2024, https://doi.org/10.1007/s10270-024-01191-z.

120. M. Dumas, L. M. Rosa, J. Mendling, and A. H. Reijers, *Fundamentals of business process management*. Springer, 2018.

121. A. F. Ghahfarokhi, G. Park, A. Berti, and W. van der Aalst, "Ocel standard," 2020.

122. A. F. Ghahfarokhi and W. M. P. van der Aalst, "A Python Tool for Object-Centric Process Mining Comparison," 2022. [Online]. Available: https://arxiv.org/abs/2202.05709

123. A. Berti, "Filtering and Sampling Object-Centric Event Logs," 2022. [Online]. Available: https://arxiv.org/abs/2205.01428

124. W. M. P. van der Aalst and A. Berti, "Discovering Object-centric Petri Nets," *Fundam Inform*, vol. 175, pp. 1–40, 2020, https://doi.org/10.3233/FI-2020-1946.

125. G. Li, E. G. L. de Murillas, R. M. de Carvalho, and W. M. P. van der Aalst, "Extracting Object-Centric Event Logs to Support Process Mining on Databases," in *Information Systems in the Big Data Era*, J. Mendling and H. Mouratidis, Eds., Cham: Springer International Publishing, 2018, pp. 182–199.

126. W. M. P. van der Aalst, G. Li, and M. Montali, "Object-Centric Behavioral Constraints," 2017. [Online]. Available: https://arxiv.org/abs/1703.05740

127. A. Goossens, J. De Smedt, J. Vanthienen, and W. M. P. van der Aalst, "Enhancing Data-Awareness of Object-Centric Event Logs," in *Process Mining Workshops*, M. Montali, A. Senderovich, and M. Weidlich, Eds., Cham: Springer Nature Switzerland, 2023, pp. 18–30.

128. W. M. P. VAN DER AALST, P. BARTHELMESS, C. A. ELLIS, and J. WAINER, "PROCLETS: A FRAMEWORK FOR LIGHTWEIGHT INTERACTING WORKFLOW PROCESSES," *Int J Coop Inf Syst*, vol. 10, no. 04, pp. 443–481, Dec. 2001, https://doi.org/10.1142/S0218843001000412.

129. J. Kleijn, M. Koutny, and M. Pietkiewicz-Koutny, "Regions of Petri nets with a/sync connections," *Theor Comput Sci*, vol. 454, pp. 189–198, 2012, https://doi.org/10.1016/j.tcs.2012.04.016.

130. S. Ghilardi, A. Gianola, M. Montali, and A. Rivkin, "Petri net-based object-centric processes with read-only data," *Inf Syst*, vol. 107, p. 102011, 2022, https://doi.org/10.1016/j.is.2022.102011.

131. R. Hull *et al.*, "Business artifacts with guard-stage-milestone lifecycles: managing artifact interactions with conditions and events," in *Proceedings of the 5th ACM International Conference on Distributed Event-Based System*, in DEBS '11. New York, NY, USA: Association for Computing Machinery, 2011, pp. 51–62. https://doi.org/10.1145/2002259.2002270.

132. A. Meyer, L. Pufahl, D. Fahland, and M. Weske, "Modeling and Enacting Complex Data Dependencies in Business Processes," in *Business Process Management*, F. Daniel, J. Wang, and B. Weber, Eds., Berlin, Heidelberg: Springer Berlin Heidelberg, 2013, pp. 171–186.

133. V. Künzle and M. Reichert, "PHILharmonicFlows: towards a framework for object-aware process management," *Journal of Software Maintenance and Evolution: Research and Practice*, vol. 23, no. 4, pp. 205–244, Jun. 2011, https://doi.org/10.1002/smr.524.

134. D. Fahland, "Describing Behavior of Processes with Many-to-Many Interactions," in *Application and Theory of Petri Nets and Concurrency*, S. Donatelli and S. Haar, Eds., Cham: Springer International Publishing, 2019, pp. 3–24.

135. R. Hull, "Artifact-Centric Business Process Models: Brief Survey of Research Results and Challenges," in *On the Move to Meaningful Internet Systems: OTM 2008*, R. Meersman and Z. Tari, Eds., Berlin, Heidelberg: Springer Berlin Heidelberg, 2008, pp. 1152–1163.

136. G. De Giacomo, X. Oriol, M. Estañol, and E. Teniente, "Linking Data and BPMN Processes to Achieve Executable Models," in *Advanced Information Systems Engineering*, E. Dubois and K. Pohl, Eds., Cham: Springer International Publishing, 2017, pp. 612–628.

137. H. A. Reijers *et al.*, "Evaluating data-centric process approaches: Does the human factor factor in?," *Softw Syst Model*, vol. 16, no. 3, pp. 649–662, 2017, https://doi.org/10.1007/s10270-015-0491-z.

138. A. Berti *et al.*, "OCEL (Object-Centric Event Log) 2.0 Specification," 2024. [Online]. Available: https://arxiv.org/abs/2403.01975

139. A. Goossens, J. De Smedt, and J. Vanthienen, "Object-Centric Event Logs: Specifications, Comparative Analysis and Refinement," 2024. [Online]. Available: https://arxiv.org/abs/2405.12709

140. M. L. van Eck, N. Sidorova, and W. M. P. van der Aalst, "Multi-instance Mining: Discovering Synchronisation in Artifact-Centric Processes," in *Business Process Management Workshops*, F. Daniel, Q. Z. Sheng, and H. Motahari, Eds., Cham: Springer International Publishing, 2019, pp. 18–30.

141. E. H. J. Nooijen, B. F. van Dongen, and D. Fahland, "Automatic Discovery of Data-Centric and Artifact-Centric Processes," in *Business Process Management Workshops*, M. La Rosa and P. Soffer, Eds., Berlin, Heidelberg: Springer Berlin Heidelberg, 2013, pp. 316–327.

142. A. Rebmann, J.-R. Rehse, and H. van der Aa, "Uncovering Object-Centric Data in Classical Event Logs for the Automated Transformation from XES to OCEL," in *Business Process Management*, C. Di Ciccio, R. Dijkman, A. del Río Ortega, and S. Rinderle-Ma, Eds., Cham: Springer International Publishing, 2022, pp. 379–396.

143. A. Goossens, A. Rebmann, J. De Smedt, J. Vanthienen, and H. van der Aa, "From OCEL to DOCEL – Datasets and Automated Transformation," in *Process Mining Workshops*, J. De Smedt and P. Soffer, Eds., Cham: Springer Nature Switzerland, 2024, pp. 70–83.

144. D. Bano and M. Weske, "Discovering Data Models from Event Logs," in *Conceptual Modeling*, G. Dobbie, U. Frank, G. Kappel, S. W. Liddle, and H. C. Mayr, Eds., Cham: Springer International Publishing, 2020, pp. 62–76.

145. B. Knopp, M. Pourbafrani, and W. M. P. van der Aalst, "Discovering Object-Centric Process Simulation Models," in *2023 5th International Conference on Process Mining (ICPM)*, 2023, pp. 81–88. https://doi.org/10.1109/ICPM60904.2023.10271944.

146. X. Lu, M. Nagelkerke, D. v. d. Wiel, and D. Fahland, "Discovering Interacting Artifacts from ERP Systems," *IEEE Trans Serv Comput*, vol. 8, no. 6, pp. 861–873, 2015, https://doi.org/10.1109/TSC.2015.2474358.

147. M. L. van Eck, N. Sidorova, and W. M. P. van der Aalst, "Guided Interaction Exploration and Performance Analysis in Artifact-Centric Process Models," *Business & Information Systems Engineering*, vol. 61, no. 6, pp. 649–663, 2019, https://doi.org/10.1007/s12599-018-0546-0.

148. D. Fahland, V. Denisov, and Wil. M. P. van der Aalst, "Inferring Unobserved Events in Systems with Shared Resources and Queues," *Fundam Inform*, vol. 183, pp. 203–242, 2021, https://doi.org/10.3233/FI-2021-2087.

149. S. Esser and D. Fahland, "Multi-Dimensional Event Data in Graph Databases," *J Data Semant*, vol. 10, no. 1, pp. 109–141, 2021, https://doi.org/10.1007/s13740-021-00122-1.

150. D. Fahland, "Process Mining over Multiple Behavioral Dimensions with Event Knowledge Graphs," in *Process Mining Handbook*, W. M. P. van der Aalst and J. Carmona, Eds., Cham: Springer International Publishing, 2022, pp. 274–319. https://doi.org/10.1007/978-3-031-08848-3_9.

151. E. González López de Murillas, H. A. Reijers, and W. M. P. van der Aalst, "Connecting databases with process mining: a meta model and toolset," *Softw Syst Model*, vol. 18, no. 2, pp. 1209–1247, 2019, https://doi.org/10.1007/s10270-018-0664-7.

152. I. Osman, S. Ben Yahia, and G. Diallo, "Ontology Integration: Approaches and Challenging Issues," *Information Fusion*, vol. 71, pp. 38–63, 2021, https://doi.org/10.1016/j.inffus.2021.01.007.

153. D. Djurica, A. Jabbari, J. Mendling, and J. Recker, "Effective presentation of ontological overlap of multiple conceptual models," *Decis Support Syst*, vol. 187, p. 114327, 2024, https://doi.org/10.1016/j.dss.2024.114327.

154. C. W. Gunther and H. M. W. Verbeek, "Xes-standard definition," 2014.

155. J. L. Peterson, "Petri Nets," *ACM Comput. Surv.*, vol. 9, no. 3, pp. 223–252, Sep. 1977, https://doi.org/10.1145/356698.356702.

156. T. Slaats, D. M. M. Schunselaar, F. M. Maggi, and H. A. Reijers, "The Semantics of Hybrid Process Models," in *On the Move to Meaningful Internet Systems: OTM 2016 Conferences*, C. Debruyne, H. Panetto, R. Meersman, T. Dillon, eva Kühn, D. O'Sullivan, and C. A. Ardagna, Eds., Cham: Springer International Publishing, 2016, pp. 531–551.

157. M. Snoeck, W. Lemahieu, F. Goethals, G. Dedene, and J. Vandenbulcke, "Events as atomic contracts for component integration," *Data Knowl Eng*, vol. 51, no. 1, pp. 81–107, 2004, https://doi.org/10.1016/j.datak.2004.03.007.

158. W. M. P. van der Aalst, "Toward More Realistic Simulation Models Using Object-Centric Process Mining.," in *ECMS*, 2023, pp. 5–13.

159. M. Pourbafrani and W. M. P. van der Aalst, "Data-Driven Simulation In Process Mining: Introducing A Reference Model."

160. C. Verbruggen and M. Snoeck, "TEC-MAP: A Taxonomy of Evaluation Criteria for Multi-modelling Approaches," in *Enterprise, Business-Process and Information Systems Modeling*, H. van der Aa, D. Bork, H. A. Proper, and R. Schmidt, Eds., Cham: Springer Nature Switzerland, 2023, pp. 259–273.

161. C. Verbruggen and M. Snoeck, "TEC-MAP: a taxonomy of evaluation criteria and its application to the multi-modelling of data and processes," *Softw Syst Model*, 2024, https://doi.org/10.1007/s10270-024-01198-6.

162. A.-W. Scheer, "Architecture of Integrated Information Systems (ARIS)," in *Business Process Engineering: Reference Models for Industrial Enterprises*, A.-W. Scheer, Ed., Berlin, Heidelberg: Springer Berlin Heidelberg, 1994, pp. 4–16. https://doi.org/10.1007/978-3-642-79142-0_1.

163. B. Lantow, K. Sandkuhl, and J. Stirna, "Enterprise Modeling with 4EM: Perspectives and Method," in *Domain-Specific Conceptual Modeling: Concepts, Methods and ADOxx Tools*, D. Karagiannis, M. Lee, K. Hinkelmann, and W. Utz, Eds., Cham: Springer International Publishing, 2022, pp. 95–120. https://doi.org/10.1007/978-3-030-93547-4_5.

164. R. Noel, J. I. Panach, M. Ruiz, and O. Pastor, "Stra2Bis: A Model-Driven Method for Aligning Business Strategy and Business Processes," in *Conceptual Modeling*, J. Ralyté, S. Chakravarthy, M. Mohania, M. A. Jeusfeld, and K. Karlapalem, Eds., Cham: Springer International Publishing, 2022, pp. 255–270.

165. M. de Leoni, P. Felli, and M. Montali, "Integrating BPMN and DMN: Modeling and Analysis," *J Data Semant*, vol. 10, no. 1, pp. 165–188, 2021, https://doi.org/10.1007/s13740-021-00132-z.

166. J. Krogstie, G. Sindre, and H. Jørgensen, "Process models representing knowledge for action: a revised quality framework," *European Journal of Information Systems*, vol. 15, no. 1, pp. 91–102, 2006, https://doi.org/10.1057/palgrave.ejis.3000598.

167. F. D. Davis, "A technology acceptance model for empirically testing new end-user information systems: Theory and results," Massachusetts Institute of Technology, 1985.

168. H. J. Nelson, G. Poels, M. Genero, and M. Piattini, "A conceptual modeling quality framework," *Software Quality Journal*, vol. 20, no. 1, pp. 201–228, 2012, https://doi.org/10.1007/s11219-011-9136-9.

169. F. D. Giraldo, S. España, W. J. Giraldo, and Ó. Pastor, "Evaluating the quality of a set of modelling languages used in combination: A method and a tool," *Inf Syst*, vol. 77, pp. 48–70, Sep. 2018, https://doi.org/10.1016/J.IS.2018.06.002.

170. R. Bendraou, J.-M. Jézéquel, M.-P. Gervais, and X. Blanc, "A Comparison of Six UML-Based Languages for Software Process Modeling," *IEEE Transactions on Software Engineering*, vol. 36, no. 5, pp. 662–675, 2010, https://doi.org/10.1109/TSE.2009.85.

171. W. Luo and Y. Alex Tung, "A framework for selecting business process modeling methods," *Industrial Management & Data Systems*, vol. 99, no. 7, pp. 312–319, Jan. 1999, https://doi.org/10.1108/02635579910262535.

172. C. M. Chiao, V. Künzle, K. Andrews, and M. Reichert, "A tool for supporting object-aware processes," in *2014 IEEE 18th International Enterprise Distributed Object Computing Conference Workshops and Demonstrations*, IEEE, 2014, pp. 410–413.

173. K. Andrews, S. Steinau, and M. Reichert, "Enabling Process Variants and Versions in Distributed Object-Aware Process Management Systems," in *Information Systems in the Big Data Era*, J. Mendling and H. Mouratidis, Eds., Cham: Springer International Publishing, 2018, pp. 1–15.

174. K. Andrews, S. Steinau, and M. Reichert, "Enabling Fine-Grained Access Control in Flexible Distributed Object-Aware Process Management Systems," in *2017 IEEE 21st International Enterprise Distributed Object Computing Conference (EDOC)*, 2017, pp. 143–152. https://doi.org/10.1109/EDOC.2017.27.

175. C. M. Chiao, V. Künzle, and M. Reichert, "Enhancing the case handling paradigm to support object-aware processes," 2013.

176. P. Soffer, B. Golany, and D. Dori, "ERP modeling: a comprehensive approach," *Inf Syst*, vol. 28, no. 6, pp. 673–690, 2003, https://doi.org/10.1016/S0306-4379(02)00078-9.

177. J. Krogstie, "Quality of Modelling Languages," in *Model-Based Development and Evolution of Information Systems: A Quality Approach*, J. Krogstie, Ed., London: Springer London, 2012, pp. 249–280. https://doi.org/10.1007/978-1-4471-2936-3_5.

178. P. Fettke and P. Loos, "Ontological evaluation of reference models using the Bunge-Wand-Weber model," *AMCIS 2003 Proceedings*, p. 384, 2003.

179. M. Estañol, A. Queralt, M.-R. Sancho, and E. Teniente, "Specifying Artifact-Centric Business Process Models in UML," in *Business Modeling and Software Design*, B. Shishkov, Ed., Cham: Springer International Publishing, 2015, pp. 62–81.

180. C. M. Chiao, V. Künzle, and M. Reichert, "Towards schema evolution in object-aware process management systems," 2014.

181. M. Estanol, A. Queralt, M.-R. Sancho, and E. Teniente, "Using UML to specify artifact-centric business process models," *BMSD*, pp. 84–93, 2014.

182. P. Bernus and L. Nemes, "A framework to define a generic enterprise reference architecture and methodology," *Computer Integrated Manufacturing Systems*, vol. 9, no. 3, pp. 179–191, 1996, https://doi.org/10.1016/S0951-5240(96)00001-8.

183. M. Estañol, A. Queralt, M. R. Sancho, and E. Teniente, "Artifact-Centric Business Process Models in UML," in *Business Process Management Workshops*, M. La Rosa and P. Soffer, Eds., Berlin, Heidelberg: Springer Berlin Heidelberg, 2013, pp. 292–303.

184. F. D. Davis, "Perceived usefulness, perceived ease of use, and user acceptance of information technology," *MIS quarterly*, pp. 319–340, 1989.

185. V. Venkatesh, J. Y. L. Thong, and X. Xu, "Consumer Acceptance and Use of Information Technology: Extending the Unified Theory of Acceptance and Use of Technology," *MIS Quarterly*, vol. 36, no. 1, pp. 157–178, 2012, https://doi.org/10.2307/41410412.

186. J. Krogstie, O. I. Lindland, and G. Sindre, "Defining quality aspects for conceptual models," in *Information System Concepts: Towards a consolidation of views*, E. D. Falkenberg, W. Hesse, and A. Olivé, Eds., Boston, MA: Springer US, 1995, pp. 216–231. https://doi.org/10.1007/978-0-387-34870-4_22.

187. J. Krogstie and H. D. Jørgensen, "Quality of Interactive Models," in *Advanced Conceptual Modeling Techniques*, A. Olivé, M. Yoshikawa, and E. S. K. Yu, Eds., Berlin, Heidelberg: Springer Berlin Heidelberg, 2003, pp. 351–363.

188. Y. Wand and R. Weber, "An ontological model of an information system," *IEEE Transactions on Software Engineering*, vol. 16, no. 11, pp. 1282–1292, 1990, https://doi.org/10.1109/32.60316.

189. D. Karagiannis and H. Kühn, "Metamodelling Platforms," in *E-Commerce and Web Technologies*, K. Bauknecht, A. M. Tjoa, and G. Quirchmayr, Eds., Berlin, Heidelberg: Springer Berlin Heidelberg, 2002, p. 182. https://doi.org/10.1007/3-540-45705-4_19.

190. V. Künzle, B. Weber, and M. Reichert, "Object-aware Business Processes: Properties, Requirements, Existing Approaches," University of Ulm, 2010.

191. R. C. Nickerson, U. Varshney, and J. Muntermann, "A method for taxonomy development and its application in information systems," *European Journal of Information Systems*, vol. 22, no. 3, pp. 336–359, May 2013, https://doi.org/10.1057/ejis.2012.26.

192. *ISO: ISO/IEC/IEEE 42010:2011 Systems and software engineering — Architecture description.* Accessed: Mar. 09, 2023. [Online]. Available: https://www.iso.org/standard/50508.html

193. M. Bernaert, G. Poels, M. Snoeck, and M. De Backer, "CHOOSE: Towards a metamodel for enterprise architecture in small and medium-sized enterprises," *Information Systems Frontiers*, vol. 18, no. 4, pp. 781–818, 2016, https://doi.org/10.1007/s10796-015-9559-0.

194. D. Harel and B. Rumpe, "Modeling Languages: Syntax, Semantics and All That Stuff, Part I: The Basic Stuff," Weizmann Science Press of Israel, ISR, 2000.

195. H. C. Mayr and B. Thalheim, "The triptych of conceptual modeling," *Softw Syst Model*, vol. 20, no. 1, pp. 7–24, 2021, https://doi.org/10.1007/s10270-020-00836-z.

196. A. G. Kleppe, "A Language Description is More than a Metamodel," in *4th International Workshop on Software Language Engineering, ATEM 2007*, 2007.

197. P. Höfferer, "Achieving business process model interoperability using metamodels and ontologies," in *ECIS 2007 Proceedings*, 2007. [Online]. Available: http://aisel.aisnet.org/ecis2007/174

198. J. Ruiz, E. Serral, and M. Snoeck, "Evaluating user interface generation approaches: model-based versus model-driven development," *Softw Syst Model*, vol. 18, no. 4, pp. 2753–2776, Aug. 2019, https://doi.org/10.1007/s10270-018-0698-x.

199. J. Börstler, N. bin Ali, M. Svensson, and K. Petersen, "Investigating acceptance behavior in software engineering—Theoretical perspectives," *Journal of Systems and Software*, vol. 198, p. 111592, 2023, https://doi.org/10.1016/j.jss.2022.111592.

200. M. Snoeck, "Object and System Behaviour," in *Enterprise Information Systems Engineering: The MERODE Approach*, M. Snoeck, Ed., Cham: Springer International Publishing, 2014, pp. 127–147. https://doi.org/10.1007/978-3-319-10145-3_6.

201. D. Calvanese, M. Montali, M. Estañol, and E. Teniente, "Verifiable UML Artifact-Centric Business Process Models," in *Proceedings of the 23rd ACM International Conference on Conference on Information and Knowledge Management*, in CIKM '14. New York, NY, USA: Association for Computing Machinery, 2014, pp. 1289–1298. https://doi.org/10.1145/2661829.2662050.

202. M. Estañol, M.-R. Sancho, and E. Teniente, "Verification and Validation of UML Artifact-Centric Business Process Models," in *Advanced Information Systems Engineering*, J. Zdravkovic, M. Kirikova, and P. Johannesson, Eds., Cham: Springer International Publishing, 2015, pp. 434–449.

203. K. Sandkuhl, J. Stirna, A. Persson, and M. Wißotzki, "Overview of the 4EM Method," in *Enterprise Modeling: Tackling Business Challenges with the 4EM Method*, K. Sandkuhl, J. Stirna, A. Persson, and M. Wißotzki, Eds., Berlin, Heidelberg: Springer Berlin Heidelberg, 2014, pp. 75–86. https://doi.org/10.1007/978-3-662-43725-4_7.

204. K. Sandkuhl, J. Stirna, A. Persson, and M. Wißotzki, "Sub-models of 4EM," in *Enterprise Modeling: Tackling Business Challenges with the 4EM Method*, K. Sandkuhl, J. Stirna, A. Persson, and M. Wißotzki, Eds., Berlin, Heidelberg: Springer Berlin Heidelberg, 2014, pp. 87–147. https://doi.org/10.1007/978-3-662-43725-4_8.

205. The Open Group, "Archimate." Accessed: Feb. 02, 2022. [Online]. Available: https://www.opengroup.org/archimate-home

206. K. Sandkuhl, J. Stirna, A. Persson, and M. Wißotzki, *Enteprise Modeling: Tackling Business Challenges with the 4EM Method*. Springer-Verlag Berlin Heidelberg, 2014. https://doi.org/10.1007/978-3-662-43725-4.

207. D. Calvanese, M. Montali, F. Patrizi, and A. Rivkin, "Modeling and In-Database Management of Relational, Data-Aware Processes," *Lecture Notes in Computer Science (including subseries Lecture Notes in Artificial Intelligence and Lecture Notes in Bioinformatics)*, vol. 11483 LNCS, pp. 328–345, 2019, https://doi.org/10.1007/978-3-030-21290-2_21.

208. M. De Jaegere, A. Waegeman, C. Verbruggen, A. Simonofski, and M. Snoeck, "MERODExBPMN," Leuven, 2023.

209. B. Ternes, K. Rosenthal, and S. Strecker, "User interface design research for modeling tools: a literature study," *Enterprise Modelling and Information Systems Architectures (EMISAJ)*, vol. 16, pp. 1–4, 2021.

210. A. Bobkowska and K. Reszke, "Usability of UML Modeling Tools," in *Proceedings of the 2005 Conference on Software Engineering: Evolution and Emerging Technologies*, NLD: IOS Press, 2005, pp. 75–86.

211. J. Pietron, A. Raschke, M. Stegmaier, M. Tichy, and E. Rukzio, "A study design template for identifying usability issues in graphical modeling tools.,"

212. J. Ruiz, E. Serral, and M. Snoeck, "Unifying Functional User Interface Design Principles," *Int J Hum Comput Interact*, vol. 37, no. 1, pp. 47–67, Jan. 2021, https://doi.org/10.1080/10447318.2020.1805876.

213. J. Ruiz de la Peña and M. Snoeck, "Exploring the effectiveness of learning UI design by feedback ENable user interface simulation: the FENIkS approach.," 2018.

214. D. Norman, "The Psychopathology of Everyday Things," in *The Design of Everyday Things*, D. Norman, Ed., Basic Books, 1988, pp. 5–22.

215. P. Doncaster, "The UX Five-Second Rules: Guidelines for User Experience Design's Simplest Testing Technique," 2014, *Morgan Kaufmann Publishers Inc.*

216. J. Brooke, "Sus: a "quick and dirty'usability," *Usability evaluation in industry*, vol. 189, no. 3, pp. 189–194, 1996.

217. J. R. Lewis and J. Sauro, "Item Benchmarks for the System Usability Scale," *J. Usability Studies*, vol. 13, no. 3, pp. 158–167, May 2018.

218. K. Rosenthal, B. Ternes, and S. Strecker, "Understanding individual processes of conceptual modeling: A multi-modal observation and data generation approach," *Modellierung 2020. Bonn: Gesellschaft für Informatik*, pp. 77–92, 2020.

219. V. Amaral de Sousa, C. Burnay, and M. Snoeck, "Artifact-Centric Modeling and Implementation of Blockchain-Enabled Business Processes," *Business & Information Systems Engineering*, 2024, https://doi.org/10.1007/s12599-024-00885-4.

GPSR Compliance
The European Union's (EU) General Product Safety Regulation (GPSR) is a set
of rules that requires consumer products to be safe and our obligations to
ensure this.

If you have any concerns about our products, you can contact us on

ProductSafety@springernature.com

In case Publisher is established outside the EU, the EU authorized
representative is:

Springer Nature Customer Service Center GmbH
Europaplatz 3
69115 Heidelberg, Germany